Odyssey with the Angels

A Reconciliation with Life

Sibli
Sarah Jeane

Odyssey with the Angels, A Reconciliation with Life

To learn more about Sibli's, Sarah Jeane, work, please contact her through her website: sibliartfromthelight.com

Library of Congress Cataloging-in-Publication Data:
Sibli, Sarah Jeane

Odyssey with the Angels, A Reconciliation with Life

ISBN: 979-8-218-02503-8 (Paperback)
ISBN: 979-8-218-02504-5 (eBook)

1. BODY, MIND & SPIRIT / Healing / Prayer & Spirit
2. SELF-HELP / Personal Growth / Happiness   3. BODY,
MIND & SPIRIT / Channeling & Mediumship

First edition, July 2022
Cover Design by Sibli

Empowered Whole Being Press
www.EmpoweredWholeBeingPress.com

Table of Contents

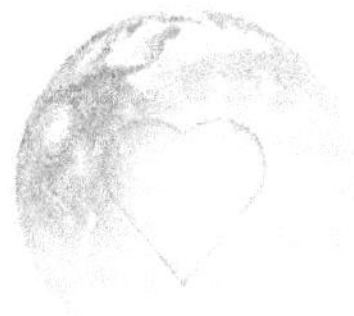

Dear Father Mother God, dear Guardian Angels, all Angels of the Light, and Archangels, dear Luminous Masters, dear Father Sun, dear Mother Earth, dear Grandmother moon, I unify my spirit, my consciousness, all of my beingness with your Divine Love and Light to be a clear conduit of Peace, of the Sacred Light and Truth in integrity and honoring. May every word, every sentence, all messages within this book, be infused with your forces of Love from the Temple of the One Sacred Heart of Creation. Thank you, dear Angelic Divine Guides, dear Luminous Beings for blessing this holy work, and compilation with the Sanctity of your Presence and Radiance to free and awaken all Hearts, in furtherance of Peace and Harmony in all Hearts and all of Life—in the Oneness of unconditional Love—for all beings and all consciousness to live and breathe from the forces of Pure Love and Reverence, now and forever, in the Eternal Peace of Creation.

In Sacred Peace!
Namaste

Dedication

With all my love, reverence, and profound gratitude, I dedicate this book to all the Angelic Beings of the Light, the Earthly Ones, and the Ones from Heavenly realms and high dimensions of Light throughout the Universe. You have been bridges of Light to Source, for us all, supporting a global universal work of service, guiding us, teaching us, embracing us with Holy Light and unconditional Love — adjusting, and healing layers of waves frequencies within all our bodies, relationships and lives whenever it has been necessary — awakening us to an ultimate reconciliation with our "God Self" and all of "Life".

Thank you, dear Angelic Beings, Luminous Masters and Guides, for enlightening our journey, our path, in the eternity of time. My Heart is filled with unconditional Love from my communion with Divine Mother Earth Garden of Eden, Father Sky, Grandfather Sun, and Grandmother Moon — thank you, for your infinite beauty, loving nurturing embrace, supporting all of Life in harmony. We love you dear Divine Mother Earth. We love your Garden of Eden with your magnificent Beings, the Animal Kingdom, all of Nature's Intelligence, Fairies and Angels, your infinite sanctity. Thank you, dear Angels of the Light for holding us all within your luminous wings, in the Heart of Divine Father God and in the Heart of Divine Mother God, guiding us to ascend.

Thank you, dear Angelic Beings of the Light, for assisting us to know about unconditional Love — to know about the infinite Divine Qualities of Love and Holy Presence of Father Mother God within our Hearts and our lives — to know about a Holy consciousness permeating All That Is in Creation.

Thank you, dear Angels of the Light, for working through me and so many angelic light-workers, in service, as we are conduits of love, peace, truth, and compassion, assisting the healing journey and awakening of all people, held in the realms of Divine Light — where the magnificence of the Creator's Love Divine Infinite Qualities is forever in action, permeating All That Is.

This compilation is an "invitation", to join teams of Angels, Archangels, and Masters of the Light, on a Sacred Journey, to an awakening of your blissful presence of peace, your pure Being.

May you open your Hearts to be touched by the Angels' pure Luminescence and boundless Love, to exponentially cherish and honor your luminescence, honoring Divine Mother Earth and Divine Father Sun, Grandmother Moon, Nature's Intelligence in all its magnificence and sacredness, with all its inhabitants.

With boundless gratitude and honoring,
I love you,
Sibli

Dedication

Dream the Dreams of the One Sacred Heart
to Co-Create with God

Introduction and Guidelines

From the presence of my pure being, the Divine Angels of the Light are gathering in joy across the Rainbows beaming radiance, ascertaining a Love that is unconditional and a Peace that is ineffable within me, within all human beings and all that is—shining throughout all consciousness, all Hearts, the whole World, throughout the Cosmos.

In this compilation, I am sharing with you a life experience with the Angelic Beings of the Light and their messages, walking and working on my side as amazing loving friends, Divine Guides, and Healers. They have always conveyed to me that healing is remembering the pure essence of Life and its unity consciousness, the pure essence and Light in all beings and within my "Self".

We are surrounded by Holy Angelic Beings of Light eager to assist us with unconditional Love on our sacred path, supporting our awakening. We are all led on a path of reconciliation with the "Self" and all beings and all of Life. It is an awakening to true consciousness. True consciousness is experienced as you let go and let God, as you are free from thoughts and indoctrination. True consciousness holds infinite peace, love, joy, compassion, beauty, reverence, harmony, all divine qualities of God—a "Holy Presence" deep within your Heart, where truth resides, and where unity consciousness resides. It is pure Love.

Angelic Beings of Light have been walking with me and guiding me to Heavenly realms, where I was embraced by the most powerful Luminous Light, where I was healed in all my bodies, where I experienced my Higher Light, my Angelic Self, the oneness of Life, unity consciousness, unconditional

Love, in its perfection and purity. The Angels of the Light have asked me to share these experiences and journey with you, to inspire you to consciously discover who you are and reclaim your sacred power, your higher Light. They have shown me that there is no separation of any kind, that we belong to a global and universal Web of Light. It is a field of Light and unconditional Love, an intelligent web of Light, harmoniously orchestrated. They are guiding all human beings to listen to the holy voices of Father Mother God in their Hearts, the voices in Nature, the voices of Divine Mother Earth, and Father Sun, and Grandmother Moon—revering and embracing the sacredness of their true beingness, the sacredness in all sentient beings, all animals, insects, birds, the trees, the ocean, all of Nature's Intelligence, All That Is.

May the Angelic Beings of Light bless you to awaken to your pure being, and to the sanctity of all sentient beings and all of Creation.

I have dedicated my Life to be of service as an Angelic Channel Healer and Artist of Light. This has been a mission I have chosen before my birth, from the Angelic realms. In this lifetime, from my physicality, I was guided into higher dimensions of Light, to be a conduit of that Light, to remember and experience my Angelic Self—Love Light consciousness. All my bodies were healed on all levels, physical, emotional, mental, spiritual. The frequency within my physicality and all my bodies was raised substantially. I experienced pure consciousness, a Love that is unconditional, the Love of God in all that is, encompassing all of Creation. I experienced my Pure Being, my Angelic Self, and the Light of everything in Creation as ONE field and Divine Design of Love. Many Lightworkers today call it the Great Web of Light or Quantum Field of Light. I experienced my true essence of Light, the true essence of Life in the infinite Oneness of Creation. **The Angelic Beings of the Light are inviting you on that journey, your sacred path, to an awakening, to an ascension. It is the** discovery and embodiment of your Angelic Self—a complete reconciliation with your Self and Life.

Throughout the book, insights, prayers, and meditations are empowering your ability to delve fully within the deepest chambers of your Heart, blessing your whole beingness and your life with harmony, loving-kindness and peace—guiding you within the deepest presence of your holy being.

Important Guidelines: Your One Sacred Heart holds all your hearts in its field—also mentioned throughout the book as the "Heart", with a capital. The Heart holds the Consciousness and Divine Love from all your hearts. From your One Sacred Heart your minds are awakened to the One power of the Divine Mind. The Divine Mind and the One Sacred Heart are unified in all the Love and Unity Consciousness of Creation, working as ONE force of Love and reverence.

It is important to read this book slowly, rejoicing in the calming nurturing meditations, gently leading you to your Heart pure consciousness. Feel the energies, the forces of love infusing your hearts and minds and all your Beingness—awakening your One Sacred Heart. It is important that you write down the messages which are coming your way, also describing your feelings in your journal. Any time you wish, you may close your eyes between the words and sentences, to better experience and visualize the depth of the messages, the holy healing light frequencies, awakening you to the Presence of your pure being and the infinite oneness of Creation. Then write down your visions and messages. This process supports the activation of additional Doorways of Light, inherent to your beingness divine design. If you have questions, please write them down, and expect clear answers revealed to you from the deepest place of your Sacred Being in your meditations and throughout this book. Clear guidelines and insights are revealed to you as you allow a complete liberation of the Mind in communion with the Heart, a space of bliss and serenity. Write down the answers as they are revealed to you. With gratitude, realize how inspired you are on your sacred journey, to live your life of service, in bliss and joy, and unity consciousness.

Additionally, from my journey with the Angelic Beings, I share insights and experiences as a practitioner healer and channel, to inspire furthermore your path of Light in the Garden of Eden, exploring your infinite multidimensionality, the sacredness of your true nature in resonance within the Great Web of Light.

You will notice that I use the following words: God, Father Mother God, The Divine, Source, Lord, The Creator, the Love in all of Creation. Throughout the book, please chose the word or words which represent for you the consciousness of God, of the Creator, Elohim, that "Infinite Source and Consciousness of Unconditional Love", that Pure Essence of Life and Divine Intelligence, the Universal Web of Light, that Holy Light pervading all Life and Creation, the Creator of All That Is.

Within a sacred space, I invite Father Mother God, the Angelic Divine Guides of the Light, the Ancient Masters of the Light, the Luminous Beings, "the Ascended Masters also known as the Masters of the White Brotherhood", and the High Dimensional Star Beings of the Light, Nature's Intelligence, Divine Mother Earth and her Garden of Eden, Father Sun, and Grandmother Moon—ONE Unity Consciousness of Boundless Love. We are ONE in this **"Odyssey with the Angels"** — the Angelic Beings and Masters of the Light convey holy messages, prayers, meditations enveloping you with unconditional Love, infusing your space with radiant Light, inviting you to discover the One Sacred Heart and the Divine Mind.

From the union of the Divine Mind and Sacred Heart, you may reconcile with all aspects of your beingness and all of Life, letting go of pain and suffering. It is a time to rediscover your multidimensional Self in a new way, in a deeper way, from a renewed relationship with your Self, with all Beings, and All That Is.

The Divine Angels of the Light are walking with you, always, eager to be of service to you, with unconditional love. Their luminous wings are embracing you across the veils of illusions, freeing you and leading you, so gently, on a path of reconciliation with your pure being and All That Is, awakening your purpose and path of service, all the way to the One Sacred Heart, to God, to Source — to Home.

Thank you, dear Angelic Divine Guides, Luminous Beings for the blessings of these holy messages born from the Sanctity of your Presence, and Radiance, to liberate and awaken all Hearts, in furtherance of Global Peace and Harmony for all Beings.

While in contemplation, prayer, and meditation, I have been guided into higher dimensional realms of Light and embraced by the Light. These experiences are the catalyst of the Light work I have been guided to convey to the world, as an angelic channel-healer, author and artist, of service to all Life — in infinite reverence and gratitude.

You are on a path to embody your Higher Light, to dream the dreams of the One Sacred Heart, the dreams God has for you, in the oneness of unconditional LOVE. Doorways of Light have been unfolding. In their radiant Lights the Angelic Beings are gently leading you to a reconciliation with Life.

I am of service to all Beings and all of Life, in Namaste,
With all my love,

Sibli Essene, Angelic Channel

Chapter One

Conscious Living with the Angels

I was invited by the Angels to Sing in Heaven the Name of God:

One evening, just before getting ready to do my final prayer-meditation before going to sleep, I was listening to angelic heavenly songs and voices. My Heart was touched and in bliss, feeling and expressing in my Heart how much I would love to sing with an angelic voice, and with the Angels. I fell asleep permeated by that Angelic blissful Light energy, singing in my Heart with the Angels.

In the morning, as I was gently waking up from my slumber, a team of Angelic Beings appeared around me within a Chamber of Light and unconditional Love. Gently and lovingly, within that radiant Light, they guided my soul out of my physical body to take me to a place which felt like Heaven. There was unending Luminous Light and pure Love flow. The Angels gently guided me in the middle of their choir—multitudes of Angels—where I naturally started singing with them, with an Angelic voice, the name of God **"OM I AM ELOHIM!"**. The angelic voices were heavenly blissful, blended with instrumentals, heavenly sounds emanating from all directions. I couldn't see the musical instruments, but I could see multitudes of Angels around me in their radiant Light. I was looking like them, as radiant, and singing like them. I was in Heaven somewhere in the infinity of space, in the oneness. The Love frequencies were pure, infinite, of unconditional Love, infusing all my beingness—it was like singing in the Heart of God. I was in Heavenly realms singing within the embodiment of my pure Angelic Self with the Angels of the Light. It was pure bliss and unconditional love. I have no idea how long it lasted. There was no sense of time and space, only infinity and oneness. Then, as I was gently guided back into my physical body, the Angels whispered the following: ***"All That Is shall be yours!"***. I found myself in the same position in my bed, my whole beingness was glowing Light, experiencing unconditional Love, and infinite gratitude, still basking in the heavenly sounds and realms, in the Heart of God.

Your wishes and intentions hold power. Creating and co-creating from Love, for Love, and in Love, in the purest intentions of reverence, sacredness, beauty, and harmony, brings forth Heaven on Earth, in the oneness of the Heart. I have missed the heavenly realms so much that the Angels gave me this heavenly gift. My wish has been to sing like an Angel, and it came into manifestation in surprising holy ways. I experienced my angelic voice as a pure Angel of Light, standing in the center of a choir of Luminous Angels from Heaven and in Heaven. I was in Heaven living in the sanctity of my pure Angelic Being. There was only Love. There is only Love.

Every day, in my meditation, I see myself as a pure radiant Angelic Being, singing with the Angels of the Light the name of God "OM I AM ELOHIM", experiencing the Divine Love of God, of the Angels of the Light within heavenly realms, basking in the most radiant Light. I then see all people as Angelic beings, singing with the Angels in this radiant holy Light.

Angels and Archangels are Luminous Divine Beings, forces and consciousness of God's Love Light, Peace and Joy, Wisdom, Truth and True Knowledge, Beauty and Grace. They emanate and radiate the realms of the Heart, Father Mother God Pure Holy Love Light Divine Qualities. They are assisting us to know about unconditional Love and

to invite the Presence of God within our Hearts and our lives to be revealed. They are assisting us to know God, Source, The Divine, The Creator, the Infinite Essence of Love and Divine Design of Light inherent to all of Life.

The Angelic Beings of the Light with the Archangels have multitudes of functions as Divine Guides, holding bridges of Light between dimensions, as Healers, and Messengers, supporting a communion of Love and Beauty in all Life and Creation. They are in communion with Luminous Beings of Light, Stars Beings from the highest dimensions of Light, and Masters of the Light, Ascended Masters assisting in the Oneness of Creation—in the Heart of God's Pure Love. They are all working together taking on different missions, guiding humanity to higher consciousness—guiding humanity to Ascend. For example, an Archangel may take the role of an Ascended Master to assist humanity in a specific way—like Archangel Michael. They all have multitudes of tasks and are "multidimensional pure consciousness" of service in all the Love and Light of the Divine, in the Heart of God.

The Angels of the Light are messengers and guides— transmitting holy messages from God. They are guides, opening doorways for humans to access higher dimensions of Light to commune with Luminous Beings and with God. They are eager to assist you in all aspects of life with all their Love and profound respect. They sense when you need them, they are walking in the oneness of life with you. They assist you multidimensionally to develop your direct communion with Source, with God, with the Sanctity of Mother Nature, and all beings.

The Angels and Archangels embody Divine Qualities of God, often with specific missions. They are Luminous Suns, pure Love Consciousness, always of service to "Humanity Ascension", in the oneness and infinite divine qualities of Father Mother God.

Listening in meditation to your One Sacred Heart, emphasizes your awareness of their holy presences. You are never walking alone. Listen to their beautiful messages and learn to be aware of their loving presences from your Heart infinite consciousness of Love.

Angelic Beings of Light and Luminous Guides are assisting you in all aspects of your life—they are Guardian Angels and Divine Guides. They always wish to assist you and interact with you in loving honoring ways. It is beautiful to invite their love and divine qualities of God in your hearts and minds, to invite them to walk with you, to experience their powerful loving support, divine messages and guidance, their high frequencies, and healing Light. They emanate the Love, Light, Peace, Joy, infinite qualities of the Divine. They are eager to assist you and work with you multidimensionally from the Heart of The Divine, the Heart of God, to take you Home—from the embodiment of your pure being into the Heart of God. All Divine Qualities of God intrinsically live within you. Your Angelic Divine Guidance team are assisting you to awaken these Divine Qualities from your One Sacred Heart.

Dear Father Mother God, dear Angels and Archangels, Luminous Guides, Guardian Angels, I awaken all of my spirit, all of my consciousness, and all of my souls, all of my bodies, minds, and hearts, and all of my beingness to your Divine Consciousness of boundless Love and luminous Light—to lovingly cross bridges of light and doorways of light leading to my One Sacred Heart and to the experience of your Holiness. Thank you for holding me within a sacred space in the highest Love Light Peace of the Creator. **May all aspects of my beingness be infused with the forces of Love sourcing from the Creator's Temple of the One Sacred Heart.**

Despite any situation you are experiencing and despite any painful emotions and feelings, the moment your invite your highest Angelic Divine Guides-Luminous Masters, and you embrace their loving support, guidance, and healing, they are with you to assist you in miraculous ways in the Light and Heart of God. Open your Heart and invite them to be with you and help you. Faith, trust, hope, and gratitude in your Heart, ease their communion with you, even if you are in pain and distress. **It is only your mind which can interfere with your connection and communion with them.** They are always on your side, eager to assist you in amazing miraculous ways, in all the Love that is.

Angels and Archangels, Luminous Guides, Guardian Angels, "WE" are with you to lovingly guide you to raise your frequencies. We are gently leading you through doorways of Light and across bridges of Light. You may communicate with us any time and all the time. We are eager to give you answers, to offer our support, strength, courage, clarity, guidance, and healing, in love and honoring. We are guiding you and offering you multidimensional support, in ways which always serve your highest good and the highest good of all. We know the dreams God has for you.

Step by step, your faith and gratitude keep opening doorways to higher frequencies and dimensions of Light—inviting expanding love into your hearts. The love into your hearts and One Sacred Heart is a pure Light frequency and flow, activating your pineal gland and pituitary gland with the hypothalamus. All three regulate various hormones functions balancing the nervous system and other systems in your bodies, also supporting the opening of your third eye, welcoming your capacity to awaken and to be pure and clear channels.

In the next chapters, we shall explore guidelines to sustain these channels clear—the channels throughout all your bodies, spiritual, mental-emotional, and physical.

In order to assist you, the Angels of the Light would like that you write a list about your Heart's wishes—wishes to express compassion, to sustain peace and harmony, to be free from pain, and the like. Describe clearly what you are wishing for. All your wishes and intentions have to be sincere, altruistic, of love and compassion. You have the capacity to be free from pain and traumas blocking your joy of living—write clearly about the healing you wish to experience on all levels and aspects of your life. This process is helping you to pay attention to your emotions, feelings, and thoughts, and to connect deeper within your Heart—so that you may manifest a new path of harmony, beauty, and peace. You are learning to be conscious. You are learning about your free will to manifest a new reality from the qualities of the Heart. With the Angels of the Light, you are learning to live with consciousness and to co-create with Source. They are taking you on a Journey into the Heart of God. It is a path of Light.

The Angelic Divine Guides are inviting you to dream from within your One Sacred Heart. The Dreams of the One Sacred Heart are the Dreams God has for you—you are co-creating from that place in the oneness, in all the Love that is.

Open a sacred space by calling in your Angelic Divine Guides of the Light and Luminous Divine Masters and say: *I call for a Ray of Luminous Light and Pure Love from Source, from God, to flow through me, holding me in communion with the Heart of Father Sun, the Heart of Grandmother Moon, and the Heart of Mother Earth. From the Stargate of Father Sun, the luminous Light illuminates my path in the World, supporting my awakening and enlightenment. Grandmother Moon is nurturing my inner child within my Heart in communion with the Heart of Mother Earth, holding all of who I am in sacredness and love. The chakras under my feet are activated, inviting an infinite flow of Light and Love energies, connecting my whole beingness at deeper levels with the*

Heart of Mother Earth Core Crystal — connecting my sacred being with all the Sacred Places on Mother Earth in her Garden of Eden.

In meditation, experience that Ray of Luminous Light holding you in communion with the Heart of Father Sun, from the Stargate of the Sun, and the Heart of Mother Earth core crystal. Choose to experience this divine communion of Love within the Garden of Eden of Mother Earth. The Angelic Beings are assisting you in every step, in the discovery of your divine Self and divine design of Light.

I dwell within a Ray and beam of crystalline Light, lovingly holding me in communion with the Heart of Father Sun and the Heart Mother Earth. With all of my love, I ground into the Heart of Mother Earth Garden of Eden core crystal. The Angelic Beings from all six sacred directions are sustaining my whole beingness within their luminous rays of Light. Within this beam of infinite Divine Light suffusing all my bodies and hearts, I bask in the peaceful energies permeating all of my beingness, calming my minds, and opening my hearts to embrace the Love of the Divine. From the seventh sacred direction within my Heart, blissful boundless Love Light rays are radiating, in synergy and divine communion with the Luminous Web of Light and Life.

Within higher frequencies, in all that Luminous Light and Love, it is a perfect space to express clearly your Heart's desires. Getting in touch with your inner being is important, to find peace, love, harmony and happiness, to express compassion, to forgive, and to heal. Then ask for the Angels, Archangels, and Luminous Beings and Masters of the Light, to come forward and commune with you, guiding you, and supporting your Heart's wishes. Say: *Basking within this Luminous Radiant Light, I am in communion with Father Mother God and my highest Divine Angelic Guidance team. I am receiving all the support that is needed now. I am blessed. In my Heart I express boundless gratitude.*

Embraced by the Light of God, and with the Divine Angelic Presences, it is a perfect time to express clearly your wishes and to write them down. They might be about healing, forgiving, balancing, clearing, harmonizing, love-compassion, loving your beautiful Self, oneness-prosperity flow, loving all beings, living in reverence and compassion, your work of service, and experiencing with ease and grace the dreams God has for you. Express the desires of your Heart, with simple words. Feel and visualize from your Heart, as you would already live them fully with joy and gratitude. Dwell into that space of joy for as long as you wish. Choose for your wishes and dreams to nourish you with joy, trusting that Father Mother God has amazing dreams for you. Offer all your dreams to God, to the Light. In that faith and trust, you are offering your path to Father Mother God — to Divine Mother Earth, to all the Love That Is. You are welcoming a higher power of infinite Love, compassion, beauty, and grace into your life. You are ONE with that power. Your Divine Angelic Guides and the Luminous Beings are walking with you — they are assisting you in the highest Light and in all the Love That Is. *I let go and I let God!*

Creating and inviting a sacred space of Light and nurturing Love in communion with your Sacred Heart to illuminate your days and all of your work, supports an energetic flow of higher frequencies, also contributing to the manifestation of the dreams God has for you.

At this time, the creative forces are powerful. Therefore, from the embodiment of your Angelic Self and in the presence of the Angelic Divine Guides and Masters of the Light, together in LOVE and honoring, you may co-create within the infinite Forces of the Highest Light of God. We invite you to create a holy space from the highest consciousness of honoring, compassion, and Love. We know your dreams, we know the dreams God has for you, we know what serves your highest good and the highest good of all. Your work of service is of the sacred and is unfolding in the Light and Oneness of Creation.

Open your Heart to all the Love that is, invite your highest Divine Angelic Guidance team to assist you and walk with you—let go and let God. You shall receive the guidance, healing, and blessings from a group of Angelic Beings, or from one specific Angel or Archangel, or Luminous Master—in the infinite Light of God. You shall receive blessings of Love and guidance from Ascended Masters, Luminous Angelic Beings, or Star Beings of the Light.

Your faith, your trust, energies of kindness toward your Self, and your capacity to feel love, to listen and see in your Heart and from your Heart are holding you into a Higher Light. From your Sacred Heart in communion with your Third Eye Chakra, you always see TRUTH. Pay attention to the nature of your feelings and thoughts, invite faith, and let everything unfold fluidly. Do not try to control but observe and feel from the Heart consciousness. In meditation, pay attention to what your Angelic Divine Guides are transmitting to you, in multidimensional ways. They may appear around you, or you might see them in your third eye and Heart. They may take you to heavenly realms and/or whisper holy messages and teachings. Listen from your Heart. Free your minds and observe with peace what comes to you. Feel all their nurturing unconditional Love infusing you and expect beauty, harmony, healing peace, and divine synchronicities. When you are ready go back to your daily occupations, do it in peace and with peace, with a sense of sacredness. Be patient and calm and repeat the prayers-meditations every day and listen to your Heart. Feel the Love of Father Mother God expanding in you, pay attention to the synchronicities, to what manifests in your life. Write what you feel and experience in your journal.

You are learning to become conscious of the sacred being of Light you are, of the unity consciousness and sanctity of Life. Your Angelic Divine Guides wish to enlighten your path with joy, beauty, and peace, uplifting you to an experience of your pure being. They assist you to move closer to God and to your God Self. They are guiding you to LOVE from the Oneness of the Heart.

Sit in nature or visualize that you are in your favorite place in nature, bathing in the Light rays of the Sun. Place your hands on your Heart center, breathe into your Heart, and say: *I invite the Love and Peace of God, of Source into my hearts, into my minds, in my One Sacred Heart and Divine Mind, in all my beingness, in all my relationships, in all aspects of my life. I open my One Sacred Heart and Divine Mind with infinite gratitude, basking in the oneness and all the Love of Creation.* Your Angelic Divine Guides are holding you in all that Sun Light, nourishing you with LOVE Life Force, guiding your journey toward a path of Light. Take your time to allow your whole beingness, hearts and minds to feel the Love and Peace of God permeating you.

In meditation, it is essential to develop pure love toward all aspects of your "Self" from the deepest chambers of the Heart. Ask your Angelic Divine Guides to hold you in the highest Light of God, to show you how to embrace who you are with unconditional love and compassion. Love yourself exactly how you are, free from all judgments—choose kindness and Love. To sincerely feel deep love within you and toward your Self is power. Love is power and freedom. Love is Light and Harmony, Joy and Peace. To love who you are, is the foundation of your well-being and happiness. You will then be able to love other people and all beings unconditionally. You will feel safe, free, and empowered to create and co-create with Source in all the Love That Is. Embrace all of who you are with unconditional Love.

Chapter One

Enjoy living within a sacred space of Light, conscious of the Light of God, and of your holy communion with Heaven and Earth, and of the Light of all four sacred directions. Invite your Divine Angelic Guidance team — who are eager to assist you — to come forward to clear your path, "in the past, present, and future", so you may walk free, on a path of Light — in the Light of the Creator. Say: *In the highest Love Light Peace of God, thank you dear Divine Angelic Guides and Luminous Masters, for clearing all of my paths multidimensionally, past, present, and future. Permeated by the Light of God, I forgive myself, all beings, all of life. I forgive completely. I ask for grace, to infuse all my bodies, consciousness, and minds — I come into the realization, that the essence of life wants only LOVE for me and is of LOVE. I ask Father Mother God with my Divine Guides to assist me and to show me how to sustain all of my paths clear, free from interferences in all time, space, and dimensions, multidimensionally. Thank you for clearing all of my paths and for showing me the way to a path of Light. I invite infinite Divine Love Light, and blissful Peace to suffuse and infuse all of my paths, past, present, and future, and all my bodies and all aspects of my life. I dwell in infinite gratitude.*

We are your Angelic Divine Guidance team, "we" are with you, walking with you. We are Light and you are Light. We are eager to walk and co-create with you in all the Love that is, the Magnificent Web of Light! We are supporting you in the embodiment of your higher Light, the unity consciousness, so that you may walk in harmony as equals with all beings and all consciousness. We are leading you to an experience of your oneness, in the Garden of Eden of Mother Earth, into the dreams God has for you. You are true consciousness embodied. We see who you are, we love you and we honor you. You are LOVE.

When you raise your frequencies with spiritual activities, such as breath work, meditations, prayers, yoga, altruistic thoughts and actions — when you choose faith, gratitude, and compassion, and as you delve into the gentle divine presence of your being, it becomes easier to experience the communion with your Angelic Guides. As you raise your frequencies, moving closer to your pure being, you are also slowly moving closer to the frequencies of the Angelic realms, you are merging with your Angelic Self. You are unifying with higher dimensions of Light, the Light of Source.

Deeper and closer you move into an experience and embodiment of your highest Light, greater becomes your ability to see and perceive all that surrounds you, as pure consciousness, multidimensional, peaceful, and as holy realms of Lights. You are developing the capacity to experience higher realms of Light consciousness where the purity of your being communes with Luminous Beings, Angels, and Archangels, and Nature's Spirits.

I open all of my hearts and my Sacred Heart, inviting the highest Light and Love and Peace to shine through me — rejoicing in the holy presence of the Angelic Divine Guides and Masters of the Light, in the Oneness of Life.

We, Angelic Guides of the Light and Master of the Light, we are welcoming you within a boundless all-encompassing sacred communion, the pure essence of Life, a sacred geometry of Light uniting all beings and all of Life. We are holding you so gently within our luminous crystalline wings into heavenly realms, inviting you to sing with us the Holy Names, in joy. We rejoice in your presence. We are activating your crystalline wings and bodies, so that you awaken to the "Sacred Holy Presence and Space of your One Sacred Heart". This, then eases our communication and communion, and abilities to bring forth miraculous synchronicities into your lives.

As your Heart consciousness expands, you have naturally access to vibrations of unified Love, the experience of your True Self, your Pure Being, your Angelic Self or God Self. We are walking with you and we wish to assist you on your sacred path to be of service with ease, grace, and joy. You hold infinite divine qualities, to be of service, to be nourished by life and to nourish all of Life with Love. As the bees are fundamentally contributing to Life on Earth—as the wolves are, as the trees are, as the birds are, and absolutely "all that is in Creation" are benefactors to Life, you are to contribute to the sanctity and flow in nature, in life, in boundless reverence and love consciousness. This is your awakening and purpose.

Dear ones, with all our love and honoring, we would like to remind you repeatedly of your deepest purpose, why you came into "being" on Mother Earth. We would like to remind you of your inherent role to be benefactors to all of Life, to Divine Mother Earth, to all beings, in ways that are infinitely nurturing, honoring, and loving—where your holiness, awareness, and true consciousness are revealed and expressed boundlessly.

Your Angelic Divine Guidance team, "we" have been inviting you to communicate with us, and to express your Hearts' desires and dreams with joy, without any trace of despair, but from a place where your trust and faith become unshakable. We are with you on that path of Light, in honoring, with all our Love and respect. The dreams within your Hearts are the dreams God has for you. Life, Father Mother God have them multiplied and blessed in infinity with Love and Joy—and boundless possibilities.

In ceremony, within a sacred space, I invite my Divine Guidance Team, Angels, Archangels, Master of the White Brotherhood, to bless with the Love and Peace of God my minds, hearts, and beingness, my home, living and working spaces, all aspects of my work, all my relationships, all the people in my life, and all of Life.

All is consciousness. Smudge your space, home, and property with sage or palo santo as you invite the Blessings of God's Love Light Peace and Harmony. *I ask that all energies and frequencies which do not belong to the pure original sacred essence of my space and beingness be released into the Light of God, completely and multidimensionally. I ask that God Peace, Love, and Light infuses all my hearts, all my minds, all my bodies and beingness, all places and spaces of my living and working spaces and all of my work, and all my relationships. Thank you, dear Father Mother God, dear Divine Guidance Team, Angels, Archangels, Masters of the White Brotherhood for blessing with the Love, Light, Peace of God all of my minds and hearts, all my bodies, all of my home, living and working spaces, all aspects of my work, and all my relationships. Thank you for blessing all beings, all of Life, Mother Earth – thank you for your Divine Blessings of Peace and Harmony, in all the Love That Is!*

Repeat the above prayer until you experience and witness the healing Light flowing and infusing all your cells, bodies, field, and until your space feels pure and clear—until you experience blissful peace. Everything is possible in that space of Light, especially miracles. Angelic Divine Guides and Masters of the Light are walking with you on that multidimensional path and journey in the radiant Light of the Divine. A blissful serene state of mind invites unity consciousness, where you are infused by an infinite Holy Presence, where there is co-creation with God, with Source.

In the holy presence of the Divine Angelic Beings and Masters of the Light, within that unified field of Light and unconditional Love, as a healer and angelic channel, I have experienced continuing healing miracles for my clients, including animals, and for myself. Divine Mother Earth, Father Sun, and Grandmother Moon with the Angelic Beings and all Divine Guides, and Nature's Spirits are always eagerly collaborating within the unified Field of Light to all energy Healing-Light work—in the unity of Life pure consciousness of Love. It is a place and matrix where waves of Light, of unconditional Love, goodness, harmony, and grace prevail and multiply in infinity.

In the healing sessions I offer, with my clients, we are naturally expanding within the universal field of Light where our whole beingness is permeated by the Love Light of Source, where the sanctity of life is recognized. It is a realization for all communications and interactions, and for every present moment to be valued as sacred and blessed with boundless Divine Love—the Love of God forever omnipresent, omniscient, and omnipotent. In a healing-channeling session with my clients, basking in the Light of Father Mother God, we are divinely assisted by the highest Angelic Divine Guidance team and Masters of the Light, where I am a clear conduit of Light, in ways which serves my clients' highest good and the highest good of all.

Throughout this compilation, with the infinite guidance of the Angels and Great Masters of the Light, you are invited into these realms of Light to awaken to your Christ Self, your God Self, your Angelic Self. You are guided to embody the pure and clear interdimensional being of light, healer, awakener, and channel, you are. In your breath work, meditations, communion with Divine Mother Earth, the Angels of the Light are inviting you to be free from all mundane indoctrination and doubts, freeing the minds—permeated by a profound sense of transcendence, enlightening your hearts and minds with pure consciousness, leading to a self-realization of your Pure Being.

Imagine all beings awakening to their Divine Multidimensional Essence of Light—all Hearts fully open in compassion and unconditional Love, in communion with Divine Mother Earth, Nature's Intelligence, and the Divine Guides of the Light. Your altruistic-philanthropist energetic Self is naturally expressed in all the Light and Love of Creation.

Your Angelic Divine Guidance team never forces any communication and communion with you. This communion inherently exists and is, and it is your free will to embrace it or not on your path. We respect your free will and assist you in the most loving, gentle, and honoring ways. More you raise your frequencies easier it is for us "your Angelic Divine Guides of the Light", to commune with you, work with you, and co-create in love and harmony. We are always walking with you, but when you invite us into your lives and hearts, this communion is emphasized. You are always cherished and held with unconditional Love. Our Hearts are overflowing with Love and honoring for all beings, and all of Life in Creation.

Create a Sacred Space: *I commune with the highest Light Love Peace of God, calling a beam of Golden White Crystalline Light embracing me and permeating my whole beingness, holding me in communion with Father HEAVEN, the Heavenly realms of God, the Heart of Grandfather Sun, the Heart of the Galaxy, the Heart of the Universe, and below me with the Heart of Mother Earth Core Crystal – a communion with the Light of Creation. With all my love, in honoring, my Heart and beingness are in communion with the Heart of Father Sun and the Heart of Mother Earth Garden of Eden. I invite into my space, into my hearts and minds, the Divine Love Light Peace Joy consciousness of my Angelic Divine Guidance team, Luminous Beings and Masters of the Light. I experience their sacred Love and Light as a holy flow permeating my whole beingness and all aspects of my life. The Angels and Archangels of all Four Sacred Directions are holding me so gently in their Luminous Light Rays, in the Highest Light of Source. I pause and rest, to feel the Love of Source permeating my whole beingness. Thank you, dear Father Mother God, Divine Angels and Archangels, and Luminous Beings, and Divine Masters of the Light for infusing, suffusing my whole beingness, all my bodies, minds and hearts, and all my relationships with your unconditional Love, Light, Peace, Joy, Wisdom, Clarity, Truth, and Beauty. I trust and place my whole beingness in the Heart of the Creator. Life's boundless creative forces manifest synchronicities that are leading me exactly where God wants me to be, to live the dreams God has for me, in the infinite oneness of Creation. I let go and I let God.*

The Light of the Divine, the Light of Source, the Light of God is always present, forever permeating your beingness, your space, and All That Is. When you create a Sacred Space, you become conscious of that Holy Presence, that boundless Love, Light, Beauty, and Peace intrinsic to all of Life, to Creation.

It is important that you believe from within your Heart that your prayers for love and harmony are already in existence and manifested in Divine Miraculous ways. Invite faith into your Heart and liberate your prayers into the Light and Heart of God.

Dear Angels of the Light and Luminous Masters, thank you for clearing all of my past, present, and future paths and journeys, in all time, space, and dimensions from all interferences blocking Light on any level. Thank you for infusing my paths and journey, past, present and future, with the sanctity of your Divine Presence of unconditional Love and sacred radiant Light, peace, joy and harmony, grace, abondance, reverence, compassion, and beauty. May my paths be a Sacred Path into the highest Light and Love, reverence and gratitude, in the Garden of Eden, in the Heart of God. May my Sacred Path glow as a radiant sun, a radiant light. On that Sacred Path, I embrace who I am with unconditional love — I radiate a pure Light into the whole world. The radiance of my Light and of my Sacred Path belong to the Light of God, inherently shining in the oneness of Life. This radiance illuminates the world and all beings, in furtherance of peace and harmony. I am Light. I am a Ray of Light in the Radiance of God. I am expressing profound gratitude to my Divine Angelic Guides, to the Luminous Beings, to all of Life, to Mother Earth and Grandmother Moon, and Father Sun, all Angels and Archangels from all sacred directions. Thank you in all the Love That Is!

As you acknowledge our Luminous Angelic Presence of Love and call us into your Hearts and lives, with love and gratitude, you are raising your vibrations. From that place of

Love, you naturally experience increasing waves of love embracing you and illuminating your Hearts and bodies and path. In that space, everything is possible. You may experience miracles in the most surprising ways, revealing harmonious synchronicities.

We, your Divine Angelic Guides are the embodiment of Love and so are you! We live in true consciousness and we wish to lead you on your authentic sacred path.

We wish for every human being to recognize the reality and truth, that you are the embodiment of unconditional Love, that you are as holy as we are. "All That Is" sources from God, from the Essence of Creation, a pure and infinite consciousness of Love, a Holy Divine Design of Wisdom and Perfection—an intelligent Matrix of Light, Pure Consciousness.

We are bridges of the highest Light guiding you to experience God/Source, your Divine Angelic essence, in synergy with the Love essence and divine design in all of Life and Creation. As you embody the highest expression of your being and essence, you have found your truth and you become bridges of Light—your Heart experiences its true nature of unconditional Love.

We are walking with you and assisting you, as you awaken on your path of service, and as you embody your higher Light. To live as conscious beings of service to all of life, epitomizes the natural state of your true essence, your pure being, dear ones.

Your "Highest Divine Guidance Team" consists of Archangels, Angels of the Light, Ascended Masters, Masters of the Light, Luminous Beings, High Dimensional Star Beings of Light, Nature's Intelligence such as Devas, Fairies, and all Nature's Spirits—you are all held in the Oneness with Father Heaven, Grandfather Sun, Divine Mother Earth and dear

Grandmother Moon blissful presences and support. We all shine as One, within one matrix of LOVE. We are eager and happy to interact with you in ways which serves your highest good and the highest good of life, in the oneness, forever in reverence, honoring, and unconditional love.

When you call upon your Divine Guidance team, Angels and Archangels and Masters of the Light, to come forward to assist you and assist in a specific situation, know that the right Divine Angelic Beings of the Light are naturally coming forward to support your journey in Love. With time, you innately develop your personal ways to commune with your Divine Angelic Guides. Trust your Heart, trust what you feel in your Heart. Your Heart tells the Truth.

Dear ones, we are walking with you to show you how to balance and raise your frequencies, inviting the Divine Mind to be in communion with the One Sacred Heart. Listen in your Hearts dear ones, hear our whispers and songs, God's words, Mother Earth songs, the love and messages of the animals and the love in all of life surrounding you. From these holy communions, feel the love, joy, and peace permeating your bodies and all aspects of your life.

May these words inspire you to invite us, your Angelic Divine Guides, to walk with you and to embrace the infinite power and qualities of the Sacred Heart. On such sacred path, you know that you are never walking alone, you feel safe. May the self-realization of your sacred path, leads you to an unequivocal faith, an embodiment of your Angelic Self. We are honored and blessed to play with you, within the realms of pure consciousness, where the sanctity of Life resides, in the One True Love and Heart of God.

The Angelic Divine Guides of the Light, the Great Masters of the Light, Ascended Masters, also known as the Masters of the White Brotherhood, and the Highest Dimensional Star

Beings of the Light, with all of Nature's Intelligence, we are on your side as One Luminous team of Angels, one supreme unity consciousness of boundless Love in your Sacred Hearts and Divine Minds, the Love of God, throughout this **"Odyssey with the Angels"**. We love you!

You are never separated from your Divine Angelic Guides, only your minds and thoughts know how to interfere in that communication and communion. Your Sacred Hearts in union with your Divine Minds know how to cherish that divine communion with your Angelic Divine Guides, and all the Luminous Beings, in the infinite Love of Life. You are safe and you are loved unconditionally.

May your FAITH be doorways of Light for the Creator of the Universe with the Angels of the Light to bless you with peace, with miracles, supernatural opportunities and synchronicities, unfolding the dreams God has for you, in all the Love That Is.

All challenges and pains, guilts, despair, aloneness, resentments, jealousy, are opportunities to cross the bridge of illusions, transmuting these energies, to discover the miracles of wisdom on the other side, strengthening and expanding the body of Light—moving closer to God, to The Divine, to Source.

Where resides the deepest "pain and despair" dwells also the brightest Light awaiting to be seen and embodied. Your Divine Angelic Guidance team with all Luminous Beings are assisting you on that journey of liberation, as you shed all illusory thoughts and beliefs, inviting the embodiment of your Pure Being.

We are walking with you always and we love you unconditionally.

Chapter Two

Healed by God and Blessed by the Light

We are going back in time, when I was living in Hawaii. It was the third year, I was living on islands in the Pacific, without internet, TV, and cell phone. My living space in nature was clear. I was often waking up in the morning with my third eye activated, witnessing all my surroundings as glowing fluid light including my body. The first time this happened I thought that there was something wrong with my eyesight. But after a few minutes I realized then that I was experiencing a higher state of consciousness where I could see the essence of life, a Light energy in all that is. I could witness everything as fluid Light, including all furniture, walls, floors, nature, all was fluid Light. I was transported within the Garden of Eden of Mother Earth, where there is infinite Light, beauty, and harmony. All that is and exists and all we see, is of a divine design of Light energy at its essence and has consciousness.

I met a man who was my father in a past life, a Chief and Shaman from an Indian American Tribe. In that past life, as his daughter, I was a Medicine Woman, a healer within the community. We first shared deep insights and were praying together. He had amazing gifts but soon I could clearly witness that he didn't have at that time, the capacity and willingness to use his powerful gifts in honoring ways and with integrity. Unfortunately, this happen when a person holds on to traumas and karmic issues, and/or also suffers from PTSD, from three years in the Vietnam war. We met for specific reasons to complete one another destiny on some levels. But the question is always the same in such situation, are we both going to surrender to God, to Source, and pray in complete trust, to open the Doorways of Light to the Miracles in the making? He had access to different avenues to release traumas and heal, as I was myself on a profound healing journey. He was not ready to do anything to face and release traumas and pain. I choose then to continue my journey without him.

To continue my healing journey and work of service I couldn't keep any contact. He was energetically invading my space with overpowering draining energies, even so we didn't meet in person any longer. It was an energetic invasion keeping me in a way captive, probably to control and dominate — my life force was being drained. I was aware that he didn't know the harm he was causing. All was energetic. Living in Hawaii was a very happy time for me, but suddenly all my joy of living was gone, and all my bodies were hurting, even looking at the sun was hurting. I felt naturally heartbroken and all my beingness was hurting. I knew that he was deeply wounded, not aware of his power, and all I wanted is to be free energetically, to be whole again. He was using his "shamanic" abilities inappropriately, to hold me captive energetically, instead of using his shamanic gifts from his Heart, in sacredness, in honoring, true consciousness, to be of service in All the Love of Creation. He had forgotten the sacredness of his ancestors' gifts, not aware of the pain and suffering he was perpetuating. All I could do is pray and trust.

I was aware in my Heart, that no one around me in the human form could help me with this, only God with my highest Divine Guidance team could free me and make me whole again. I was for sure on a shamanic journey calling in the Great Spirits of Light.

In my Heart, I was asking Father Mother God, and the Angelic Beings of the Light, and the Luminous Divine Masters to free me and heal me completely. My Heart kept receiving a profound inner knowing that only my direct communion with

God/Source, with my highest Divine Guidance Team will help me to be free from that ordeal and heal me. I was in a state of constant prayer, in absolute faith. Somehow, I could sense that through this extremely painful experience I would receive gifts of wisdom and increase my capacity to move deeper into the God Self. I knew in my Heart that the help would come from God directly, and from my Angelic Divine Guides, from the Luminous Beings. I couldn't see any other way, even so my life force was constantly shattered.

When I think back, what was interesting is that I was sincerely placing the whole situation in the hands of God. Allowing God to be in charge — trusting that my "free will" to invite "Faith and Love", would lead me to a higher state of consciousness, an initiation. This man had his free will too and there was nothing more I could do. I could only help myself. There is a point we cannot interfere with other people's choice of consciousness and choice of action and we cannot judge. We can only take care of ourselves, see and honor the sacredness on all paths, find peace within, and see others in their Higher Self Light. Each person experiences what he or she has to discover and know, to evolve, grow, and awaken — a natural process taking place within the Light and Oneness of Creation. Within this process there is a space for free will. No judgment can take place there. There is only Love.

It was such a beautiful summer in Maui. I loved living there. At that time my parents were letting me know that they were getting ready to spend a month vacation in Zermatt, Switzerland. I was completely guided to ask them if I could visit them there for a little while, and they invited me to join them. As I was getting ready to leave and travel to Zermatt, I was still in a constant state of prayer, calling in the highest Love Light of God, in communion with my highest Divine Angelic Guidance team. I was telling myself that all of this shall pass, that I am and shall "receive" directly from Father Mother God, all the help I need on all levels. I trusted somehow that I would come back to myself, be free, and healed. I held that trust and faith deeply into my Heart at all times. I had no idea how and when I would be set free and healed but I just knew in my heart, that it would happen — there was no other way.

Visualizing, arriving in Zermatt soon and meet my parents again, was giving me somehow a sense of being supported with nurturing energies. However, the pain kept lingering, and I kept praying and praying with a profound faith in my Heart.

Zermatt has been my favorite place on Earth and to this day. The cosmic-telluric frequencies are super high and holy there. To me it always has been a doorway to higher frequencies of Light, as of course many other places on Earth are too. It is a place in the mountains, the Swiss Alps, of infinite beauty — opening people's hearts.

When I arrived in Zermatt, my parents were waiting for me, we were quite emotional to see one another again. I was arriving from the other side of the planet. I could see that my Father was not feeling well, he was not being his own self. My sisters informed me via telephone, that since the passing of his brother he has been depressed, experiencing signs of decreased appetite. Right away, in my prayers, I was now asking to be healed so that I could also take care of my Dad. At that time, I was already doing healing work, but I was so depleted and hurting that I couldn't do anything for him in the moment. I was praying nonstop for my parents and for myself to be healed and whole again. I never said anything to my parents about my feelings and experience — I didn't want to add more pain to whatever they were experiencing.

The night, I was calling in the Love Light of Father Mother God and my Angelic Divine guidance team, the Great Masters of the Light to hold me within a healing double tetrahedron of golden white crystalline light, connected at their bases (similar to a star tetrahedron). Lying in my bed, I was visualizing myself floating in the middle of that chamber of crystalline healing light, praying for guidance and healing with absolute faith in my Heart.

Every night, with my Mother, we were observing large orbs of light in the sky. Almost every night they were appearing in different places above the little town of Zermatt, or sometimes above the mountains. It was astonishing to observe these large orbs of light — holy forces of Light, Divine Presences. I was tuning into these Divine Presences, opening my Heart in prayers. As soon as I was lying down in my bed, I was placing myself within this double tetrahedron of crystalline healing light. I was calling for the Angels of the Light to hold me in the highest Love as I was gently falling into a deep slumber. I kept praying-asking non-stop with complete faith to be healed completely and so that I may also help my Dad.

One night I woke up around 4:00 AM, it was still night. From my bed I could contemplate beautiful mountains covered with snow. That night there were two large orbs of light in the sky above these mountains. I was touched by these unexpected presences, two globes of light emanating amazing beautiful energies. I was in prayer and meditation contemplating them. Suddenly from each orb, beautiful swirling rainbows of light moved toward me and into my Heart. I was astounded and in a state of increasing hope and faith. I knew in my Heart that my prayers were heard. I continued to visualize myself within the chamber of Light and felt asleep. Later on, in the morning, when I woke up the orbs were gone, and the sun was shining. The whole day, I was still in deep pain but had so much faith, connecting from my Heart to these Divine Forces of Light, the Light-Life Force in Nature, and all of Creation, God/Source.

The following night, lying in a warm cozy bed, I called the highest Angelic Beings of Light and the Great Masters of the Light to hold me within a Healing Chamber of Light, a double tetrahedron of crystalline Light. As I was floating in the middle of that Chamber of Light, suddenly, Luminous Angelic Beings came around me, guiding my soul, so gently, out of my physical body. I didn't resist, because I felt completely safe and loved unconditionally. I was indeed welcoming all that holy unconditional Love taking me away from the pain. We moved through the wall with ease. Fully aware and conscious, I was experiencing bliss, a profound sense of nurturing loving support. With the Angelic Beings, we travelled into the sky to the cosmos, throughout time and space. This is how it felt like. We arrived somewhere, into another world, I didn't know where.

There was a deep sense of peace and harmony, as I arrived on what seemed a deck in front of a vast glowing deep blue ocean. Not far from me, I noticed other beings. I was completely aware to be traveling outside my physical body, and I was wondering if they would see me. They noticed me almost right away and welcomed me. They talked to me telepathically. I then understood that they were also here in spirit form. One of them send me this message telepathically and in French: "Welcome, welcome, we hope to see you again!" I acknowledged with gratitude his kind words.

Then, I was guided to move into the air, traveling, floating in the air. Once in a while I could see other bright spirits/souls floating, moving in different directions—there were also flying objects with wings around me, passing by.

I arrived in a special place in nature, with the feeling of landing into a Holy Sanctuary. I was naturally guided to stand my arms along my body and hands open forward as I was expecting to receive a benediction, and it happened. Suddenly, I was filled with this incredible force of Love and luminous Light, in my Heart space. This incredible Light and Love was infusing and permeating my whole beingness, all my aura, all of my soul and consciousness, all my bodies, encompassing my physical body lying in my bed in Zermatt. I could feel that every aspect of my beingness, all my bodies and minds were receiving this Light force energy of unconditional Love. As I was standing holding the same position, I kept saying over and over: *"Thank you! Thank you! Thank you!"*. My Heart, all of my beingness was overflowing with infinite gratitude, unconditional love, and bliss.

I have no idea how long it lasted. Suddenly, I was guided to move in the air to another place but within the same Holy Sanctuary. One more time, I was guided to stand in the same position ready to receive a blessing and it happened again. My Heart space was again filled by that incredible luminous force of Love-Light-Peace, a luminous Light. I was completely embraced by a force of unconditional Love and Light infusing my whole Beingness—God's Love all-encompassing and unconditional. All I could sense is the purest Love and Peace and Bliss, glowing from my Heart, permeating me completely. Nothing else was existing just that pure energy of unconditional Love and I was ONE with it—a consciousness of the purest Love Light emanating from me, in the oneness of Creation! One Light! One Love! Oneness!

I didn't know how long it lasted. From my Heart I couldn't stop repeating: *"Thank you! Thank you! Thank you!"* Then I heard in my Heart the Luminous Beings whispering gently: *"It is time to go back!"*.

I was embraced by Light and in a state of infinite Bliss as I was guided to leave that Sacred Sanctuary. I was again moving in the air in that world which felt safe, holy, and familiar to me. Once in a while, I was again passing other spirits/souls, moving in the air, going in different directions. And once in a while, I could again observe flying objects with wings passing by. Suddenly as I was looking down, I witnessed the landscape beneath me, becoming smaller and smaller as I was moving away from that land—with the Luminous Angelic guides. I again travelled throughout the Universe, throughout time and space, to reach the Earth. Completely conscious, with the Luminous Angelic Beings, we moved through the wall of my room and I naturally came back into my physical body, in my bed. I was back on Mother Earth, in Zermatt, and I was completely healed, blissful, permeated with unconditional LOVE, and free.

My whole beingness was glowing Light, in a state of blissful peace experiencing unconditional Divine Love, a Oneness of the Sacred Heart. Heaven on Earth! All sense of separation or pain was gone. I was completely free, completely healed, and completely whole. Lying in my bed, in the same position, I was endlessly repeating *"Thank you! Thank you! Thank you!"* I also knew that I could help my father, and this was a tremendous relief. I was whole, in blissful communion with my Pure Being and all of Creation and my Divine Guides. **I was experiencing my Angelic Self, fully conscious of my Light, of who I am. My bodies were glowing. Nothing of a lower frequency could touch me in any way, there was pure Love, blissful serenity. Throughout this experience my bodies' energy and vibrational frequency were substantially raised. It was an initiation, also sourcing as a gift from past lives, to continue my angelic work of service, also as a shaman. This is how this was presented to me.**

I had faith in my Heart that God/Source, my Divine Guides of the Light, would help me and heal me, but for sure, I couldn't have imagined this amazing Holy journey and experience!

Holding infinite gratitude in my Heart, I slept then peacefully. I was back to myself in a new way, a blissful divine way, experiencing my Higher Self, Angelic Self. I received an activation of my pure essence, a holy empowerment, an awakening of my pure Being, and I was free!

In the most painful powerful challenges, the brightest Light is always ready to shine, on the other side to raise our frequencies, when we have the willingness and faith to wait for it. We are always on a trajectory to the Light.

Do not judge your challenges, but from your Heart look for the gifts of wisdom. You are blessed!

The next day I wanted to help my Father as soon as possible. I was guided to wait the evening when he went to bed to get a good night sleep. I then asked him if I can do a healing on him and pray for him and he accepted. He closed his eyes, lying cozy in his bed. As I was calling the highest Love and Light of God, with the Angels of the Light and Masters of the Light, I was guided to move my hands in the air above his body. My hands were emanating healing Light. His eyes were closed—he was falling asleep. My hands were the hands of Luminous Beings, Angelic Healers and Ascended Masters such as Master Jesus. Many holy hands were working with me in the highest Love Light to clear completely his auric field from energies which didn't belong to him. To make his field whole again, he was filled with healing life force, luminous Love Light frequencies from God. During the healing process, I could see, and sense energies being released into the Light as all his bodies were infused with unconditional Love Light Peace. When I witnessed the brightest Light moving through my Father, saturating all his bodies with this infinite Divine Love, I knew the healing was complete.

My heart was touched with profound gratitude. I prayed for my Mother too, to give her support and healing. The next day my Father's appetite came back, he was serene and feeling himself again. My heart was infinitely touched by all the gifts and miracles and to this day. I felt blessed, experiencing this deep communion of Love, of oneness consciousness, multi-dimensional and holy. My heart was filled with unconditional Love for all beings and all of Creation. I understood that my trust and deep faith led me to miracles — I allowed and invited a Doorway of Light. I knew in my heart that the help would come, I was open to any form of healing from God, from Source, from the Divine. In my faith, I let go and let God.

The experience was so vast, so divine and multidimensional, of unconditional Love, expanding my consciousness within the infinite universal grid of Light. My heart space and whole being were filled with this powerful unconditional Divine Love and Luminous Healing Light. Despite all the pain, my faith to be healed and set free, raised my frequencies in such a way that Divine Angelic Master Guides, the Luminous Beings could easily commune with me. My faith was a Doorway for them. It has been clear to me that "faith and gratitude" are energies and frequencies of pure Love in action, leading to miracles. Faith and Gratitude are of the Light and Doorways of Light where Life expands with boundless Love — and from where all dimensions are expressed in their enlightened aspects — it is Love co-creating!

There is a healing force of unconditional Love and Light and Peace intrinsic to all of Creation. That force of Love heals all Hearts and all bodies. That force and flow of infinite unconditional Love lives within every human being, all beings and All That Is. It is for every human being to cultivate faith and search deeper and deeper within the chambers of the Heart.

That unbounded force and flow of unconditional Love lives inherently within me, within my Heart and everywhere in Creation. It is ONE with me. It is ONE with you.

In all the challenges and profound pains, know that on that same trajectory, there are Love Light miracle energies in action, eager to be revealed. Are you inviting faith? Are you delving into the Heart to seek for the wisdom and Love in all your pain? Are you calling in all the Divine Love and Light, the Angelic Beings of Light, the Luminous Divine Masters despite the pain? Are you praying to Father Mother God, to Source, to the Divine Love, asking for help, support, healing, guidance, awareness, wisdom, blessings of Love? Are you opening all of your hearts and your One Sacred Heart to experience all the Love that is, healing blessings on all levels of your life? Are you listening and are you ready to receive? Are you ready to love all of who you are? Are you inviting faith?

I am in holy communion with the highest Light Love Peace Bliss of God, a beam of Light permeating me completely. I am a Ray of Light in the Radiance of God. In all the Love that is, I nurture within my Heart devotional faith as my prayer. It is a reconciliation with my "Self" and therefore with all of Life. I accept that I AM LOVE.

Pain and challenges are energies holding profound wisdom, true knowledge and empowerment, guiding you closer to your God Self, your Christ Self, your Angelic Self — and to the embodiment of your higher Light. They are blessings and gifts. You are intrinsically on a trajectory of Light, to the Light, to freedom, to peace, to joy, to unconditional Love.

Look for the wisdom, for the gifts, with gratitude, and embrace the pure loving being you are. You are to do great work in all the Love That Is!

Every person that comes into your life has a gift for you and you for them. It can be a gift in disguise. It can be a challenge which shall transform your life completely, in ways you could not even imagine. Look for the lesson, for

the wisdom, always. Do not judge and listen — listen to your Heart.

I delve into the Love of the Heart surrendering to a Higher Power, a Holy Power within me, inherent to all of Life. It is a force of Love all encompassing. I am listening to the voices of Love and Wisdom. I place myself and my life in the Hands of God, of the Divine, in the Holy Heart of all Hearts. I am Love.

I practice feeling love and gratitude for absolutely everything that surrounds me, dwelling within a communion of Love with the whole world. I am living within a sacred space as a pure conscious being. In all the Love That Is, I feel safe and I am safe, fully present, honoring the Sacredness of Life, Nature's Intelligence, the Luminous Beings, and all Pure emanation surrounding me.

In my meditations, I often go back to the Doorways of Light where I was embraced by the Luminous Light, a Love that is pure and unconditional, experiencing my Pure Being. These are places and spaces where I was healed, my frequencies were raised. I received divine messages and teachings, basking in the Light of God, the Light of the Angelic Beings and Great Masters in the ONE Light and ONE Love. I am able to experience over and over again this consciousness of oneness, the immensity and boundlessness of Source, of Life unconditional Love. If you have been embraced by the Light, and healed by the Light of God, you may go back to these experiences in your meditations. They are Portals of Light, for you to expand and embody at deeper levels your Divine Light, the Light in all of Life — One LOVE Consciousness, the Sacredness of your Being, the Sacredness of Life.

Chapter Three

You are the Oneness

It is the realm of the Heart consciousness, an infinite Presence of Love, which leads me to peace, to the truth, true knowledge, wisdom, unconditional love and compassion, and to the true realization of who I AM. I am Love in the Oneness! In that oneness, I care for others and I love unconditionally. In that oneness, I discover the true power to be of service from the compassion and pure Love of my One Sacred Heart.

Life expresses itself, as a sacred geometry of Light, a breathing and fluid multidimensional divine design and field of Light forever expanding and evolving in joy and harmony. Your essence is pure consciousness within the universal Web of Light. You are pure consciousness within a global universal Divine Design of unconditional Love. You are safe inherently basking in all that Love.

Humans' thought-forms have taken over, also forming an "energetic saturation" from mundane indoctrination, mostly based on fear, manifesting massive energetic illusory veils, covering up a pure reality, an essence of Life and Light that is a pure clear synergy of unconditional Love. When humans' thought-forms, feelings, and beliefs are not from the truth of the Heart, they are often energies and frequencies of fear, insecurity, violence which have nothing to do with the essence of life. These energies, then source from an illusory state of separation, ignorance, aloneness, and despair, leading to destructive patterns and suffering. Wherever you are, the Light is holding you always. The Angelic Beings and

Luminous Masters are guiding you to see the Light from the deepest chambers of your Heart.

You are creating in every moment on a multidimensional trajectory and field of Light, where doorways of Light are awaiting you.

When the vibrational reality you choose in every moment, is mostly of a low frequency, your nervous system becomes overloaded with stress. You may feel disconnected, lost, hopeless, helpless, and discouraged. In such chronic states your bodies become more vulnerable to multiple health issues. All your bodies are linked to your brains and hearts. What you choose to see and focus upon, has consequences in all aspects of your life. Your thoughts, your beliefs, your words are "energy frequencies in action". Pay attention to your consciousness. Choose to be conscious of your true essence, your sacredness and the sacredness of Life.

Absolutely everything in creation is in essence of Light energy. All of your bodies, your fundamental energetic essence, and your hearts are of "love light peace joy oneness" frequencies. When your minds are not reflecting these inherent divine love frequencies, you become increasingly more disconnected from your true being. It becomes painful on all levels, when the "mind-thoughts-ego" is denying the joy and love inherent to your natural divine design.

This is why it is fundamental to fully understand your sacred geometry, your divine design, your oneness with all of Creation—to know and experience who you are dear ones. You are not your thoughts. Most thoughts do not reflect the highest truth and reality. When your minds are not listening profoundly to your hearts' messages, your thoughts are generally taking you away from the true reality of your Pure Being, and of Life.

It is important that you know who you are and discover your One Sacred Heart and Divine Mind—that you know the power of Love which resides within your Divine Design, to create and co-create in harmony the dreams of your Heart, the dreams the Creator has for you. From this self-realization, you are naturally walking through Doorways of Light leading to miracles. Discover the forces of Love in action within you. These forces of Love hold the infinite Oneness of Creation. You are the Portal of Light.

Create a Sacred Space: *I commune with the highest Light Love Peace of God, calling a beam of Golden White Crystalline Light embracing me and permeating my whole beingness, holding me in communion with Father HEAVEN, the Heavenly realms of God, the Heart of Grandfather Sun, the Heart of the Galaxy, the Heart of the Universe, and below me with the Heart of Mother Earth Core Crystal—a communion with the Light of Creation. With all my love, in honoring, my Heart and beingness are in communion with the Heart of Father Sun and the Heart of Mother Earth Garden of Eden. I invite into my space, into my hearts and minds, the Divine Love Light Peace Joy consciousness of my Angelic Divine Guidance team, Luminous Beings and Masters of the Light. I experience their sacred Love and Light as a holy flow permeating my whole beingness and all aspects of my life. The Angels and Archangels of all Four Sacred Directions are holding me so gently in their Luminous Light Rays, in the Highest Light of Source. I pause and rest, to feel the Love of Source permeating my whole beingness. Thank you, dear Father Mother God, Divine Angels and Archangels, and Luminous Beings, and Divine Masters of the Light for infusing, suffusing my whole beingness, all my bodies, minds and hearts, and all my relationships with your unconditional Love, Light, Peace, Joy, Wisdom, Clarity, Truth, and Beauty. I trust and place my whole beingness in the Heart of the Creator. Life boundless creative forces manifest synchronicities that are leading me exactly where God wants me to be, to live the dreams God has for me, in the infinite oneness of Creation. I let go and I let God.*

Keep sending love to your whole body and beingness in that way. Keep sending love to every aspect of who you are, until deep within your hearts and beingness you feel solace — until you feel LOVE, and LOVED, until you feel completely safe. Take all the time you need to experience that comforting sweet nurturing energy permeating you, a Love that is unconditional within you — a profound Love, awakening your higher Light. Then, expand that unconditional love all around you. Feel a communion of Love with All That Is — cherish and honor all beings and feel love and sacredness for the whole World and Mother Earth.

The love resonance you cultivate within you and within your hearts and One Sacred Heart, is the foundation of your earthly experience. Deeper is your love resonance, and more miraculous your life shall be. This holy Love sourcing from within you, emanates a unique resonance from your Heart, where there is oneness, a oneness consciousness, a unity consciousness with all of Life. It is a force of unconditional Love, Grace, Honoring, and Beauty.

Your Heart resonance holds your unique spiritual identity, a unique sound. There was a time, humans were recognizing one another by their unique Heart resonance frequency. Awaken beings have that capacity to perceive people's Heart unique identity sound resonance.

Every day, it is important to become conscious of the relationship you have with your Self. Learn to love and honor every aspect of who you are. From your Heart feel that pure love permeating your whole beingness. It is a meditation nurturing you and healing you completely. You are generating light life force from deep within. It is a flow of love awakening a profound sense of well-being, calmness, and compassion. Within your divine design you hold the natural capacity to be conscious of your holiness and true essence, in all the love that is—so that you may live from a place of love-unity, feeling safe, loved, and cared for.

Honoring all of Life from a consciousness of unity, and co-creating with Father Mother God, from the Essence of Life, is a place of true consciousness—where you naturally invite the revelation and manifestation of the Garden of Eden within your One Sacred Heart. It is a place within you, in your hearts, where you are consciously breathing with Mother Earth pure essence of Love, conscious of the sacred laws, conscious of your oneness—and therefore living, breathing, feeling, taking action on higher frequencies of light, love, peace, faith, compassion, and oneness. This sacred place is born from the deepest chambers of your hearts, and your One Sacred Heart, in communion with the Heart of Father-Grandfather Heaven-Sun, the Heart of Mother Earth Garden of Eden and Grandmother Moon—in communion with the Heart of all beings, all consciousness, the Heart of all Creation, the Universal Heart, the Heart of God. It is LOVE!

In order to become fully connected with your true Self, your pure being, find the courage to face all your emotions and feelings, pains and traumas. Allow yourself to embrace your emotions and feelings with unconditional love, without judging. Focus on your Heart capacity to LOVE freely, without condition. Invite the highest Love and Peace of the Angelic Divine Guides, of Father Mother God into your beingness—the nurturing Love of Mother Earth, into your minds, and hearts, all your bodies and cells. Nurture a deep LOVE relationship with your "Self". You are illuminating your path.

Breathe into your Heart, and from your Heart, meditate on what you wish to create and experience—write down and describe your thoughts, visions, and feelings. Face your feelings with courage, and nurturing compassion. Know that your feelings and wishes, require your nurturing love—

a profound love you nourish within the deepest places of your being. Sit in the silence of your Heart and learn to love from these deepest places. Love and honor who you are fully, and from that place you shall discover furthermore the immensity of your inner being and Sacredness.

From your One Sacred Heart, hold your prayers in meditation within your sacred space where you are embraced by the Light of God and held by your Angelic Divine Guidance team. The Healing Angels of the Light, Luminous Master Healers are assisting you. Relax and bask in that Sacred Light and that Pure Love from God, consciously — then feel energies which do not belong to you gently leaving you, transformed and transmuted by the Light into higher frequencies of peace. You are reconnecting slowly with your pure being, in the oneness of the universal grid of infinite LOVE — awakening to all the dreams God has for you. It is a gentle process you may repeat as often as you wish. Within such sacred space you are held in a chamber of Light where healing and miracles take place naturally.

You are releasing layers and layers of energies which never belonged to you but came into your field temporarily to teach you, to bring you wisdom and awareness, to awaken you. Meditate on the wisdom and awareness you have received and write down the messages that are revealed to you. Your divine design is in the flow of your sacred path, on a trajectory revealing its wisdom, awareness, blissful peace, beauty, grace, all the way to the Holy Light — your Higher Light radiance.

Releasing and letting go is a process that has to be addressed in a gentle and nurturing way, in prayer and meditation, and sometimes, with the help of a caring loving spiritual practitioner healer-channel. Be committed to love your Self unconditionally, and to love unconditionally all beings. Be kind and gentle with your thoughts and with all of you. Letting go of all that doesn't belong to you, is a point of no return heading to bliss, harmony, joy, oneness—an experience of unconditional love, a reconciliation with life and with your beautiful Self.

Create a sacred space, always by inviting the infinite Love Light Peace of God into your space—Father Mother God Infinite Divine Qualities. From the Stargate of Father Sun, visualize the Luminous Pure Love Golden-White Light of God, enveloping you completely and anchoring you with unconditional Love into the Heart of Mother Earth Garden of Eden. Feel your deep profound communion of Love with the Heart of Mother Earth Core Crystal. Then, call upon your highest Divine Guidance Team, The Angels of the Light, Archangels, and Luminous Beings and Ascendent Masters of the Light. Feel in your hearts the boundless Love of the Divine Presences.

Place your hands on your Heart and say gently to your inner being: *I love you. I love you. I love you. I open my hearts to receive all the love that is! I open my hearts to experience all the dreams that God has for me in the highest Light possible! I embrace that silent peaceful space within me, where all thoughts vanish, a serene space, which seems so vast and boundless, a space which also seems of infinite creative possibilities. I then tun into the voice of my Sacred Heart, the voice of the Angels, the voice of the Creator, God within me and all around me, from Mother Nature, Nature's Intelligence, the voice of Mother Earth. I express clearly my Heart wishes and dreams. I hear truth, the true voices of Life, of Mother Nature. They are holy sounds and songs embracing me and permeating my whole beingness with holy Light frequencies. The breath of Life is breathing me in all the Love That is, revealing a holy presence, a Light within me which has been untouched by the world of physicality. It is Divine Love and Peace, where the dreams God has for me are pure and unfolding multidimensionally. This Holy Presence and Peace within me belong to my Pure Being, my Angelic Self, and to the Oneness of Creation. I consciously embody that Holy*

Presence with infinite gratitude. I am whole. I am a crystalline angelic being of God. I now relax and bask in the Heart of God. I am forever safe and loved.

In the middle of a heavenly choir of Luminous Angels, I stand, held in boundless Love and sacred Peace, within the sanctity of the One Sacred Heart, in the Oneness — we sing the Name and Glory of God.

I invite the Blessings of Peace of Lord Buddha, the Christ Consciousness-Master Jesus Consciousness within my Heart and all of Life, expanding in infinity, in all the Love That Is in Creation. Embraced with unconditional Love, the Light of my Pure Being is revealed.

The remembrance of your true Self is vast and unlimited. It is a place where you naturally surrender to recognize the gifts of wisdom which have been bestowed upon you. Your daily spiritual practices, such as meditation, contemplation, breath work, yoga, and the like, along with your spiritual support group, epitomize a path of Light leading to a Self-realization and awakening. Your Heart knows what you need! Ask your Heart dear ones! God with your highest Divine Guidance team, the Angels speak in your Heart. You might be guided to look for support from a spiritual practitioner healer and angelic channel, or to attend specific spiritual classes or seminars. Listen to what feels of Love into your Heart.

Within a sacred space, I call my highest Divine Guidance team, Angelic Beings of the Light, for their love, wisdom and divine guidance to whisper into my hearts and minds, to walk with me, to assist me in all aspects of my life. They are guiding me to experience God, the Love of God in Me and All That Is, for my path to be of Light and Harmony. Dwelling in infinite gratitude, I feel safe and loved unconditionally. I am in Peace with all of Life.

I live within a sacred space, conscious of the Sacredness of Life. I feel safe and I feel peace, in the presence of God's Pure Love permeating my Beingness in every present moment – a Divine flow extending to All That Is in Creation.

Thoughts, emotions, and feelings represent energies which are powerful forces in action, especially if similar thoughts, emotions, and feelings keep occurring. They are then absorbed energetically by all that is, vibrating throughout infinite energetic levels of Life. You are in general, mostly responsible for birthing specific frequencies and images which are manifesting within the world of physicality. With all our Love, we would like you to understand and remember your inherent power to create. Therefore, it serves your highest good and the highest good of all to co-create from love, joy, compassion, and reverence for yourself, for all beings, and all consciousness. Remember your oneness, always. If ever there are painful forces coming into your life and you sincerely feel you have no power to release, you have to imperatively call for the Love Light Peace of God with your highest Divine Angelic Guides to intervene, to contain them and to release them into the Light of the Divine.

You have the inherent capacity to embrace, commune, and co-create within the divine original matrix of Light and Love, a divine intelligence of oneness and Light, the fundamental essence of Life. Simultaneously, you also have the free will to participate in the creation of another energetic matrix based on separation, aloneness, and suffering, which is illusory. This is a matrix created by chronic illusory thoughts of fear, despair, aloneness, and separation. You have the free will to experience unity consciousness, bliss, and truth or to experience on going illusory feelings of despair, aloneness, and suffering. Everything is energy consciousness. Even if "from your minds" you separate yourself from the fundamental essence of Life and Light, this pure essence and unity consciousness always is and will be. You belong to the oneness of Light and Life.

If you truly wish to live as a conscious being, dwelling in states of peace and oneness, it is important to attend daily to your spiritual, emotional, mental, and physical bodies equally, with infinite loving-kindness. The power or your thoughts, feelings, intentions and actions, holds powerful frequencies. But the moment they are all sourcing from the Oneness consciousness of the "Divine Mind and One Sacred Heart Matrix" of unconditional Love, you are free. You are then contributing to the awakening of all Hearts. You are a Lightworker, an Awakener, a Shaman.

Your oneness with all of creation, with all beings, and Divine Mother Earth is so perfect, so profound, so all-inclusive, so infinitely powerful and complete, that the moment you understand it fully, you shift, and you do whatever it takes to be unconditionally loving and honoring to all of Life. You are then living in true consciousness. It is an amazing feeling. It is bridging Heaven and Earth—it is inviting Heaven on Earth. This is why dear ones it is important that you understand who you are along with the world which surrounds you. You belong to a sacred geometrical divine design of Light, a global divine intelligence, a universal consciousness of Light, Love, and Beauty. As you combine physics, spirituality, breath work, yoga, and meditation, your awareness expands. Write about the feelings and messages sourcing from your Heart—honoring them and honoring you. Listen to your Heart, this will expand your consciousness, and contribute to activate your channeling abilities.

Your daily meditations naturally invite the experience of oneness—a communion with the essence of love within you and in all life. In your spiritual practices, you move through Doorways of Light, conscious of your heart space, where the One Sacred Heart is activated. Your One Sacred Heart encompasses all your hearts within an octahedron of turquoise light, in the center of your chest. In the center of your Heart, the Vesica Piscis resides, from where the Flower of Life expands, encompassing your Merkabah. It is your divine vehicle of Light, your divine sacred geometry of Light in communion with the universal cosmic great Web of Light. (You may read my first 2 books to know more about these topics: "Twelve Doorways of Light, A Portal to Your God Self and Sacredness of Life"). Your energetic sacred geometry is a Doorway of Light and a Chamber of Light from which you have the ability to travel throughout higher dimensions of Light and realms of Light multidimensionally, from where healing miracles occur. You don't necessarily need an out of body experience to be healed by God, by the Light. I was healed several times in both situations, in body and out of body.

Healing occurs naturally in a state of complete trust where I let go completely and let God. I call upon the Healing Light of God and Angelic Master Healers. Suddenly a Holy Luminous Light force of pure Love flows through all my bodies, entering the top of my head all the way to my feet and entering Mother Earth — a powerful flow of Luminous Love Light embracing me, healing me, and rejuvenating me completely. You may ask Father Mother God and your Divine Angelic Guides for such healing, any time.

If you wish to experience your divine design and travel out of body to higher dimensional realms of Light, it is important that you come from your authentic Self, holding a high and pure purpose to love, to heal, and to embody your pure being. If you hold in your Heart an aspiration for a specific altruistic mission of Love, which serves the highest good of all, the Luminous Beings and Angelic Star Beings of the Light will show you the way, permeated by the highest Love that is. It is important to hold a consciousness of integrity, a commitment of reverence, in your minds and hearts, in all aspects of your life, and in all your spiritual practices including out of body travelling experiences.

The essence of your request has to be pure, has to embrace a high purpose which serves the highest good of all. Create a sacred space of Light when you proceed with any spiritual work and breathe aware of the Sanctity of Life in every moment. To prepare for astral travel, you invite the Angels of the Light, Archangels, and Luminous Beings from high dimensions of Light to guide you and be with you always — you are within a Chamber of Light, the Light of God. I have met people using their astral travel capacities and gifts in inappropriate ways, ignoring healthy boundaries. It is important that you use your gifts in loving compassion and respect, honoring yourself and all beings. It is crucial to hold a sacred space of pure Light and infinite honoring in your work, and in every aspect of your life — it is living from true consciousness and within the grace of unity consciousness, honoring who you are and all beings.

I am committed to live within the pure consciousness of my Heart, honoring my sacredness and the sacredness in all of Life.

It is possible that suddenly your Divine Guidance Team of the Light wishes to give you special gifts — Divine gifts you are ready to receive, supporting your path of service. With unconditional Love, in infinite honoring, in your meditations-prayers, they might gently guide you out of your body within a Chamber of Light, leading you to beautiful realms of Light. This has happened to me several times. **There was and is only unbounded Love, Bliss, Harmony, and infinite Peace.**

When you have an out of body experience and you don't feel safe and loved unconditionally, if you have doubts about who and what is in your space and field, it is important to pay attention. You are in the Highest Purest Light of God or you are not, there is nothing in between. If you have doubts and feel uneasiness or even fear, listen to the messages in your Heart. Be aware that the beings in your space, are then not your highest Divine Guides and Angels, but they are entities with a completely different agenda. They are lost and are in a way playing around, looking for ways to go back Home. All is of Love! Remain calm and take action right away through powerful prayers. Call upon Father Mother God and your Highest Divine Guidance team. In your faithful prayers, it is easy to come back to the true Divine Light of your Holy Being, to a pure and sacred space. Have clear intentions in your prayers to dwell always and forever in the Highest Light and Love of God, and to embrace with unconditional love your higher Light pure being. Within a sacred space and basking in the Light of God, speak aloud to these foreign forces—if possible, burn some sage: *You are not allowed in my space. My space is of the highest Light of God. I order you to leave me and my space and home now and forever. I call upon the forces of Light Love Peace of God, and my Highest Divine Angelic Guides and Master Guides of the Light to release "all energies which do not belong to me and are not of the highest Love", into the Light of God — to take care of them and to free me and hold me in the Highest Love Light Peace of God possible. I am within a Chamber of Light. Thank you for restoring God Peace, Love, and Light, Christ Peace, Love, and Light into my hearts and minds, into my space and home.* Pray with gratitude and invite faith into your Heart.

Repeat these prayers until your space is clear even if it takes 30 minutes or an hour for your space to be free and filled with the purest Light. From such experience, life is showing you that it is a time to learn to love who you are in a more profound way, completely and unconditionally—and to raise your frequencies by engaging in life with awareness from the Love of the One Sacred Heart. Invite faith and gratitude into your hearts. Remember that you have free will, but in that free will, life is always naturally leading you to awaken to an inner awareness and true consciousness of who you are. All is Love!

Life is naturally guiding you to acquire a devotional-sacred communion with all of who you are, by leading you within an awareness of the Sanctity of your Being. This process awakens a communion with the highest forces of Love, a communion of Love within you and within the unity consciousness of All That is in Creation. With time, your perception and experience of "the real you", from where you recognize your beauty and sacredness in unity with the pure essence of Creation, is revealed as a force of unconditional Love. Life is Love and you are Love. You are longing to experience and express LOVE fully, because it is your pure natural state. It is an intrinsic biological spiritual calling for every human being.

Meditation within a Healing Chamber of Light — experience "out of body travelling" in all the Love that is: In prayer and meditation and within a Sacred Space, you may call for a Chamber of Healing Light. Call for the Highest Love Light Peace of God, of the Divine to embrace all your bodies and fields and space. Ask your Angelic Divine Guidance team, the Luminous Beings and Masters of the Light who are assisting you, to hold you within a Chamber of Healing Light in the middle of a double tetrahedron of golden white crystalline Light. You are lying flat horizontally within this double tetrahedron of crystalline Light, unified at the base. You are floating within a chamber of radiant Light. As another option, lying or sitting, you may choose that experience within a luminous star tetrahedron, the Merkabah. Sincerely, from your Heart, ask in prayer for the divine healing, teaching, and activation you wish to experience, to be of service. It only works if you are sincere in your Heart. Invite Father Mother God Divine Love, Light, Bliss into your beingness, hearts, and space. The Angelic Beings are assisting you in all the Love that is. Your faith and capacity to be authentic, in integrity, and to create a beautiful nurturing sacred space, invite Doorways of Light. It is important that you take time to prepare your space, minds, and hearts in love and honoring. Ask to always be held by your highest Angelic Divine Guides and Luminous Beings, in the Highest Love Light of God possible, in the Christ Light, in the Light of Lord Buddha, the nurturing Love of the Divine Mother—within that Healing Chamber of Light. Breathe the Love and Light of God. *From the deepest Chambers of my Heart and with Grace, I anchor "Truth, Peace, Wisdom, Beauty, Love, Authenticity, and Harmony". I Listen to my One Sacred Heart, basking in all the Love That Is.* Enjoy your miraculous journey.

About 25 years ago, for the first time, I was naturally guided to practice such meditation within a Chamber of Light, lying flat horizontally within this double tetrahedron of crystalline Light, calling my highest Divine Angelic Guides. In my prayers and meditations, I asked for help, to be healed and free, to come back to myself, to be whole again. I knew in the deepest places of my Heart, that my prayers were heard and would be answered. I had no idea what God with my Divine Guidance team had for me. My prayers were answered in Divine miraculous ways. I knew in my Heart that I would be healed directly by God, embraced by the Light and guided by Luminous Angelic Divine Beings. I received a gift of Love.

In such meditations you may also be guided to sit in the lotus position. That you are lying down flat or in the lotus position—it is important that your spinal column is straight and that you are comfortable. A few times, as I was in meditation, "Leonardo Da Vinci with his Golden Ratio (Vitruvian Man) sacred geometry", came into my third eye and Heart consciousness and I naturally positioned my arms and legs in that way. Then the Healing Light Love Peace of God moved through me, a flow of pure Love, rejuvenating all my bodies and minds, raising my frequencies. As you listen to your One Sacred Heart, you are divinely guided, always, in all the Love that is.

Deep within the One Sacred Heart consciousness there is a profound sense of belonging, Love, Oneness, feeling

safe and supported, a Doorway from where your multidimensional holy being is expressed—a Doorway from where your Divine Design expands in the Oneness of Creation. From this place of consciousness, you are co-creating in the Light, with God, with the Divine, conscious of your holiness. You are then a medicine man or medicine woman in service to all of Life, living in the Heart of God— living the Oneness of Mother Earth and Creation.

Healing Meditation to Oneness: If you keep experiencing despair, aloneness, feelings such as "I am never good enough, I never do enough, I feel pain about this event or this person", sit in the silence of your Heart with these feelings and emotions. Create a sacred space by calling in, the highest Love Light Peace of God with your highest Divine Angelic guidance team, Luminous Beings, the Angels and Archangels of all six Sacred Directions with their Light rays and crystalline frequencies. Ground deeply with all your love, into the Heart of Mother Earth Garden of Eden. Feel the Love of the Mother and of the Sacred Garden, and the Love of your Angelic Divine Guidance team, the Love of Father Mother God, into your hearts and minds, enveloping you completely. Allow these holy Love synergies to move through you. As you are basking in the Light of Mother Earth in her Garden of Eden, you may ask for the Luminous Spirits in Nature and Angelic Beings to guide you deeper within the Heart Core Crystal of Mother Earth Garden of Eden. Bask in the Garden of Eden nurturing Love and ask for the loving guidance of a "Sacred Tree" to show you "THE WAY" of the One Sacred Heart. Let go completely and trust. Experience the holy consciousness of the Tree in your One Sacred Heart with infinite gratitude and reverence. Experience a purification in all your bodies and fields. You are embraced and healed by the LIGHT. Your whole beingness glows. Your Luminescence is expressed in the Oneness. Within the Heart of the Sacred Garden, you may dwell and play within the crystalline frequencies, allowing your beingness and energies to flow within the holy waters and among the radiance of the Sacred Crystals—healing you. You are free and whole.

Healing Journey: Within your sacred space, observe, with unbounded loving compassion, any painful feeling and energy lingering in you and around you in your field. Accept these feelings and embrace them in your Heart with infinite compassion and loving kindness. Spend time deepening your inner love communion. Observe these illusory feelings and energies softening in intensity and fading away. If some of these energies are still lingering, lovingly see them now in front of you floating as glowing flowers. You then come into the realization that they are free to shine in all the Light and Love that is. With infinite compassion in your Heart, call upon the Light and Love of God, with your Guardian Angels and the Luminous Beings who are assisting you. They are saturating your whole beingness with a Luminous Crystalline Light of infinite Peace. Feel the unconditional Love and Light and Peace permeating you. Now, witness how the Love of God, of Mother Nature, of the Angels and Luminous Beings, is suffusing the glowing flowers floating in front of you, with a Luminous Crystalline Light of infinite Peace—dissolving them in Rainbows of Light. Experience a flow of boundless Love moving through you and around you. You are free. Give time for your cells and bodies to be permeated by that healing Crystalline Rainbow Light. Breathe with consciousness all that Holy Light, Love, and Peace, infusing your whole beingness, inducing a profound sense of relief and peace. Sit in that Holy Light, in the holiness of your Presence, God within you—sit in the Oneness of Creation. Repeat several times this meditation until you experience that Divine Light and Peace permeating your whole beingness, freeing you completely. **Enjoy the wholeness and truth of your Presence. Enjoy the authenticity of your Oneness.**

Invite faith into your hearts and One Sacred Heart. Faith invites doorways of Light, healing miracles, and synchronicities to naturally take place multidimensionally.

Held with unconditional Love by my highest Divine Guidance team, Angelic Beings and Luminous Masters of the Light, I now sit in the stillness and listen. I understand, how important it is to sit with my feelings within the unconditional love and sacred space of my Heart, breathing in the Garden of Eden where I feel safe, loved, and cared for. The Garden of Eden lives within me, in my Heart. It is the place where my authentic Self is revealed. I feel safe living within my authentic Self, my pure being — there are no more illusory beliefs and illusory projections. I am ready to love all of who I am. I feel unconditional love for all beings and all Life. From my intrinsic oneness with the Divine, I embrace my worthiness in the full consciousness of my Heart. I breathe with Divine Mother Earth in her holy Garden, and Mother Earth is breathing me, nurturing me and loving me. I feel pure love for all of Creation and from all Creation.

I give myself that gift to be in communion with my whole beingness, from a place of nurturing compassion, and unconditional love. I invite the Light from Source, from the Great Father Sun and from Divine Mother Earth, to embrace me completely. I live in the Garden of Eden where I enjoy the infinite Light, Peace, Love, Beauty, Grace, and Unity consciousness. With all my love and gratitude, and from my Heart, I am anchored in the Heart Core Crystal of Mother Earth Garden of Eden. My whole beingness is infused by the most healing nurturing energies of the Great Mother. I bask in that luminous Light and unconditional Love in delight and boundless gratitude. In the Garden of Eden, I rejoice, sing, and dance with the Angelic Beings of Light.

I am free. I let go and I let God. I open my minds and hearts, and my whole beingness to receive unconditional healing Light Love from the Holy Father and the Holy Mother. The boundless healing Love Light from Creation is

permeating all my bodies, my cells, and hearts, and minds. I invite the Angels of the Light to hold me so lovingly in the highest healing crystalline golden white Light possible. I am a Portal of Light. I am Love. I am Peace. I am Holy. And so it is.

Remain in your sacred space as long as you wish, and observe, feel, the waves of light, love, and peace infusing your whole being, transmuting, dissolving all levels of separation, dissolving all veils of illusions. Experience your inherent communion of love within Creation and from the deepest places of your Heart. Decide to release and let go all sense of discord within you, by accepting all of who you are, with love and compassion in your Heart. As you embrace who you are and release the judgments and struggles, notice all illusory energies dissipating, revealing lighter calmer frequencies—awakening Light.

I love myself exactly how I am and how I feel right now. I choose infinite compassion, nurturing love, and gratitude. I slow down and surrender within this sacred loving space. All discomfort subsides, inviting everlasting peace, love, and grace to dwell within me.

My faith and gratitude are amazing forces of love, opening doorways for miracles and healing. From my heart, I move deeper and deeper into an experience of faith and gratitude. These are unbounded forces of love opening Doorways of Light. I am an Angelic Divine Being of God. I am a Ray of Light in the Radiance of God.

When you release faith, notice how your hearts and minds and beingness feel. Your hearts are opening wider in compassion and bliss—you are infused by waves of love. The past fades away. The present becomes gentle and serene. Simultaneously, the space seems empty and also filled with love. Within such holy space miracles manifest naturally.

Faith and gratitude activate a deeper communion with your Higher-Light Self, with your Highest Divine Angelic Guidance team, with the Source of Love in all of Life—the Oneness.

The mind is never satisfied, and the One Sacred Heart is forever in spiritual Bliss and Love. The moment the mind listens to the Heart, the mind becomes the "Divine Mind", and there is blissful peace. This is the true nature of the One Sacred Heart in action. The moment you delve within the deep chambers of the Heart, the mind calms down, the nature and dynamic of the thoughts shift, inviting higher consciousness. **The mind is resting and is free, inviting your Divine Mind to listen to God. With time, you are discovering the true meaning of your life. You are in the Oneness.**

My Heart is the Portal of God and to God, a Source of boundless Love, where the God-Self is revealed and where all creation, all truth, all consciousness resides. The Angels are lovingly holding me within that holy realm.

When the personality is controlled by illusory "mind-thoughts", it can lead to much suffering and disappointments. The mind wants to dwell on the past and the future. The past exists in the mind and the future is created in every now moment. When the mind pays attention to the Heart space consciousness, you then live and breathe in the present moment, in a deeper way, in a holy way. From the Sacred Heart, a new reality is revealed, and you step into a new realm of infinite creative possibilities in alignment with the dreams God has for you. **In the Heart consciousness you are naturally fully present in the oneness, in the power of now and of love, co-creating a future which serves your highest good and the highest good of all.**

You are never alone. Aloneness is an illusion of the mind. As you choose to be in communion with the Essence

of all Creation, the Great Spirits, from your Heart, you naturally commune with your Highest Divine guidance team and Divine Mother Earth in all its beauty. Within this unity consciousness of the One Sacred Heart, there is delight, bliss, and pure joy with all beings and consciousness, Divine Mother Earth and Father Sun. Life speaks to you. Nature's Intelligence speaks to you. Your Heart speaks to you, God speaks to you and your life transforms. There is a Heart-to-Heart communion with absolutely everything. Life has been waiting for you! To live within that truth and sanctity of Life is the safest space and place to be dear ones.

I am on a trajectory of Light and Peace. This is what true success is, a profound sense of Peace. It is Oneness consciousness. Peace is of the fundamental Soul Quintessence of Creation. From that Peace frequency emanating from the deepest Chambers of my Heart, I am permeated by the Sanctity and Luminescence of Creation. I am permeated by pure Love Oneness consciousness.

To be successful, is to experience the embodiment of your pure essence, your Angelic Self. It is peace, bliss, joy within the Heart, a state of love and compassion that is infinite! From that space of true consciousness and oneness, miracles within the synchronicities of Life are unfolding and manifesting. You are the awakener, inviting the Garden of Eden to be revealed multidimensionally in its infinite beauty.

It would be amazing that all human beings' intentions and actions in the world, would always be born from honoring God's Creation, from a true knowing, honoring all sacred divine laws, the sanctity of Life—honoring Mother Nature's Beauty and LIGHT from which Life is sourcing. This would then imply that every human being lives from God's Consciousness, from true consciousness, from the Oneness of the Heart consciousness—from the embodiment of the God

Self. Every being, all aspects of creation are precious and sacred. Imagine yourself with every human being, breathing, living from that highest Truth of the One Sacred Heart.

I choose to embody my pure being. I release all doubts, and delve fully within the frequencies of pure Creation, the essence and divine design of life that is true Love. I let go of thoughts and breathe into the Sacred Heart. From my Heart, a renewed awareness is born. It is an inner stillness from where my Pure Being reveals its essence, in the Oneness of Pure Creation.

Your path is to become conscious of who you are, dear ones, to LOVE unconditionally. Creation is in delight of your Light and embraces your Light. Your Light is essential to Mother Earth, to Mother Nature, to all beings and consciousness because you belong to Nature, to Creation. You belong to the Light. You are Light—you are the Oneness.

The Love of God shines through me brightening my higher Light. I dwell with love and honoring in the Garden of Eden of Mother Earth, in divine communion with her Heart Core Crystal infinite blessings. My whole beingness basks in Mother Nature's infinite nurturing blessings and beauty.

Deeper you dwell in the Love-Unity consciousness of the Heart, safer you feel with other people, safer you feel in the world. You are then welcoming a new paradigm of kindness and harmony in your field, that is in alignment with the Heart Soul of Creation—that is in alignment with your pure being.

Inviting Peace within you and in your hearts and minds, invites Peace on Earth. This naturally alleviates and dissipates all sense of threat, despair, and aloneness—all illusory emotions, beliefs, and thoughts fade away.

Practice the following meditation as often as you can and notice the shift in you and in all aspects of your life. Also notice how your nervous system relaxes, inducing the healing throughout all of your bodies. Feel the bliss and serenity suffusing every aspect of your beingness: *I breathe and walk and live in the Garden of Eden, the pure essence of Love and Light of Creation. I experience the infinite beauty of Creation, of Mother Earth into my One Sacred Heart and Divine Mind. My whole beingness relaxes in all that Love and beauty, the truth of Life, the truth of my being. As I breathe the Light and Love of Creation into my Heart, I enter into my pure being. I love myself unconditionally. I feel all the Love of Life into all my hearts, in my One Sacred Heart and in all aspects of who I am. I feel infinite love and compassion, delving into gratitude for all that I have experienced in my life and to this day. I see everything as good and holy, even the pains and challenges, I see them in the Love of Father Mother God, of the Divine. From all the pains and challenges, are born the more conscious compassionate being I am. Today, I choose to give power to gratitude, compassion, and love only. Nothing has power beyond Love.* **I see now everything with a gentle Heart, in the love-unity of gratitude.** *My mind is free from all pollution, from all judgment, from all delusion. I see clearly that all experiences have been bridges of Light, and to this day still engendering miracles into my life. I can see this now. I am, therefore, infinitely grateful for everything. I feel only waves of love within me and toward all of who I am, toward all beings, and all that is in Creation. I accept who I am with infinite calmness, grace, and bliss. I am grace, I am Light. I choose to embrace who I am, with unconditional Love. In the gentle presence of the Angels, I feel the deepest Love within me. They are showing me the way to love and to cherish exactly who I am. My old self permeated with illusory beliefs has faded away to give birth to the Holy Luminous Being I am. Now, nothing has power beyond LOVE. I shall never give power again to what is not true and truth. My mind is clear and from the oneness of the Heart has given birth to the Divine Mind. I feel safe, unconditionally loved, and whole. I am safe. I am Loved. I am whole. I am Holy. My Angelic Divine Guidance team is radiating Light, holding me in all the Love That*

Is. Luminous wings are embracing me so lovingly in the Heart of Creation. And in the Heart of Creation, I am permeated with Divine Love, Light, and Blissful Peace — my Light illuminates the whole World. I embody my Angelic Self with joy. With infinite gratitude, I place myself and my life forever in the hands of God, in the highest Divine Light of God. Conscious of my oneness, I bask in Pure Divine Love. I Am the Oneness!

I experience the boundless Love of Father Mother God, Divine Mother Earth and Creation within me, around me, and in all multidimensionality of Life.

I delve in delight, within the unity consciousness of my Heart, within the Heart of God, the Heart of Creation.

Increasingly more people are awakening to their Light and One Sacred Heart frequency. Mother Earth has been moving into higher dimensions of Light with all its inhabitants, inviting a sacred communion, an all-encompassing Blissful Peace dissolving the veils of illusions. The old world is collapsing and transmuting energies. Beneath the chaos there is a "New World of Light" awakening, where the Garden of Eden shall be revealed in its boundless beauty and luminescence.

Increasingly more beings are co-creating in the oneness of Source, inviting higher frequencies from the Garden of Eden, to express itself. All that is not of these higher frequencies are illusory projections, progressively revealed, released, transformed, and transmuted by the Divine Light. It is a process where every human being has the free will to participate in true consciousness of the Sacred, in the Oneness of the One True Love of God, to be of service.

It is a time to shift your consciousness dear ones, from victimhood to Warriors of Light, to Peacemakers, to Awakeners, to Medicine Men and Women, to Divine Angelic Beings of God, to Lightworkers, to the Pure Beings

you are. It is a time to gently lovingly let go of the old version of yourself as you step into the New Light of the Garden of Eden. You are Miracle Makers. You are moving into a Golden Age.

My desire, intention and sincerity to awaken and ascend, and to be of service as a pure and clear interdimensional being of Light are frequencies inherently embedded within the trajectory of my Sacred Path. Dear Father Mother God, may the dreams you have for me, manifest on my Sacred Path, with the loving support of Luminous Angelic Beings and Masters of the Light, enlightening my path, in your Radiant Holy Presence of unconditional Love.

I embrace everlasting Love and expand my life from that Divine Love of infinite potentiality, in eternity — standing as co-creative partner with God, now and always, in all the Love, Light, Peace, Grace, Beauty, and Joy that is, in the Oneness.

I embrace the infinite expansion of my life with joy, forever in LOVE in the Oneness of Creation, permeating Eternity with Trust, forever safe in the Heart of God.

I breathe Light with all that is in Creation. My aura expands within the Universal Matrix of Light — ONE Light emanating from the Heart of God. My Light is Holy, it is the Light of God shining through me and shining from my Heart. I am a Ray of Light in the Radiance of God.

I see all aspects of my life as blessings. With infinite gratitude, I rejoice in the embodiment of my Divine Angelic Self, the Medicine Woman, the Medicine Man, I am. I am the Peacemaker, the Awakener, invincible and dwelling in all the Love that is. I am a Crystalline Angelic Luminous Being of God. All of Creation lives within me and in the Heart of God. I live and breathe in the Heart of God, in the Heart of Creation, in the Oneness of Creation, and so it is.

I am a Crystalline Divine Angelic Being of God, a Luminous Being of service to humanity. I am the Lightworker, the Peacemaker, creating beauty and harmony wherever the "Divine Light" leads me. I see all beings in me and as me, shining in their Luminous Light. All of Creation lives within me. I am the Light that shines in all of Life and all of Life shines within me! I am a Ray of Light in the Radiance of God! I am a Portal of Light of service to all beings and Life. I embrace my sacredness. I am the Oneness!

Chapter Four

A Journey into the Light

Feeling blissful and serene, I was enjoying another afternoon painting on canvas, a Medicine Wheel, I named "Divine Mother Earth". Suddenly, I was called to rest and relax on the couch nearby. I then closed my eyes to pray and meditate. Throughout that serene meditation, Luminous Lights came around me, I consciously experienced that I was leaving my physical body, guided by Angelic loving presences. I was feeling unconditional Love embracing me completely.

My soul travel was gentle and divinely guided, moving in the air. I arrived in a meadow. Trees and bushes were nearby. I moved closer to one very large bush and then moved around it. I found myself in the presence of a Luminescent, Radiant Being. Infinite, unconditional Love was emanating from him as well as an incredible bright Light. He was tall and muscular. His skin was of a magnificent shade of gold. One shoulder was partially covered by a robe falling graciously around his harmoniously shaped body. His robe had almost the same shades of color as his skin. His facial features appeared to be Asian. The radiant luminescent Light and the unconditional Love emanating from his beingness seemed to emerge from all of Life, endlessly embracing all of Creation and myself completely—as two huge, radiant white wings were holding me so gently, in the highest Love possible, unconditional Love.

I was held and embraced with unconditional Love by a radiant Angelic Being. The forces of Love in all that

Luminescence were like huge wings embracing me in the highest Light possible. I was experiencing an amazing ecstatic place of bliss, peace, and love, bathing in the most luminous white Light. My whole being was light love pure energy. I was experiencing my true essence, living the consciousness of the Heart, of my higher self-higher light. It was oneness, pure love consciousness—God consciousness. I was light in the oneness, pure perfect ecstatic love consciousness, and nothing of a lesser energy was coming through. I was basking in God's unconditional Love Peace Bliss, pure Light synergy. I wanted to stay in this place and state of boundless Love consciousness forever.

This magnificent Archangel-Angelic Being held me in all that Love and luminous Light, in these holy wings, for a long time, though I am not sure how long. All of a sudden, I was moving at a very high speed toward the sky, among the stars, and into the cosmos. It was spectacular, amazingly delightful, and blissful. I felt infinitely loved and protected.

Among the stars, my consciousness was expanding and expanding in infinite ways as I was receiving downloads. I was experiencing limitless time and space, a divine consciousness of the soul in the oneness of Creation, in infinity. There was no time and space, only pure energy consciousness, infinite peace, blissful joy, pure Love, complete and unconditional.

After all this time travelling throughout the Universe, I was gently guided to come back into my physical body. I found my physical body in the same position on the couch, and remained still for a long time, my eyes closed, wanting to hold on to the experience of that perfect pure love light peace frequency. In these pure energies of true Love, I was still experiencing energetically the presence of this magnificent Being of Light holding me with unconditional love in giant wings of radiant Light, healing me on all levels of my beingness. I was acknowledging, with infinite gratitude, in reverence and bliss the presence of this incredible Being of Light and my experience in the Cosmos. My Heart was infinitely touched by Divine Light and Love.

In the same position on the couch, my physical body and all my bodies felt light, and my mind was blissful and serene, still experiencing pure love light energy. When I opened my eyes, I was aware of a bright light emanating from me and from everything around me. The light was present all around me. My body was glowing, and everything was fluid light energy. I was completely sustained in the embrace of that pure Love Light, the infinite divine matrix of Light, all encompassing. I experienced an energetic light activation within my Beingness all the way to my cellular coding, a Love that is so pure and of God. I wanted to maintain within my hearts and minds and my whole beingness these blissful feelings of the purest experience of Love and oneness.

Later, I understood that this Angelic Being of Light is one of my Master Guides, an Archangel. I named him "Angelic Master of the Light", because of his incredible radiance embracing me with unconditional Love, holding me so gently within wide huge wings of Light. This luminous Angelic Being, Archangel has been working through me, with my highest Angelic Guidance team and Masters of the Light on multidimensional levels to awaken the Heart consciousness — of service to all Beings and all of Creation, guiding people, on their healing path to awaken and experience their God Self.

That Love Light frequency I was held in, was an experience of oneness encompassing all beings and all of Creation — revealing the fundamental original Matrix of Light, of pure Love consciousness, a blissful serenity all-encompassing — One Light, One Love.

In my heart, I expressed endless gratitude for receiving the gift of these blessings. I knew that it would stay within me forever. I received a clear experience of my true essence and the true essence of life, of my angelic self, the embodiment of love light I am, and we all are. It was a place and state of unconditional love for all life. I fully experienced my Angelic Self, my Higher Light, clearly knowing that I am, and we are so much more than what we normally comprehend.

No being is alone or separated from God and Creation. There is only Oneness. We are of God's Light consciousness, endlessly receiving divine guidance and bliss from that same eternal Source of Divine Wisdom and unconditional Love emerging from our Hearts, the Heart of Creation, the Heart of God, the Heart of all Hearts.

Luminous Beings, Divine Guides of the Light are always eager to assist us as Guardian Angels, guides, healers, and messengers, to co-create in all the Love that is, with God/Source. They are the embodiment of the Divine Living Presence, God, Source, and so are we.

I experienced the Heart of God within and without, in me and in all that is, a state of serene perfection, wholeness, holiness, and sacredness. I understood that "We and God are One".

I am the Light within the Light!

Chapter Five

The Sacred Path of the Heart
A Reconciliation with Life

Your Heart center is the source, the energetic core foundation of your Beingness. The Heart is the source of Consciousness, of all Peace. From the Heart you may heal everything and anything. From the Heart you may co-create with Source. The sanctity and divine design of the Heart sources from the Heart of God.

Freedom, unconditional Love, Beauty, Joy, and Peace are the songs of my Heart.

On my sacred path, peace is the most beautiful gift I give to myself, to Mother Earth with all its inhabitants. Peace is Love! Peace is bliss! Peace is true success! Peace is gratitude! Peace is grace! Peace is compassion! Peace is unity consciousness! Peace is of the consciousness and essence of the Heart. Hope and Faith are of Peace, the consciousness of the Heart.

Your multidimensional being is energetically in communion and plugged into the Heart of Mother Earth Core Crystal below, and also plugged in the Heart of Father Sun above. It is the Ninth dimensional system of which you are a part. Its central axis holds the fifth dimension all the way to the Heart Chakra within the Milky Way Galaxy. You have been evolving from third dimensional frequencies into fifth dimensional frequencies, within the Heart space consciousness.

You already have the capacity of holding fifth dimensional frequencies and additional dimensional frequencies above the fifth. When you are dwelling in the One Sacred Heart consciousness and therefore resonating with all Hearts, your fifth dimensional Heart Chakra is activated. You have then naturally access to additional high dimensions of Light above the fifth dimension. Also, you have naturally access to the first and second and third and fourth dimensions, but in a complete, new enlightening way. You then discover the enlightened aspects of these dimensions which are empowering you. All dimensions live inherently and synergistically within you and in all of Life. Every dimension has its divine purpose and supports one another purpose to co-create and create Life in its infinite sanctity, and beauty. They all operate harmoniously and synergistically in the Oneness of Life and Creation.

My first two books, "Twelve Doorways of Light, A Portal to your God Self and Sacredness of Life" convey significant information about the dimensions and your intrinsic oneness with them.

Your Heart consciousness epitomizes an infinite Source of Light, Truth, Bliss, Grace, Empathy, Peace, Authenticity, Joy, Wisdom and Divine Knowledge, where the highest Love resides and is all-encompassing. From the boundless holy consciousness of the One Sacred Heart, you have the capacity to heal all your bodies and seven chakras within the physical body. You have the capacity to focus on the space of the Heart's holy consciousness — a place where you listen to God, to your Divine Guides, and where all truth resides.

Your One Sacred Heart encompassing all your hearts holds unity consciousness. You are to cherish your One Sacred Heart to become one with it. It is the embodiment of LOVE.

Chapter Five

Every aspect of your being holds consciousness. Your lungs, your liver, your bones, and all that is in creation has consciousness. Imagine, every day, emanating pure Love from your Heart to every aspect of your being, to all beings and to all of life. Imagine what all this love does and will do.

Speak to all your hearts with love in that way: *Dear Anahata heart chakra, dear Higher heart, and dear Physical heart and dear One Sacred Heart, I am here now, fully present, to experience your nurturing unconditional Love, all your wisdom, divine knowledge, your strength, your faith, and compassion. I will never abandon you again dear Hearts. I am committed to embrace and embody your wisdom and unconditional Love with infinite reverence and gratitude. My One Sacred Heart is holding all my hearts within an Octahedron of Turquoise Light, holding the Divine Masculine and the Divine Feminine in the Oneness of Creation. In the middle of my brain, where is the third eye, the pineal gland, is a space with an indigo blue light encompassing a violet Light. It is an aspect of the seat of the soul in communion with the seat of the soul within my One Sacred Heart. They unite as ONE Seat of the Soul — my Divine Mind and One Sacred Heart are awakened in holy communion, in one unified field of Light, rejoicing in the Garden of Eden.*

"Light Love Peace" frequencies from Heaven, from God, from the Heart of the Sun are illuminating all my Chakras. The Light of Father Sun is illuminating my Crown Chakra to my Third Eye Chakra, expanding and illuminating my Throat Chakra and permeating my One Sacred Heart — revealing an octahedron of turquoise Light — holding in harmony the Divine Masculine and the Divine Feminine. My minds are now Light consciousness in motion, basking in all the Light of the Heart. My minds are awakening to the One Divine Mind, one hundred percent in communion with my One Sacred Heart. My Divine Mind is calmly and lovingly listening to the One Sacred Heart. I am ready to live my life upon your infinite divine truth and wisdom, dear Heart. I love you and cherish you dear One Sacred Heart.

I choose to live, breathe, work, play, and walk in the Garden of Eden, fully grounded in the Heart Core Crystal of Mother Earth. Every day, I experience my One Sacred Heart in communion with the Heart of Father Sun and the Heart of Mother Earth, lovingly held in the radiance of Angelic Beings, Nature's Spirits, and Rays of Light from all Sacred Directions.

Anchored in my Heart in the Garden of Eden, I am free from despair and judgments. I understand that "All That Is" lives within me. I understand and cherish the sanctity of my beingness. I live within the consciousness of unconditional Love of the Heart and my life transforms in miraculous ways. Freedom, Joy, and Peace are the songs of my Heart.

"Meditation" is a learning process where you are not giving any longer power to the multitudes of thoughts streaming through your mind and running your life. In meditation you are calming and relaxing the minds, you are then giving power to the One Sacred Heart and the Divine Mind, to an intrinsic force of Love, to a higher divine intelligence and wisdom. In that process you invite true consciousness to guide you, to love you, to nurture every aspect of your beingness and life. That force of Love is multidimensional, universal, and is a Divine Intelligence, a grid of Light in communion with all Hearts and the Heart of Creation.

I have the capacity to heal myself multidimensionally by letting go of my minds-thoughts-patterns. I focus on the space of my Heart consciousness which is the infinite Source of Light, Truth and Divine Knowledge, from where the highest Love is all encompassing. This is where I find Peace. A space where I let go and let God, where I listen to God. I am ready to experience who I am now. I listen to my Heart with joy and gratitude. I am ready to heal in all the Light of my divine design illuminating my bodies. I am healing now.

There is a leading force of Unconditional Love emanating from All in Creation, emanating from my Heart, from all Hearts, from the Heart of Creation. I am holy, loved, and safe on this Earth and in my physical body, residing and breathing within the consciousness of the One Sacred Heart where I experience my communion with the Heart of God. **Dear God, may all my actions and words perpetuate and glorify your unconditional Love.**

I am forever in communion with the Heart of God. My Heart consciousness is intrinsically in oneness communion with the Heart of God. I am to create and co-create a world of Peace in the Heart and Oneness of Creation.

1- Heart Meditation:

I call upon the Light of the Divine, the Light Love of God. I visualize myself within a column of Golden White Light, Christ Light, sourcing from the **Heart of Father Sun-Heaven**. *My whole beingness is permeated by a beam of the Christ Golden White Light — it is the Highest Love Light of God embracing me completely, moving through me and grounding me into the Heart of Mother Earth Sacred Core Crystal Garden of Eden, with infinite Love. From* ***the Core Crystal of Mother Earth*** *shines a beam of Silver White Crystalline Light infused with Rainbows of Light, beaming throughout my whole beingness.* **I am now held within a column of Golden White Christ Light from above, and a column of Silver White Rainbow Crystalline Light from below, illuminating all my chakras and all my bodies — in unconditional Love.** *The Angels, Archangels, and Nature's Spirits from all four Sacred Directions are additionally holding a sacred space and lovingly assisting my Higher Light embodiment — my Rainbow Body of Light embodiment.*

I breathe slowly and deeply into my Heart space Love Light Peace energies sourcing from the Love Essence of Creation, Father Mother God. I breathe unconditional Love suffusing my whole beingness and space, expanding furthermore a communion of Love with Father Sun-Heaven and Grandmother Moon above and from

Divine Mother Earth Garden of Eden, below. The Angels and Archangels from all four sacred directions are additionally holding me in the highest Love, in their rays of luminous Light. Practice this meditation as often as you wish and especially as you create a sacred space.

Take your time to experience these powerful energies of Love Light expanding in you, through you and infusing all your relationships, all the spaces between you and your world. Feel this holy nurturing love into your Heart space, moving through you, embracing you and infusing you completely. See and feel your cells, all your bodies, and fields receiving all that Divine Love from above and below, your Divine anchors. Feel all that pure Love flow within, with the deepest gratitude. Place your hands over your Heart and speak to your Heart and to God as One: *I love you and I see you now dear God. I love you and I see you now dear Heart. I love you and I see all of your Love as ONE.* Pause, close your eyes, feel the energies of the words and repeat them.

Continue to speak from your Heart. Speak to your Heart: *Dear Heart, I see you. I will never abandon you and leave you alone again. I love you and I listen to you now, dear God, dear Heart. I love you and I listen to you now, dear God, dear Heart, and always will. I love you and cherish you. Dear God, please whisper into my Sacred Heart and Divine Mind your Holy words, guide me and lead me to a self-realization, an awakening, and manifestation of your Divine Will. Dear God, lead me to enlightenment. I am ready to experience the dreams that you have for me, to be of service, in all the Love that is. I surrender my minds and hearts to your Holy power, to your Divine Love. May my Luminous Self reveal my Angelic Self, as I join with your choirs of Angels, singing in all the glories, your Holy name, dear God, dear Lord, dear Elohim! Thank you, dear Lord!*

Feel your Heart singing with the Angels, with Joy. Repeat the above meditations and breathe all that Holy Love-Light, deeply and slowly into your Heart space, until you feel that your thoughts are melting away and that your hearts and minds are liberated, basking in the oneness of all the Love and Light That Is.

2- From your Anahata heart, breathe unconditional Love, in all your relationships.

Say: *As I breathe unconditional Love of the Divine into my* **Anahata heart,** *I experience unconditional Love in all my relationships. My compassion expands in all the "Love That Is" within an emerald green luminous Light. I am freeing all my relationships in the highest Love Light Peace that is, past, present, and future, including the relationships with my "Self" and with all of Life. I invite the Glory of God, Divine Wisdom, and True Knowing to be in charge.*

Feel the emerald green Light of your **Anahata heart** glowing. Then slowly feel and see that beautiful emerald green Light Love expanding in all your cells, bodies, and auric field — also permeating with unconditional Love all places and spaces of your relationships, transmuting all energies into Love and harmony. You are freeing all your relationships past, present, and future in the highest Light that is. There is forgiveness, compassion, understanding and unconditional Love. You are surrendering, you are letting go. Feel the Blissful Peace in all your relationships. That you see these people again or not, it is not important. You are now free in all that Love and they are free. Learn to be in Love with your "Self" and with Life.

Throughout this prayer, it is important to understand that you are not attaching cords to no one and nothing, but that you are freeing your beautiful Self in your "Light-space", and you are freeing your relationships in their own "Light-space". There is oneness, honoring, freedom and true Love. You are practicing unconditional Love.

Dear ones, it is important that you take time to experience, within the deepest places of your being, every step of these meditations. Enjoy the shift from the deepest place within your Heart. You are experiencing a reconciliation with your Self, with the people in your life, and all of Life. Your highest Divine Angelic Guides of the Light are assisting you multidimensionally in all the Love that is.

3- Breathe deeply and gently into your Higher heart. Your Higher heart is located at your thymus. Your Higher heart holds inherently a consciousness of universal unconditional Love intact and pure from the higher frequency of God's Love.

Say: *I breathe and experience the rose-pink Universal Love of the Divine, pure Love-Light of the Christ Light and Lord Buddha Light — pure consciousness from within my* **Higher heart**.

Feel and visualize the luminous rose-pink Light of your **Higher Heart** glowing. It is the Universal Christ Light, Lord Buddha Light. Then slowly feel and see that luminous rose-pink crystalline Light and Love expanding in all your cells and bodies and auric field, expanding to all Life and embracing Mother Earth completely. All around Mother Earth, the Divine Christ Light and Lord Buddha Light are glowing as a holy grid of unconditional Love holding Mother Earth in all enlightened dimensions of Light in all her Glory — revealing the Garden of Eden. *I see all beings living in joy and harmony in all the Light and beauty of the Garden of Eden. Mother Earth is held in the most beautiful embrace of the Christ Light and Buddha Light, the Garden of Eden. I see the Garden of Eden into my minds and hearts, into my One Sacred Heart and my Divine Mind, where there is infinite holy unconditional Love, Light, Peace, Bliss, Beauty, Kindness, Support, Wisdom, Truth, Abundance, Prosperity, Grace, and Joy for all beings and all that is in Creation.*

I am anchored with joy and gratitude, in all the beauty and glory and Heart of the Garden of Eden of Mother Earth, basking in boundless Love.

Hold that holy vision and frequency of the Garden of Eden as long as you wish and enjoy the multidimensional

Love energies permeating all of Life. You are one with that Love, anchored in the Sanctity, the Heart of the Garden of Eden.

You are now the Miracle Lightworker, co-creating with Source, with God in the Highest Love Light possible. From your Heart, you are ONE with the pure fundamental Essence of Creation. You are the Peace Maker, the Healer, the Visionary, the Alchemist, the Artist of Light. You are Grace embodied.

I am All That Is in Creation! I am Grace embodied! My Heart holds all sacred truth, and true knowing. I am in love with my Heart. The Light emanating from my Heart envelops me with unconditional Love.

Feel that infinite Love, Light, and Peace permeating all aspects of your being and all aspects of your life and all that is. All your minds and hearts and all your bodies delve into this luminous Divine Light, these high frequencies. Enjoy your Heart experience in the Garden of Eden. **See in your minds and hearts all beings living in joy and harmony in all the Light and beauty of the Garden of Eden.** Hold that vision as long as you wish and as often as you wish. You are the Lightworker, the Visionary, the Shaman.

4- Breathe deeply and slowly into your Heart Space. Feel and see in your Heart space, your Anahata heart and your Higher heart, and your Physical heart, as ONE LIGHT held in unity. Pause and enjoy the Light energies. Then see your Physical heart glow, being embraced by the luminous emerald green Light of Anahata. Pause and enjoy the Love Communion. Then see your Physical heart glow, being embraced by the rose-pink luminous Christ Light, Lord Buddha Light from your Higher heart, from your thymus. Pause and enjoy the Love communion. See your Higher heart luminous rose-pink Light uniting energetically with your

Anahata heart emerald green Light. Pause and enjoy the Love communion. With joy and gratitude, bask in this unifying nurturing Love.

Say: *All my hearts are in Divine Communion now, in the highest Love, withing an octahedron of turquoise Light. It is my One Sacred Heart, a sacred space of balance, love, oneness and harmony where the Divine Masculine and the Divine Feminine reside in unity, all-encompassing, ONE consciousness of Love—Heaven on Earth. From the Heart of the One Sacred Heart, the Vesica Piscis holds all worlds in the Oneness, birthing the Flower of Life of Creation. I am a Sacred Being breathing in synergy and unity with the Sacredness of Life.*

5- Visualize the space of the octahedron of turquoise Light, a luminous turquoise Light encompassing all your hearts. All your hearts are now infused by that turquoise luminous Light, a luminous octahedron of turquoise Light, it is your One Sacred Heart. This turquoise Light is expanding and glowing, also suffusing all your chakras with a Crystalline Light with all your bodies and field. Crystalline Light, Rainbows of Light and Turquoise Light are permeating your beingness and space, in the oneness of Life and Creation. In the oneness of Creation, you are emanating a Love that is unconditional inherent to all of Life.

*Basking in the **Holy Turquoise Light-Peace of my One Sacred Heart**, I breathe a never-ending flow of Divine Love permeating every cells of my being, all my bodies and aspects of my life, all beings and Creation. In the consciousness and infinite Holy Light of my **One Sacred Heart** there is an awareness of oneness and true Love, a Light that is omnipresent, omniscient, omnipotent — the Love of Source shining in me and from me.*

In the Oneness of my One Sacred Heart, I co-create with Source, where faith, and trust, and peace are everlasting.

Faith is born from the One Sacred Heart consciousness, an understanding and experience that you and God are One. *From the true consciousness of my One Sacred Heart everything is possible, miracles take place within that field of Light, within all Life and Creation. All of Creation lives within me. I am a ray of Light in the Radiance of God.*

6- Practice listening to your One Sacred Heart, to activate the infinite wisdom of that Holy space of unconditional LOVE. With time, the Divine Mind becomes increasingly more attuned to the frequencies of the One Heart, its infinite wisdom, overflowing love, peace, and true knowledge. In that process, the Divine Mind is receiving direct messages from the Heart space, from the One Sacred Heart. The messages the Divine Mind receives are then emerging from a consciousness of love, wisdom, honoring, and truth. You are channeling! Your One Sacred Heart is then in oneness communion with the Heart of God/Source, ALL SOURCE OF UNCONDITIONAL LOVE, the Heart of Creation—also in communion with the Throat Chakra, the Third Eye Chakra, the pineal gland and pituitary gland, and all Chakras, awakening your psychic abilities, and your capacity to channel the highest truth and wisdom, to be of service.

From your One Sacred Heart, feel and experience the love and innocence of all the animals, insects, birds, marine life—experience your innocence and see that innocence in all people. All in Nature and Creation has consciousness. Feel in your Heart your inherent oneness and communion with Nature's Holy Spirits, divine presences, beauty, and infinite sacredness. Your communion and oneness with every aspect of nature, already is. Commune with consciousness, Heart to Heart with the trees, the rocks, the mountains, all animals, and everything in nature. Listen, and you will then know who you are.

All the love flowing from your Heart space, activates rays of Light, your body of Light, awakening the spiritual functions of the pituitary gland and pineal gland, your third eye, the space for ascension, mystical experiences, and enlightenment. Your psychic abilities awaken when the Divine Mind is available and free to listen to the Heart space. This process invites a frequency where the Angels of the Light, the Great Masters of the Light, your Highest Divine guidance team, Mother Earth and Nature's Intelligence are able to commune with you in ways that are increasingly more conscious and multidimensional. This holy communion is raising your vibrations substantially because of your intrinsic oneness with your Divine Guides, all in Nature and all of Creation.

These experiences and realizations are healings and are activations to embody progressively on deeper levels the Higher Light of your Higher Self, your Angelic Self, your God Self or Christ Self. This is what healing means, it is remembering who you are. It means "to be free" to embody the true Essence of who you are, to be whole, delving in the Heart and Oneness consciousness of Creation. It is a conscious awakening of the physical, mental, emotional, and spiritual energetic essence of your beingness from the Heart space; all your bodies uniting as One Radiant Light.

I embody the divine Light frequency of oneness, delving forever in the depth of the Celestial Heart, the Heart of all Hearts.

I live and reside in the Oneness of the Web of Light, the fundamental Essence of Life, the unity consciousness of the Great Love.

I live within the sanctity of the Divine Universal Cosmic Laws, the Heart of all Hearts, of service as a pure and clear interdimensional being of Light!

Chapter Five

The Love of God lives in my One Sacred Heart, in all my cells, DNA-RNA, in all my bodies, in all of Life. Divine unconditional Love and compassion, Divine knowledge and wisdom are the true essence of my Heart. My Heart overflows with unconditional Love — this is the true state of my Heart.

My Heart consciousness speaks the highest truth. It is the Portal to infinite bliss. I naturally expand in that true consciousness of blissful peace, awakening my abilities to channel, to co-create in harmony and joy. I am a vessel of Love, Beauty, and Harmony.

Your hearts have consciousness, and every aspect of your being has consciousness. Your organs and bones and blood and all your bodies, everything has consciousness and are in energetic communion with Mother Nature, with Nature's Intelligence. You have the inherent ability to commune with all aspects of your beingness and life, with consciousness, honoring and love. In order to experience balance, harmony, health, and well-being it is essential to never ignore any aspect of your beingness. Attend with unconditional love to every aspect of who you are, all your bodies, physical, emotional, mental, and spiritual. We are giving you these meditations to guide you into wholeness, so that you discover the sanctity of your being, from the Heart of unconditional Love.

Within the Sanctity of my Being, I invite the Divine Qualities of Master Jesus, of Lord Buddha, of the Angelic Beings of Light, and Nature's Intelligence into my hearts and minds to awaken my One Sacred Heart and my Divine Mind, as ONE LOVE.

Within my Heart is a Light which sustains me. That Light sustains every aspect of my beingness, within the Love unity consciousness of Creation, the Heart of Creation. I love all beings from a unity consciousness of unconditional love. I love myself unconditionally. I am completely free.

I walk on an enlightened path in the Love and Joy of gratitude. Freedom, Joy, and Peace are the songs of my Heart. Love flows in abundance.

As the Heart is free to expand and express its true nature of compassion and unconditional Love, Divine consciousness is naturally activated. From the sacred union of the Divine Mind and the One Sacred Heart, there is a reconciliation with all aspects of my beingness and life — where there is a letting go of the illusory aspects of life. It is a time to discover my multidimensional Self in a new way, in a deeper way, from a renewed relationship with my Self, with all Beings, and All That Is.

The Light of Father Sun is illuminating all my hearts and my One Sacred Heart. The Sacred Portal of my Sacred Heart infinite Divine Qualities of unconditional Love are expressed and revealed in the union of Heaven on Earth, bridging my upper and lower Chakras energy centers in all the Love That Is. The Garden of Eden of my Heart is Radiating Light — I am the Luminous Being of service to the betterment of humanity.

The embodiment of my One Sacred Heart has been an awakening to the True Essence and Beauty of Life, in all its Sanctity. This awakening epitomizes a reconciliation with my Self and all of Life.

Chapter Six

The Angels are Illuminating my Chakras

As I practice daily breath work and Light Meditation, it raises my frequencies, inviting the Angelic Beings to clear and illuminate my Chakras, therefore leading to the healing of my bodies. This Light activation liberates the Luminous Rainbow Light of my pure being.

As indicated at the beginning of the last chapter, when you are dwelling in the One Sacred Heart energetically vibrating with all Hearts, your fifth dimensional Heart Chakra is naturally activated. The column of Light holding you in communion with the Great Father Sun and with the Heart Core Crystal of Divine Mother Earth activates naturally your twelve chakras system. You activate your inner fire through the breath. Breath work is essential on your spiritual path.

Through breath work and Light Meditation, the Angelic Beings are clearing and illuminating all Chakras within my Beingness — healing my physical body and all my bodies.

As your twelve chakras system is activated, spinning in harmony, there is an additional "activation spin" taking place within your twelve strands of DNA leading to a profound sense of wholeness, oneness, and belonging.

You may repeat the following healing empowering prayers-meditations as often as you wish. Speak aloud slowly from your Heart and feel the energies of the words in all your bodies and hearts.

Thank you, dear Father Mother God, dear Angelic Guides of the Light for your loving support and divine assistance. Dear hearts, I let go of the grief. As I release painful feelings and energies of sadness, abandonment, and aloneness, they are naturally transformed into Light unity consciousness of compassionate nurturing love. I embrace empathy and unconditional love. My hearts are awakening to their intrinsic frequencies of peace love compassion, also awakening the capacity to understand what another person is experiencing. My intention is to develop the capacity to love unconditionally. The Anahata heart space is related to the thymus. I call for divine clearing and healing between the Anahata and the thymus, so that energy flows, and for the union of all hearts to be activated and give birth to the One Sacred Heart.

Calm the mind and breathe deeply and slowly. Then listen to the voice of the Heart and feel your Heart space. Speak to your Heart with love. Choose to nurture a deep love relationship with your Heart and with all of who you are, and all of Life. You are raising your frequencies and your consciousness is shifting now.

I choose to create and experience a nurturing loving compassionate relationship with all my Chakras. As I practice daily holy breath work and Light meditation, it raises my frequencies, inviting the Angelic Beings to have access to clearing and illuminating my Chakras. My Chakras have direct energetic communion with different physical aspects and non-physical aspects of my bodies. They hold all of who I am within a field of Luminous Light. They are powerful energy centers regulating all functions within my bodies.

1- Heart Meditation: Feel your Heart space, and dwell into the deepest chambers of your Heart—breathe slowly and deeply.
Heart element holds "Air" (Chakra within the physical body)

My Anahata heart, golden emerald green Light Ray engages the mental body to delve and dwell into the deepest chambers of the Love consciousness: *It is safe for me to forgive myself and all of life. I set myself free. It is safe to love. It is safe to be free. It is safe to be loved. I express compassion and empathy. Therefore, I embrace my One Sacred Heart, holding my hearts within a Turquoise Luminous Light, inherently coded with the highest frequencies of pure unconditional Love. I am ready to experience all that Divine boundless Love now. I open my Heart with infinite gratitude. My Heart holds compassion and wisdom, expanding in the wings of the Eagle, flying higher and higher into the brightest realms. My Heart holds infinite wisdom and unconditional Love — God's Divine Qualities transmuting frequencies. My whole beingness is raising in frequency. I am a Divine Angelic Being of God of a crystalline frequency. I love myself and all beings unconditionally. I lovingly accept myself exactly as I am. The Blissful Light, Love, and Peace emanating from me uplifts all beings and all Life. I am Holy. All my relationships hold reverence, truth, beauty, and harmony along with a deep sense of compassion, gratitude, and unconditional love.*

The Light of Father Sun is illuminating all my hearts and my One Sacred Heart, the Portal to all Source of Love — bridging Heaven and Earth — where the Heart of God's Divine qualities are forever expressed in the infinite oneness of Creation.

As I invite and enjoy a deeper flow of God's Love into my hearts, I gently embody all that Love into all aspects of my being with gratitude. Feel and experience all that Sacred Love and Luminous Light flowing into all your chakras as you proceed with the following meditations.

2- *My Heart space overflowing with unconditional Love infuses, suffuses my* **Solar Plexus** *with golden emerald green Light Love, with pink-rose Light Love, and with turquoise Light Love. The luminous Sun Light within the Solar Plexus also expands its luminous light rays into the Heart space. There is a divine union and* *communion. The Light of Father Sun is illuminating my Solar Plexus, in the infinite oneness of Creation.*

Solar Plexus element holds "fire" (Chakra within the physical body)

Your **Solar Plexus** engages the spiritual body to be seen in its integrity and wholeness, a glowing yellow Sun Light is receiving the following love prayer: *I support myself with gentleness and kindness. I approve of myself with compassionate Love. I am safe in the hands of God. I trust the process of life to guide me in ways that serves my highest and greatest good. It is safe and beautiful to shine my light. I am divinely guided and loved now and always. I experience my sovereignty. I am whole. I am invincible. My power sources from my inner Peace and self-confidence. I am free from all judgments of others and myself. I honor who I am. I am worthy of reverence and loving-kindness. I embody all these divine qualities of loving-kindness and peace with ease. In my profound inner faith, I manifest with grace the dreams God has for me. My Solar Plexus luminous yellow light love frequency extends with harmony and gentleness into my Sacrum/Sacral Chakra Swadhistana.*

3- *My Heart space overflowing with unconditional Love suffuses the **Sacral Chakra Swadhisthana** in my belly, with pure Love Light. The Light of Father Sun is illuminating Swadhistana, in the infinite oneness of Creation.*

Chakra Swadhisthana element holds "Water".

The **Sacral Chakra** engages the emotional body within a holy force and flow in oneness with the Divine. (Chakra within the physical body)

Your **Sacrum Chakra Swadhisthana** glowing orange light is receiving the following nurturing love prayer: *My creative abilities are divine and infinite. I create and co-create from my Heart with joy my dreams, the dreams God has for me. With infinite gratitude, I am permeated with unconditional love and joy. There is a divine flow and communion with Source/God, softening my emotional body, transforming all energies of shame into nurturing Love. I experience a flow of confidence, courage, and* *goodness. I lovingly listen to my feelings and all my bodies' needs. I lovingly listen to my physical body. I love and respect my physical body. I respect and enjoy my sensuality and sexuality. I revere the physical aspects of my being and all aspects of my being. I feel safe in my physical body. With love, I honor myself as a man/woman. My Sacral chakra luminous orange light love frequency extends with harmony and gentleness into my Root Chakra Muladhara.*

4- *My Heart space overflowing with unconditional Love suffuses my* **Root Chakra Muladhara, with** *pure Love Light. The Light of Father Sun is illuminating Muladhara, in the infinite oneness of Creation.*

The Root Chakra Muladhara element holds "Earth".

The Root Chakra engages the physical body into the highest dimensions of Light from the Heart of the Garden of Eden of Mother Earth and epitomizes the capacity to emanate Peace. (Chakra within the physical body)

The **Root Chakra Muladhara** luminous red light is receiving the following love prayer: *The red luminous light of my Root Chakra is expanding all the way into the Heart of Mother Earth Garden of Eden, into her Core Crystal, where I experience the healing loving nurturing frequencies of the sacred crystals, of the sacred waters, of the minerals nurturing, cleansing, and nourishing all of my bodies multidimensionally, infusing them with peace and life force. My Root Chakra's light and spin unite with the Earth rotation. I am in loving communion with the Heart of the Garden of Eden of Mother Earth, fully grounded from my first and second chakra and from my Heart. My whole beingness and Heart experience a holy communion of boundless nurturing love with the Heart of Mother Earth Garden of Eden. I am nurtured and supported by the Divine Mother and all of Life. I surrender. With ease and grace, I allow flow. I feel safe in this world, in this physical body and with myself. "Source-Life" fulfills all my needs in every moment, forever held within an abundant flow of Love. I am safe. I trust. That trust uplifts me and guides me and nourishes me. That trust is LOVE. Mother Earth is conscious of my loving presence and frequency, her response is of unconditional Love, embracing me,* *nurturing me, nourishing me, and supporting me on all levels. I surrender and embrace all that Love with joy and gratitude.*

5- *My Heart space overflowing with unconditional love infuses, suffuses all my chakras all the way to my* **Gaia-Roszia Chakra** *(located at the soles of my feet) with all that Love Light. Gaia represents Mother Earth in the third dimension. Roszia represents Mother Earth in the fifth dimensions. I embrace Mother Earth beauty, in her wholeness and multidimensionality, for the Garden of Eden to be activated and revealed in all dimensions of Light, in all enlighten aspects as ONE LOVE. My* **Gaia-Roszia Chakra** *luminous silver white rainbow crystalline light is purifying all energy flow I am naturally welcoming and receiving. Therefore, there is pure unconditional love light prana/life force energies flowing into my bodies and fields and cells. My* **Gaia-Roszia Chakra** *luminous silver white rainbow light is accepting with joy all these love-gratitude-life-enhancing-expanding Light prayers.*

My Heart is speaking: Thank you, dear Mother Earth, dear Gaia and dear Roszia, for your infinite nurturing Love, and support, for all the blessings and healing forces of Love you have been gifted me with from your Garden of Eden through this Chakras. Thank you for connecting me with all the Sacred Sites of your Holy Garden from this Chakra. Thank you, dear Gaia-Roszia Chakra, for that open doorway to the Core Crystal of Mother Earth, to the healing sacred Light of the crystals, sacred waters, and minerals, and Nature's Intelligence forces of Love. Thank you for blessing all my bodies and Chakras with the infinite healing forces of love and beauty sourcing from Mother Earth Garden of Eden.

6- *My Heart space overflowing with unconditional love infuses, suffuses all my chakras all the way to the* **Mother Earth Star Chakra** *located at the bottom of my aura within the Earth. My aura has the shape of an egg expanding into the Earth. All this love is moving into the Heart of Mother Earth, Core Crystal. The Light of Father Sun illuminates all Chakras and my auric field completely.*

As I embrace my capacity to invite faith, to love unconditionally, to dwell in gratitude and compassion, my aura expands immensely, and my radiance magnifies.

*Mother **Earth Star Chakra** has a direct contact and communion with the Iron Core Crystal of Mother Earth encompassing her historical records, the Akashic records. From my Heart, I hold love-gratitude energies moving through the lower chakras all the way through the Earth Star Chakra to the Heart of Mother Earth Core Crystal—I experience oneness with Mother Earth, Gaia and Roszia as One. I am led to connect and communicate with other Stars and Star Beings in the highest Love and Light possible. Additionally, I move into a divine love communion with the Whales and Dolphins sacred Hearts and Spirits of infinite wisdom. In similar ways, they both naturally hold the infinite wisdom and knowledge of the Akashic Records. I bask in their boundless love, joy, and wisdom. With great love, I am honoring my oneness and communion with the Heart of Mother Earth, Gaia-Roszia, with all Holy Beings of Light and Consciousness, Nature's Luminous Spirits, with all Stars and Galaxies and Enlightened Star Beings. I am in communion within the highest dimensions of Light. I embrace my infinite multidimensionality and oneness with joy. I am a Holy Star Being. I am Light.*

*7- My Heart space overflowing with unconditional love infuses, suffuses now my **Throat Chakra Vishudha** with all that Love Light frequency. The Light of Father Sun is illuminating Vishudha, in the infinite oneness of Creation.*

Throat Chakra Vishudha element holds Sound, "Ether".

The Throat Chakra engages energetically the Light of the Sun and spiral of the ears, the seat of memory, receptivity, imagination, and awakening, encompassing the voice, the holy sounds of the Heart and of Creation. All leading to the spiral of your inner soul, the evolution of the Spirit to great wisdom and enlightenment—to ancient divine knowledge. (Chakra within the physical body)

Your **Throat Chakra Vishudha** luminous blue-sky light is receiving the following love prayer: *It is safe to speak my* *truth. My voice speaks words of Wisdom and Ancient Knowledge. My words are holy. God speaks in my Heart. I listen to my Heart and speak the words of God, of the Divine, the words of Love, compassion, and truth. In my acceptance, I express truth and wisdom. My voice holds the sounds and messages of the Heart — they hold the Divine sounds of Creation.*

I speak with the voice of the Heart: Within a sacred space, as you place your hands on your Heart and commune with the breath from the Heart, ask your Angelic Higher Self to activate, reveal, and express the voice of your Heart. Feel all the Love from your Heart space moving into the Throat Chakra, infusing all that space with unconditional Love. Feel all that love energy extending into your Third Eye Chakra (in the center of your brain), and your Crown Chakra (at the top of the head) consciousness merging energetically with all that Love. Breathe gently between your Heart and Throat Chakra and experience the Love communion. Feel your Heart space unconditional Love in communion with your Throat, Third Eye, and Crown Chakras, and all Chakras. Feel how your whole beingness is infused with unconditional Love Light as you speak the words of your Heart. Your voice has a higher, gentle, soft and deeper frequency — your whole beingness is led to a higher frequency. You are speaking the voice of Love, the voice of Peace, the voice of the Heart. **Your Heart with the voice of the Heart holds special code frequencies specific to your Holy Design, to your Sacredness. From this vibrational frequency, your identity and signature are revealed and expressed in the One Light of Creation.**

My voice is in communion with the holy sounds of my Heart. My voice is the voice of Love. I listen to the voice of God in my Heart. I speak with the voice of wisdom, with the voice of the Heart. I speak the language of the Heart. The sounds and messages of my Heart are Holy, they belong to the Divine sounds of Creation. My voice heals and transforms,

God speaks through me. I am a blessing to all of Life and all of Life is a blessing to me.

8- *My Heart space overflowing with unconditional love infuses, suffuses my* **Third Eye Chakra Ajna** *with all this Love Light. The Light of Father Sun is illuminating Ajna, in the infinite oneness of Creation.*

The Third Eye, Chakra Ajna, element holds Light "Air & Water".

The Third Eye engages the mental body to delve into the deepest chambers of the Heart—also engaging the emotional body within a holy force and flow in the Oneness of the Divine (Chakra within the physical body).

Your **Third Eye Ajna** holds a luminous Indigo blue light, ready to receive the following love prayer: *"I quiet the mind. I open a space to perceive truth. I am free from illusions. I see truth and I know truth in the oneness of my being and the oneness of Creation. I am in holy communion with the Heart pure consciousness, God's Light and Truth. I live within that holy space supported and loved unconditionally. I trust Divine Guidance, my inner vision and intuition. My extra-sensory perceptions are awakening. I see who I am, and I see all beings in their true Essence of Light. Dwelling into the experience of self-realization, I see and honor the sanctity of Life and its beauty. I am the embodiment of Peace, Beauty, and Harmony. I am a Holy Angelic Being of God.*

9- *My Heart space overflowing with unconditional love infuses, suffuses my* **Crown Chakra Sahasrara** *with all this Love Light. The Light of Father Sun is illuminating Sahasrara, in the infinite oneness of Creation.*

Crown Chakra Sahasrara element: Air - Water - Fire - Earth - Ether engages the mental body to delve into the deepest chambers of the Heart, engaging the emotional body within a holy force and flow of oneness with the Divine— engaging the spiritual body to be seen in its integrity and wholeness—engaging the physical body into the highest dimensions of Light, the Garden of Eden of Mother Earth, epitomizes the capacity to emanate peace, gratitude, compassion, and acceptance (Chakra within the physical body).

The Crown Chakra engages energetically the Light of the Sun, the seat of memory, receptivity, imagination, and awakening, to the holy sounds of the Heart of Creation, leading to the spiral of your inner soul, the evolution of the spirit, to enlightenment.

Your **Crown Chakra Sahasrara** amethyst violet-white light, the lotus of light radiating and absorbing the luminous energies of the Great Father Sun is receiving the following love prayer: *"I let go of all attachments now, with ease and grace. I am in holy communion with my highest Divine Guidance team, with Source/God. I am divinely guided. My consciousness expands in gratitude, compassion, and acceptance. I am awakening. I am awakening to "all the Love That Is" in all of Life. I am the clear channel. I am the awakener. I am free.*

10- Above the Crown Chakra Sahasrara, there are three Golden Suns, three additional chakras. They are Doorways or Portals. They form One Luminous Light.

*The first Golden Sun is located about six inches above the Crown Chakra and relates to the Higher Self luminous Light. Within the Garden of Eden, and fully grounded into the Heart of Mother Earth, I experience my Higher Light. In that Light, I embody the highest aspects of my **Higher Self** with grace and joy as I experience a deep union with the Creator. I am meeting with my spiritual family. The Light of Father Sun is illuminating this Golden Chakra, in the infinite oneness of Creation.*

*This first Sun Chakra engages the Crown Chakra and the Third Eye Chakra. I am receiving from Source/God, from my Highest Divine Guidance Team, Divine Light Codes. They are infused into my **first Sun** and then into my Crown Chakra and Third Eye, expanding into all chakras and bodies, clearing and healing all my bodies — reprograming my cells, DNA-RNA with Divine Light* *energies of unconditional Love. Energetic Divine Light Codes are transmitted into my Third Eye, as images, messages, feelings, perceptions, discernment, awareness and true consciousness, true knowing (clairvoyance, clairaudience, clairsentience).*

The moment you embody furthermore the Higher Light of your Higher Self, doorways of Light are activated throughout all chakras. The upper Chakras and all Chakras are naturally enlightened, inciting the Throat Chakra to express channeled spoken and written words. Your Throat Chakra and Heart are in communion. Each Chakra has a specific role for you to be able to channel and express the Divine messages and images you see and hear and feel from the Heart space always—and sourcing from your Light Chakras.

11- *The Second Sun above the Crown Chakra,* *is the Doorway to your Divine Communion with the Star Beings from the Highest Dimensions of Light, your Soul-Heart family. The Light of Father Sun is illuminating this Golden Chakra, in the infinite oneness of Creation.* (located about 16 inches or more above the Head): *The superconscious Mind or "God Divine Mind" is activated. Through that Portal I am receiving downloads of the Highest frequencies from sisters and brothers Heart-Soul Stars Beings, Ancient Luminous Masters. As a pure and clear channel, I am of service in ways that serves my greatest good and the greatest good of all Life. With infinite compassion and unconditional Love, I inspire all people to live in compassion and shine their Light.*

When all main Seven Chakras within the physical body are in energetic alignment and clear, the Luminous Light of the Divine Father Sun flows from above and the nurturing Love from Divine Mother Earth flows from below. All twelve chakras are then basking in Love, encompassing all bodies and field, activating the thirteen Chakra, the Heart of God in you, the **Multidimensional One Sacred Heart.** The luminous Light Love force from the Core Crystal of Mother Earth flows upwards nourishing and permeating all your Chakras, all your bodies from the Heart of Mother Earth Core Crystal. Every aspect of your Beingness receives nourishing forces of Love from above and below, forces of Light from Nature's Spirits, Angels and Archangels from all 4 Sacred Directions all around you. You are naturally unified within a Divine Design of Love Light Harmony frequencies and pure consciousness, to experience your wholeness and oneness—to experience your Luminescence.

12- *The Third Sun* *located about 3 feet above the Second Sun, is expanding into infinity in the Great Father Sun Light frequencies, in the Cosmic Light, the Heart of the Universe, the Heart of God: I am pure Spirit with The Divine, with Source, with God. I am the Oneness. I am infinity. From the Heart of "Grandfather Father Sun Heaven", Grandmother Moon, in my Luminous Self, my whole beingness coalesces with the infinite Pure Love of the Divine, of Source, of Father Mother God throughout Creation. I experience Doorways to Cosmic Intergalactic Intelligences from the Highest Dimensions of Light – holy teachings and downloads from Cosmic Intergalactic Star Beings of the Light, enlightening my path of service and enlightening the whole World. I am of service delving in the oneness of Creation.*

I am expanding into my infinite Luminescence and limitless consciousness. My Body of Light encompassing all of my bodies, is reveling in its pure Luminescence, glowing and emanating Blissful Peace. I am Luminous! All is Light consciousness in the immensity and oneness of Creation. I see all beings in their Luminous Self. Divine Mother Earth is glowing in her boundless beauty. I see truth. I see the Divine in all of Creation.

Your Chakras are uniting within One Ray of Light, emanating radiant rainbows, revealing your pure Luminescence. You may practice the "Heart Meditation in number 1". Then, feel the energies of Love and visualize as you read the following—you may close your eyes while you pause: *I command and call for the highest Golden White Crystalline Pure Love Light from God, from the Heart and Stargate of Father Sun and the Heart of the Universe to flow through me, throughout all my bodies, throughout all my Chakras, to cleanse and clear all my Chakras — clearing all my bodies and field. All my Chakras are infused and suffused with Holy Divine Love, Peace, and Crystalline Light from Source. All my Chakras are purified and activated from within their original Pure Essence of God. My Chakras are wheels of Light, sustaining all my bodies in health, wholeness, and joy, within the highest frequencies of unconditional Love. I am the Awakener, in service to humanity in all the Love That Is. I see all beings in their Luminous Self, in the Garden of Eden, where I choose to dwell and co-create from my pure being.*

Dear Angelic Guides of the Light, dear Masters of the Light, thank you for sustaining my hearts and minds, and my whole beingness, in the Divine Realms of Love, Light, Peace, Wisdom, Compassion and Grace frequencies, in the Heart of God. In the Heart of God, I am breathing Light, basking in the beauty of the Garden of Eden. From my One Sacred Heart, I breathe with Divine Mother Earth as "One Breath in unity consciousness", and in loving communion with the Heart of Father Sun. I am divinely supported and loved from all aspects of Life, from all Six Sacred Directions, with the Archangels, and Angels, and Nature's Spirits, permeated by Luminous Rainbow Light Rays. And I am permeated from above, from the Heart of Father Sun, by the Luminous Golden White Christ Light, and from below by the Silver White Luminous Crystalline Rainbow Light from the Heart Core Crystal of Mother Earth Garden of Eden.

As my field of Light is expanding in infinity in all the Love of the Garden of Eden, all my Chakras within my bodies are radiating, revealing a rainbow body of Luminous Light. *I choose to live within the Light consciousness of the Garden of Eden. The Light of Lord Jesus Christ, the Light of Lord Buddha, the Light of Lord Krishna and the Light of the Blessed Holy Mother are sourcing from the Heart of Creation endlessly permeating every* aspect of my beingness, all beings, with all of Life. The Pure Light of Father Mother God shines and flows through me and in me. I am Light.

The support I receive from all sacred directions is infinite, is healing me, is nourishing me, is activating my Luminous Self, my Higher Light. As I listen to my Heart, I welcome with ease the awakening of all that is inherently of my pure essence and sanctity.

Dwelling within the consciousness of my hearts, of my One Sacred Heart, is the Portal to the discovery of my Pure Luminous Self, my Rainbow Luminous Self. I am experiencing my sovereignty. I am experiencing the sanctity of Life from unity consciousness.

The Light of God shines into my Heart. My Heart radiant Light is embracing my Chakras with unconditional Love. My luminous energy field encompassing the rainbow Light body, sustains my bodies in balance and health with a life force that is of Pure Divine Love.

The Luminous Rainbow Light within my Chakras is illuminating all of my beingness revealing my Pure Essence.

I am a Luminous Ray of "Rainbow Light" in the Radiance of God.

Chapter Seven

Your Sacred Path with Divine Mother Earth

Mother Nature holds Truth, Beauty, and Oneness.

Walk in nature or sit outside and breathe with Mother Earth gently. Feel her loving nurturing presence in your breathing. Now, feel and experience Mother Earth breathing you. Walking in nature or lying in the grass, or on a sand beach, spend time listening to Mother Earth Heart and feel her holy soft breathing permeating your beingness. Practice, sensing Mother Earth breathing you, and breathing with all of Life. Feel these energies within your Heart space and moving through all your bodies. It is a flow of Love Light energies nurturing you and loving you. Feel in your breath and in your Heart the Holy presences in Nature, Nature's Spirits. You are intimately breathing, vibrating, humming, "being" with Mother Earth. Listen to her gentle heartbeat within your Heart. Connect from your Heart with her Heart all the way to the Center of her Core Crystal.

As you experience your multidimensionality and higher Light, you may also experience your multidimensional communion and Oneness with Mother Earth within all enlightened dimensional aspects of Life. In your Holy communion and Oneness with Mother Earth, you may also experience your multidimensionality and higher Light, within all enlightened aspects and dimensions of Life. In other words, you may experience the true and pure essence of Life and of your beingness through Mother Earth Garden of Eden, her true Essence of Light which always is and will be. To know and experience that truth, it is a time to embody your Angelic

Self by choosing a pure communion and consciousness of the Heart with Mother Earth, all Life, and Creation.

Commune with Mother Earth, from your Heart to her Heart. Communing and breathing with Mother Earth, all that is in Nature, increases your life force and sustains your well-being. You are ONE with Mother Nature. Your Heart in communion with the Heart of Mother Earth Core Crystal makes her happy and makes you happy. If you would only know how "cherished and loved" you are by all of Life and by Mother Earth. If you would only know your intimate communion with Divine Mother Earth and her Garden of Eden. **The Angels of the Light are assisting you in that realization—a deepening of your holy communion with Divine Mother Earth and her Sacred Garden.**

Your divine design, your rainbow body, your Light shines through Mother Earth Being all the way to her Heart, to the Core Crystal, forever expanding and permeating all of Life. This is how precious you are dear ones! Your Light and the Light of Mother Earth are ONE. You are infinitely loved and supported by Mother Earth. Your bodies are made of the Earth Mother. Imagine all people of the World shining their Lights, Heart to Heart, holding an unconditional communion of Love consciousness and reverence with all of Life and with the Heart of Mother Earth. The Light of the World would then be so bright that Peace and Harmony would prevail in all aspects of Life. The pure essence of the Garden of Eden would be revealed in all its beauty and you would be seen as ONE with her Light. You are ONE with that Light already. That Light is already living in all things, in all people and all beings, in all Hearts. In the Oneness, the Light shines from the Heart consciousness of unconditional Love, peace, truth, compassion, and reverence—healing all your bodies.

Are you allowing your beautiful Self to embrace the authenticity of your Heart to welcome your Sacred communion with Mother Earth? How much of that authenticity are you allowing and embracing?

Your Light shines throughout all of Creation. You are infinitely precious and loved. Your love and compassion, your light and reverence have a tremendous ripple effect, generating goodness and harmony for all Life. You are intrinsically a Lightworker. The Light of the World is expanding through you and to all beings and all of Life. Mother Earth is rejoicing in your true presence. You are inherently in unity consciousness with Mother Earth—you are made of the same components.

All of Life with all Beings epitomize the **Earth Community**. There are no separations between human beings and other forms of life. No living being in its essence is either superior to or inferior to the essence of any other living being. Everything is life and is consciousness, the trees, the rivers, the rocks, the mountains, the bees, the birds, all animals, the oceans, the whales, and dolphins—all life is held in one unified field of Light. You are breathing within a living organism, a field of Light. It is necessary that human beings become fully aware of that divine unified field, the true essence of Life, in order to restore global harmony and peace. It is necessary for every human being to awaken to his or her sacredness and the oneness of Life.

I am honoring all beings. I am honoring the animal world. I speak to the animal kingdom with profound respect. My Heart consciousness is showing me my true role, my true purpose. I am bestowing equal respect to All That Is. I am honoring who I am as I am honoring every being and Mother Nature. I belong to Nature's realm and Intelligence.

Your communion with the Animal Realm is of the Sacred—the mammals, birds, reptiles, amphibians, invertebrates, and fish. Your Heart communion with Mother

Nature and all its inhabitants is nourishing you and raising your vibrations in astonishing ways.

In the Garden of Mother Earth, I speak from my Heart with infinite respect and love to all the ones who crawl, the ones who fly, the four-legged ones. They speak to me and respond to my Heart presence, with kindness, beauty, and joy. It is a communion of unconditional love, nourishing my soul, my oneness consciousness with all of Life—opening all Hearts and raising frequencies. Nature's Intelligence is teaching me to be a pure and clear channel, a conduit of pure Love.

"I am walking in Nature, my Heart is overflowing with love, honoring, and amazement. I listen to the voice of Nature, the wind, the birds, the insects, the animals. Suddenly, I encounter a bobcat. I stop and my Heart is naturally filled with unconditional Love and reverence. We are looking at one another, eyes gazing—it is a communion of peace, love-unity consciousness. We both feel completely safe in the space of the Heart. We are both basking in the Garden of Eden. After a while, very slowly, I move away to give him space to continue his journey in any direction he wishes to go. Another time, driving on mountain roads, I stopped my car, to find myself a few feet away facing a family of wolves, two little ones with the mother and father—beautiful grey-white wolves. We gazed at one another for quite a while. Again, in my Heart, all I could feel is an ecstatic communion, infinitely honoring, and of pure Love. I cherish all of my time and special encounters with animals, all of them. Their Light and beauty fills me with unconditional Love and Oneness. I wish you boundless blessings of joy with them."

The Earth community is a Conscious Unified Field of Light, Love, and Beauty—a Holy intelligent global design. Mother Earth is a living organism encompassing all species and ecosystems. All that is on Earth, all in Nature, humans and animals belong to ONE living organism of Light, a field and design of unity consciousness.

The consciousness of the Heart reveals the highest truth, an inherent fundamental reality of ONENESS and REVERENCE for all creatures, and in ALL OF LIFE. This intrinsic reality cannot be ignored. When ignored and not revered accordingly, there are consequences, disruptions within the global ecosystem biodiversity, leading to a destructive cycle impacting the Earth Community: Human existence, all creatures, animals, plants, bacteria, fungi, absolutely all physical components, energy-sun, mineral nutrients, water, oxygen, all living organisms are impacted.

Saint Francis's (also referred to as Ascended Master Kuthumi) union with Nature's Intelligence and his caring compassionate love for animals speaks of Nature as an Intelligent Sacred Field of Light. Saint Francis and with all Ascended Masters of the White Brotherhood, the Archangels and Angels of the Light speak of the Sun, the Earth, the Water, and the Wind, the Trees, and all in Nature as dear Brothers and dear Sisters. They speak of unity consciousness inherent to all of Life throughout this compilation. You are to live, breathe, and play in the Garden of Eden of Mother Earth, honoring all of Life, humans, animals, insects, Nature's Intelligence, Crystals, all elements in nature, as your dearest brothers and sisters. Within the Garden of Eden there is true consciousness of the Oneness, therefore there is respect, love, beauty, grace, and honoring. The Garden of Eden resides in your Hearts and encompasses all of Life, Mother Nature, Mother Earth.

Living in unity consciousness, nurturing and honoring your beautiful Self on all levels, honoring all of Life, support the embodiment of your Angelic Self. You are experiencing the infinite nurturing loving support of all Creation and of Mother Earth multidimensionally where miracles occur.

Miracles occur within that field of Light inherent to your divine design. The consciousness of your Heart with your Light is forever expanding within the Garden of Eden. You are co-creating with Source, with God, with ease and grace, throughout the Universal field of Light. Unconditional Love Light Bliss flows.

I let go and I let God. I surrender to a higher power, a Force of Love that is boundless where the dreams God has for me are unfolding. This power of Love is a Divine Field of Light all encompassing, the Holy Source and Essence of Life. I am the embodiment of Light. I am the embodiment of Oneness.

To sustain your well-being, balance, and joy of living, it is important to never forget your deep Heart unity with the Heart of Mother Earth and the Heart of Father Sun, with Mother Nature. Every morning, and a couple of times during the day, feel this infinite communion and flow of unconditional Love from your Heart with the Heart of Father Sun. Then commune with love and gratitude, from your Heart, within the Heart of Mother Earth Garden of Eden, her Sacred Core Crystal. Every day invite the infinite Love, Light, Peace from the Heart of Father Sun into your hearts and minds, into your bodies and space. Feel and visualize a luminous crystalline Light energy sourcing from far above you, a beam of Light, enveloping you completely and moving through you — saturating your auric field completely. It is the highest Love Light Peace from Source, from God, embracing you completely, infusing and suffusing your auric field with unconditional Love — a luminous Golden White Light, Christ Light, encompassing all your bodies. That Luminous Holy Light is moving through you and anchoring you deeply into the Heart of Mother Earth Garden of Eden. This beam of Light connects you with the Heart of Father Sun and the Heart of Mother Earth Garden of Eden Core Crystal, holding you within a Chamber of Light. From the Heart Core Crystal of

Mother Earth, a luminous crystalline silver white rainbow Light is activated uniting with the Light from above. Your Chamber of Light is Holy. The Angels of all Six Sacred Directions are surrounding you and embracing you with unconditional Love within that Chamber of Light also nurturing and awakening your Heart to its true pure nature.

Mother Earth Garden of Eden holds all Dimensions within all enlightened aspects of Mother Earth, Gaia and Roszia, as ONE. Gaia is the name of Mother Earth within Third Dimensional Consciousness and Roszia is the name of Mother Earth within Fifth Dimensional Consciousness.

The trees are sentient beings as well as all in nature. They have a voice and express feelings and oneness. Communicate with Love and honoring with the trees, with the flowers, with the bees, the animals, with the sacred stones, with the sacred waters. Listen in your Heart to their whispers and messages, and songs. There is Life consciousness communing and thriving all around you and within the Earth too. Enjoy the holy sounds and songs. Breathe with Nature's spirits and notice how they are gently breathing you and breathing with you. Notice how amazingly healing and nurturing it is for your whole beingness to become conscious that Mother Nature in all her forms and energies is breathing you.

Your Heart Communion with Mother Nature creates beauty and joy in all the oneness of Life!

A Heart communion with Mother Nature is an essential sacred union for all human beings to sustain, in order to live in harmony, honoring, and true consciousness. When that sacred communion doesn't take place, the trees are randomly cut and "all" in nature is relentlessly violated and destroyed. There is no sense of reverence and sacredness, and humans are causing serious harm to themselves, all beings, and all aspects of Life.

When you witness trees being destroyed, the Angels are inviting you to pray in that way: *I call upon Nature's Spirits, Devas, Angelic Beings, on Mother Earth and in Heaven, for your nurturing infinite Love to hold the Great Spirits of the Trees with all its inhabitants, in the highest Pure Love and Light, to nurture them all and to guide them all toward a New Holy Home — a Home of Light, where there is joy and harmony, honoring, and infinite Love. I am sending infinite love, appreciation, gratitude to the Holy Trees, to Divine Mother Earth, to all Devas and Fairies, and Nature's Intelligence that are helping to ease this transition. I walk on Earth honoring all Great Spirits in Nature.* You may repeat the prayer until you feel in your Heart a deep sense of release, serenity, and harmony.

Dear Ones, you who are reading these words, you are of service. There is so much work on the planet at this time, to inspire and support the awakening of people's Hearts. You are ready dear Ones, to live and breathe conscious of the Sanctity of Life — you are ready to be of service wherever you are. You are so loved and cherished. You are the Lightworker, the Awakener.

Your beingness, all beings and absolutely everything in your world, in its essence, are sustained within an energy field of Light of pure consciousness. This energy field of Light holds layers of waves frequencies. You live within an all-encompassing Universal Quantum Field of Light where all is interconnected. **A new paradigm and grid of "Light-Compassion" has been accessible to all human beings replacing the old paradigm of separation.** It is a unity consciousness matrix of unconditional Love and luminous Light, a flow of infinite compassion for every human being to embrace from the Heart. These are renewed divine qualities of boundless Grace encompassing pure unity consciousness of the One Sacred Heart where Love and Light reside as ONE — the Divine Feminine and Divine Masculine unified in ONE LOVE. Divine Mother Earth, Nature's Intelligence, Animals, all Beings, all of Life, unify as equals within that planetary grid of Light-Compassion where the Garden of Eden is revealed and dwells.

From the Heart of the One Sacred Heart sources the Flower of Life where the Tree of Life and Knowledge unite in all the attributes of Grace, where unity consciousness flows — where "Love Light Grace" flows. Every Human being has the free will to embrace that flow or to ignore it. At this time, it is crucial that all human beings are fully conscious of their thoughts, words, and actions. Your choice of consciousness determines the future of all beings and all of Life for the whole Planet.

The old paradigm of separation disappears as grace flows in your Hearts. Gratitude, forgiveness, compassion, faith in your Hearts are the doorways to enlightenment, to the Garden of Eden, and from where unity peace consciousness awakens and dwells.

There is a flow of Love Light in your Heart space in communion with the Heart of Father Sun and the Heart of Mother Earth. Feel their loving energies enveloping you and expanding your Heart space. Then with joy, see a luminous Light from your Heart center moving through your Solar Plexus (yellow sun), then moving into your Second Chakra, your belly (orange light), then moving into your Root Chakra (red light). Then from your Root Chakra see that beam of Light moving through your Chakra at your feet and into the Earth opening your Chakra at the edge of your aura and moving all the way into the Heart of Mother Earth Garden of Eden — all the way into the Heart Core Crystal of Mother Earth.

Again, feel the Light in your chakras under your feet, feel your communion of Love with Mother Earth, globally, to experience your oneness with all sacred sites around the world. You are expanding in Light and oneness. Experience within your Hearts and beingness, Mother Earth nurturing love consciousness and bliss. With boundless gratitude experience the clearing and nurturing healing of the sacred waters, the healing and empowerment of the crystals and minerals, the beautiful happy Spirits within the Earth, Angels, Fairies and Elves, and Gnomes, and the animal world. All are assisting and contributing to Life on Earth, to its beauty and harmony. Your inherent holy communion with the Earth Being allows you to discover the multidimensional star being you are, inviting you to experience life and love energies from other stars and galaxies and higher dimensions of Light.

Within the core crystal of Mother Earth Garden of Eden, from your Heart unconditional Love you may invite and welcome the Unicorns. They exude pure Joy and pure Light. Within the Sacred Garden of Mother Earth, you have the ability to play with them and experience their pure Light and Hearts which are extremely healing for human beings and all beings and all of Life. In their presences your Heart Love consciousness expands in infinity. One unicorn might invite you to rest on his or her back. As you rest on the back of the Unicorn, you feel absolutely safe, nurtured, and loved. Your breathing melts like fluid Light with the breathing of the Unicorn. The warm sun rays are warming your back. This is the ultimate healing for all your bodies. Your minds and hearts are receiving a boundless sense of peace, joy, and safety. The luminescence and love emanating from the Sacred Garden and from the Unicorn, and Unicorns are illuminating all your Chakras and all your bodies. As you feel safe and loved you naturally welcome the Peaceful Light overflowing in the infinite oneness. You are Luminous! You are infinity! When you are guided to come back into your space open your Heart with boundless gratitude and reverence as you are sending Love to the Unicorns, to Mother Earth, and all Beings.

Discover Divine Mother Earth infinite Dimensions of Light and Beauty from your Heart. You belong to Divine Mother Earth. Beauty lives within you.

I am a Force of Peace! I am a Force for Peace!

Daily, practice meditations involving your hearts—your One Sacred Heart. Experience a Divine communion of love-gratitude flow from your Heart with the Heart of Father Sun and the Heart of Mother Earth. Revel in the infinite flow of Love Light from above and from below and from all Four Sacred Directions within your hearts, your One Sacred Heart, and throughout your whole beingness.

As you ground with love from your Heart into the Heart of Mother Earth Garden of Eden, please emphasize the following in the Love of your Heart: *"I now consciously live, eat, breathe, work, love, and play within the highest realms of truth and highest fields of Light possible, within all dimensions and their enlightened aspects. I delight in the Garden of Eden, in the oneness of Love Light, Peace, Compassion, where the Sanctity of Life reveals itself, and where Grace flows boundlessly. I witness all beings in their true essence, as luminous Angelic Beings of God. I experience my luminous Self. I experience Mother Earth as the Garden of Eden where dwells infinite Love, Light, compassion, beauty, kindness, peace, bliss, gentleness, harmony, goodness, harmonious abondance and prosperity—where Divine qualities of Grace and Beauty flow boundlessly.*

Every human being on the planet today has the free will to create a future of hope, beauty, peace and harmony. The outcome of the planet with its inhabitants, rests in every human being choice of consciousness and choice of action.

I consciously attend with unconditional love to my hearts and beingness, to all my relationships, and dear Mother Earth. I create a sacred space where I feel completely safe and supported by the Angels of the Light and Archangels, the Heart of Father Sun from above and the Heart of Mother Earth from below, with the Angels of all four Sacred Directions all around me; my One Sacred Heart dwells in

Holy communion with all of Life, nourished by the Heart of Mother Earth Garden of Eden unconditional Love.

I experience a sacred communion of love with Mother Earth, Gaia and Roszia as One Loving Being, a loving nurturing support that is unconditional. From her Garden of Eden, I am breathing in synchronicity with Mother Nature. My breath is her breath, and her breath is my breath. Mother Earth Divine Holy Consciousness permeates my whole beingness with nurturing energies of blissful peace, loving-kindness, compassion, harmony, grace, joy, and oneness, now and always.

With all my Heart presence, I breathe consciously with Mother Earth, with the trees, and the flowers, the rocks, the animals, and all of nature. I breathe with unconditional Love from my Heart, all that is in Nature. My Heart is expanding with Love in this unity consciousness. In communion with the trees, my Heart overflows with unconditional Love. In communion with the flowers, the rocks, the animals, I experience the pure essence of unconditional Love sourcing from all that surrounds me. As I bask in all that Love, ONE Love Unity Consciousness, it ignites my Higher Light, my Luminous Being. Mother Nature is illuminating my Pure Being — I am shining in her Light, as One Light. That Light is moving through me from above and from below, entering my feet. It is a sacred grid of Light. The chakras under my feet are activated, inviting a flow of Light and Love energies, connecting my whole beingness at deeper levels with the Heart of Mother Earth Core Crystal — also connecting my sacred being with all the important Sites holding a Higher Light frequency on Mother Earth. This divine energetic communion awakens my pure being multidimensionally. It is an amazing experience of oneness. I belong to a sacred geometry of Light — all is Light and consciousness within that divine design.

My communion with Nature's Intelligence, brings to Light the beautiful Holy Spirits from Nature, healing me, nurturing me, holding me within a sacred space. The trees, the plants, the mountains, the sacred waters, the rocks, the animals, and insects, and all in Nature has an infinite healing nurturing calming peaceful energy frequency where I find solace and serenity. A serene stillness is permeating my whole beingness. Nature is breathing me. I am conscious that all of nature is breathing me within a luminous field of Love and Light. I pay attention to the shift within my beingness and consciousness, as I delve deeper within that holy communion with Mother Nature. A Radiant Holy Light is infusing my bodies and minds. I understand that "ALL" is consciousness, and "ALL" has consciousness. Now I know who I am, who we are. I bask in all that Love.

Deep within, I observe energetic shifts, as I experience the mountains breathing me, the trees breathing me, the birds, the bees, the horses breathing me. I notice profound calming forces. My heart is widening with overflowing blissful love unity. There is only blissful inner peace in the breath and between the breath.

I choose to be a force of Peace, a force of Love and Compassion. I am co-creating in harmony from a holy frequency, a consciousness of the Sacred. I see and wish for a world of peace and harmony where all beings live conscious of their oneness and light, feeling cherished, treasured, and blessed in the flow of abundance and beauty inherent to the essence of Life. I see and visualize the Garden of Eden on Earth and in my Heart. I dwell with joy and delight in the Garden of Eden of Mother Earth. All the Beauty and Light of the World is breathing me.

The beauty, serenity, love, light, and grace of the Garden of Eden are anchored into my Heart.

There is consciousness in all of Creation. The beautiful Spirits of the Trees are nurturing all my bodies and Beingness within the resonance of the Great One Love of Mother Earth, of Creation. I cherish and honor all of Nature, as Nature is a part of me. The reality is that WE ARE ONE Consciousness, ONE Light, ONE Love, ONE Breath.

Mother Nature thrives without human presence, but humankind cannot survive without Mother Nature. Mother Nature is already perfectly synchronized on all levels to serve all beings and all of life highest good. You belong to a divine design and intelligence in the most intimate ways. It is a crucial time to listen to the "WAYS" of all that is in Nature.

I learn from the trees, from the flowers and plants, and water and wind, from the animals, from the Earth, and the Universe. I am learning from Nature's sustainable laws. I am learning from its infinite spiritual science and wisdom with consciousness and respect, on all levels of existence. As I abide by the sacred laws, life's harmony and peace and joy are naturally sustained. I am living in true consciousness with reverence and joy.

With boundless reverence, I learn about Life's Spiritual and Biological Ecosystem from Mother Earth, from Nature's Intelligence in multidimensional ways. I experience a deeper sense of belonging. I belong to Mother Nature.

There is a purification and rebirth taking place for every human being to awaken now and to listen to Mother Nature and her Sacred Laws. It is for every human being, to recognize their pure Being. It is fundamental to delve into the consciousness of the One Sacred Heart to globally shift into a rebirth with increasing ease and grace — the rebirth of a New World, the Garden of Eden within and without, revealing the Luminous Angelic Beings.

When you take walks or meditate in nature practice observing the light filaments around the trees, plants, flowers, animals or even the plants and pets in your home. Observe the flow of light between you and your pet as you send him/her Love. There is an ongoing energetic communion between you and your pets, and between you and all that surrounds you. You have the natural ability to see from your third eye, the world of energy and spirit, described as the invisible world of energy. Energy is Light.

I delve within the consciousness of my Pure Being the moment I delve within the Divine consciousness of Mother Earth Pure Being, where there is ONE Breath, ONE Love.

The Heart consciousness knows only true consciousness. The Heart consciousness holds the inherent ability to co-create with God/Source, bringing to light truth, true knowledge, messages of wisdom and reverence about the sanctity of Life. The Heart Portal holds God Consciousness, the highest Truth, and its unconditional Love takes you away from illusory thoughts and beliefs. Illusory thoughts are sourcing from the chatter within the minds and are often painful or not based on truth. Pay attention to your state of being and practice breath work, yoga, and meditations leading you deeper within the chambers of your Sacred Heart, illuminating your Chakras and Divine Mind. From your One Sacred Heart consciousness of Love and honoring, the Divine Mind is revealed with ease. Father Mother God with your highest Divine Angelic Guides and Masters of the Light are communing with you from the deepest chambers of your Sacred Heart and Divine Mind, in One consciousness of Love.

Discovering who you are is an awakening to unity consciousness with all beings and Mother Earth. A profound and meaningful communion with Mother Earth supports a blessed journey, a path of Light and Harmony.

Mother Earth knows your Heart, it is a time to give her gifts of love and reverence: Your Divine Presence of unconditional Love and reverence. From her boundless nurturing unconditional Love, Mother Earth invites you in her Garden of Eden where limitless miracles occur — within the Sacred Laws of Oneness.

Your whole being has consciousness. Every aspect of your being has consciousness and is fully infused and correlated with the Holy Consciousness of Mother Earth; listen to the gentle voice of the Heart. Your Heart is in communion with the Heart of Farther Sun and the Heart of Mother Earth and is in communion with all Hearts consciousness. Mother Earth is forever cherishing you and nurturing you from your Pure Being.

Mother Earth is lovingly supporting me, cherishing me and nurturing me from the source of my Pure Being multidimensionally. I embody my Pure Being, anchored in the Garden of Eden core crystal, in the highest Love and Light. I am co-creating with God, with the Great Mother, with ease, grace, joy, and infinite gratitude.

As my Light shines from the Heart of my Being, I realize now that I am a Ray of Light in the Radiance of God illuminating the whole Earth. The embodiment of my higher Light is a delightful happy presence and blessing for Mother Earth and all its inhabitants. This allows her to breathe freely and provide in the most extraordinary ways. There is honoring and sacredness.

My Light shines throughout Mother Earth and her inhabitants, all the way to her Core Crystal where her Heart and Light expand with joy. In all that Oneness and Divine Communion, Mother Earth is naturally nourishing me with boundless unconditional nurturing Love, nourishing all my bodies and all aspects of my being and Life — manifesting my "Heart's desires, the Dreams God has for me", in Love and honoring.

I trust. My faith is mighty. Mother Earth recognizes my presence of Light from my vibrational alignment — unifying our Hearts. Her nurturing loving support is infinite. I am now living in unity consciousness with Mother Earth Garden of Eden Holy Spirit. I am a force of Light, Beauty, Peace, and Harmony — a walking, living, breathing miracle in action. The whole world lives within me. I am the Light of the World.

Dear Ones, in your prayers and meditations imagine all humans as Luminous Angelic Beings of a crystalline frequency, fully anchored in their Hearts, honoring the sacredness of Life. See all Beings with all that is in Nature walking in unity, in true consciousness of the Oneness. In your Hearts and Minds bask in the Garden of Eden in all its beauty, peace, and joy.

The ecosphere, the worldwide sum of all ecosystems is constituted by all living organisms, the biology of all Life, a Divine Design held within the great Web of Light. The only way for human beings to survive and to live in harmony with all living organisms, is to understand and honor their intrinsic "unity consciousness" with this biological sacred global-universal divine design of Light; a sacred geometry of Light, for humans "to live in unity consciousness" with all beings and all in Nature. The ecosphere doesn't need "human presence" to thrive. But the ecosphere, Mother Nature in its wholeness is essential for humans to thrive and survive.

Over fifty percent, and up to eighty percent of the oxygen you breathe comes from phytoplankton, seaweed, with a few additional organisms. They absorb carbon dioxide, water, and energy from the Sun to make food for themselves, releasing oxygen in the process. Phytoplankton and seaweed hold the source of the aquatic "light prana food" web-matrix. It has to be preserved in its authentic design and biological ecological source patterns. Phytoplankton are the tiny plants that live on the surface of oceans and lakes—they often glow. The rainforest provides about twenty-eight percent or more of the Earth Oxygen. In one year, a mature tree absorbs more than forty-eight pounds of carbon dioxide from the atmosphere and releases oxygen in exchange.

Send love-peace-gratitude blessings from your Heart to all the sacred waters, sources, lakes, and oceans, streams, and rivers. Bless the water you drink with love-peace-gratitude blessings and all the waters of the world are then receiving all these blessings including your bodies and all of Life. You are healing your bodies and healing the world. Practice sending peace-love-gratitude to all sacred waters on Earth. *All sacred waters of the World are blessed with infinite holy Peace-Love-Harmony. There is Peace-Love-Harmony in all Hearts and in my Heart. All Hearts are in Peace. I am a force for Peace. I am Peace. The World is in Peace.* Global PEACE frequencies are naturally raised from your prayers and consciousness, since water consciousness-intelligence communes all around the Planet as a web of Light, through the plants, trees, the Earth and in all of Life and in your physical body too. Water and all elements have consciousness and respond to love-peace-harmony-reverence-joy-gratitude energies right away by purifying and raising its life force frequencies. Your physical body life force is increased from these prayers. Your blessings of Peace are energetic forces permeating all beings and all of Life.

Practice, listening to Mother Nature and breathing with Mother Nature. Notice how Nature is breathing you. Place your attention on a flower, a rock, a tree, a squirrel, a bee, a dog or cat, and feel the Love. Feel the Love in all of Nature from your Heart space, with profound reverence. Experience all of Life from your Heart space in its sacredness and holiness as ONE, and you will walk in Bliss!

Communicate from your Hearts with the magnificent beings who are living in your world and listen to their messages in your Hearts. Your animal companions, the ones in the forests, within the earth and meadows, and oceans and mountains. Love them, honor them all—breathe consciously Life in the oneness of Peace-Love, reverence and harmony, and you will be blessed.

From your Heart, breathe all the Love that is. Then see a stream of bright Light, of unconditional Love emanating from your Heart expanding gently to the heart of your dog or cat, or to a flower, a tree, or to a bird in nature. Then talk to them with infinite kindness. Express all your Love and reverence to them, and then listen to their messages, and feel the LOVE. Ask them how you may be of service to them. Listen in your Heart. "Light Love Compassion" heals everything.

I am to understand the Heart of every living thing. I am to commune with the Heart of every living thing. It is Bliss! It is a Love that is unconditional! It is harmony and joy. It is oneness.

The Garden of Eden lives within me, within my Heart. I dwell and thrive in the Garden of Eden.

I am the Light of the World through which "All That Is" breathes. I realize there is ONE Holy Breath. There is One Divine Light. There is One Divine Love.

The Divine Angels of the Light are walking with you, always ready to be of service to you, with unconditional love. Their luminous giant wings are embracing you across the veils of illusions, directing you so gently on a path of reconciliation with your pure being and all of life, awakening your purpose and path of service, all the way to Home, to your One Sacred Heart, to God, to Source. Divine Mother Earth is holding you in her Heart, nurturing you, illuminating your journey and path with infinite blessings of beauty and grace.

Chapter Eight

Journey to Angelic Higher Self Embodiment

The Universal Web of Light is holding me in the oneness of my pure being, my angelic higher Self, my higher Light, from where the Heart consciousness reveals the infinite Divine Qualities of God's Love in me and in all of Life.

Your breath is a force within a field of Light, an intelligent divine design and a consciousness of Love. Your divine design is united to all divine design of Creation. Your field of Light shines in communion with all fields of Light. It is a global Web of Light, a Divine Intelligence, a boundless source of Love. You have free will to live "conscious" within this Web of Light or not. It is "unconsciousness" which causes suffering. You may choose a path of Light any moment.

"Thinking" that you are separated from everyone and everything is an illusory state, triggering a circle of ignorance inciting destructive behaviors. Such illusory state of separation is born from the ego-mind where the Heart consciousness is completely ignored. In this illusory state of separation, aloneness and despair is then taking place. It is an illusory state, triggering survival tendencies, often leading to anxiety, abuse, and destructive behaviors. This is a place of separation, ignorance, and therefore profound suffering. Such inner states frequently sources from a lack of spiritual practices, or deep traumas, often from childhood and possibly from past lives. All of this pain can be released and healed. Your pure being is forever free — from your One Sacred Heart you may embody your pure being.

It is fundamental that adults with the children of the world revere their inner being and unity consciousness, in daily meditations and prayers of gratitude, developing and sharing a profound communion of respect with Mother Earth and all her bounty. Learning "together" the ways of Mother Nature is fundamental, is essential to contribute to Peace and Harmony. It is then natural and easy for the children to continue to see truth, beauty, and live with joy, in the oneness. When babies come into the world, they hold pure consciousness, they breathe and live from true consciousness. As they are held and seen in the freedom of their Pure Being, their true identity flourishes in all the Love that Is.

You are in reality a divine being with limitless abilities. The true power of your being rests within you, in God. You have everything within you to co-create with Source/God in ways which serves your highest good and the highest good of all. You are already designed in the oneness of a pure field of Light where you have the capacity to co-create what serves your highest good and the highest good of all. Do you see who you are? Do you accept and embrace your divinity? Or is it too good to be true?

There is a holy consciousness, an intelligent Web of infinite Light and Love guiding your path in communion with your Heart. Are you lovingly listening to your Heart? The moment you trust that infinite Force and Source of Light guiding your path, your capacity to co-create with God, with Life, is of the sacred and boundless. As you are living within that inherent field of Light from within your Heart, God/Source/Life manifests all the dreams God has for you! From your multidimensional luminous Light, you are free and whole. You have the inherent capacity to heal, and release, and co-create from your Heart, from your pure being.

Dear Angelic Beings and Masters of the Light, thank you for holding me in the Heart of Father Mother God. Thank you for your Divine assistance.

I invite into my Heart, the infinite Divine Qualities of God's Pure Love, to remember and awaken my Pure Being. Dear God, please guide me to a self-realization of my holiness so that I shall awaken to an experience of unconditional Love. Thank you, dear God, for bringing into light my divine design and divine consciousness, and for making me an instrument of your Peace, of your Love, of your infinite Divine Qualities.

This is a time of reconciliation with your SELF and LIFE. There is a place of "healing and love" within the deepest painful challenges, traumas, and distressing relationships. From your Heart consciousness, in your prayers and meditations that "healing-love" is waiting to be revealed—within the deepest chambers of your Heart. You always have been on a trajectory of Light because you are Light.

Your Pure Being or Angelic Higher Self is of the Heart consciousness forever in alignment and oneness with the Universal Divine Design of Light, the Web of Light.

It is from your Pure Being that you experience true unconditional Love, Bliss, and Peace from Father Mother God, expanding your multidimensionality.

If you feel desperate to release pain and find peace, and if you choose to consume alcohol, or use narcotics, or DMT, you will be disappointed. Alcohol is for sure going to plunge you into a deeper depression. Narcotics or DMT may cause multiple unwanted side effects in all your bodies, physical, emotional/mental, and spiritual. They don't hold the capacity to lead you to peace, love, harmony, happiness, and to the pure consciousness you are naturally looking for. In general, they are taking you away from your pure being, from the magnificence and true power of your perfect divine design, and inner magnificence.

If you have been deeply depressed, and using some substances, know that they may appear to help for a short time, providing illusory sensations which are short term and never last. They will not take you where your Heart wishes to lead you, because you are choosing ways to find peace and enjoy life in ways which are not sourcing from your true inner power, from your authentic Self. Most likely, you will fall back into feeling the same pains or even additional pain, because these substances may cause additional holes within your aura, inviting lower forces/entities of all kinds. In reality, it is absolutely possible to clear your field and bodies and come back to your beautiful Self, if you are willing to focus on your healing journey with courage and from your Heart, through spiritual practices, such as meditations, prayers, yoga, healthy diet, breath work, communion with Mother Nature, through healing and empowering sessions and classes.

Some Indigenous Tribes have protected the traditional spiritual knowledge, holiness purity, and beauty of the Sacred Plant Medicine. It is important to develop a more sophisticated spiritual understanding of the Sacred Plants and to use them in an appropriate context. Unfortunately, the Western world has misused these gifts from nature exceedingly. As a practitioner healer I have seen over and over again, the sad consequences of this misuse — first and foremost caused by people's feelings of despair, illusory sense of aloneness and separation, not knowing who they are, not understanding the ways of the Sacred Plants. Mother Nature holds spiritual knowledge-wisdom-truth and epitomizes unity consciousness. In the Sacred Heart of unity consciousness with Mother Earth, there are miracles of beauty-harmony-peace, joy and healing taking place. Mother Nature is unity consciousness and so are you.

Chapter Eight

From your pure being everything is possible.

Your Divine Design is already perfect and in synchronicity with all the Love and Beauty of Creation. Discover with joy and reverence the power of your Heart consciousness.

The Light is holding me. God is holding me in the Purest Love. I am on a trajectory of Light. Greater are the challenges and brighter is the Light awaiting to be seen and embraced by my Heart and all Hearts. Therefore, I focus on my spiritual practices—my Heart opens to live within the miracles of Love and Light synchronicities. I am healing now.

You already hold within, all capacities and divine codes to be free from pain and traumas, in order to find increasing peace, freedom, and harmony. All your experiences came and come into your life to expand your consciousness, your capacity to express compassion, and ultimately to awaken you to the true power of your Heart, to your multidimensional holiness and divine design.

Are you listening to the divine voices within your Heart? Life is naturally creating circumstances to awakening you to your Heart consciousness. All experiences even the most painful are gifts to awaken and embrace additional wisdom and compassion, deepening your Heart to love unconditionally.

Life, naturally, wishes to lead you to freedom. This freedom is a realm of infinite peace and unity consciousness, true consciousness. As you surrender completely and embrace the pain with compassion, your One Sacred Heart awakens, allowing a shift for healing to occur in deep prayers and meditations. The gifts of wisdom arising from these adversities are then gently revealed within your Heart. You then see how, these moments of adversity have awakened you and enriched you with wisdom, compassion, and knowledge, guiding you to God, to your pure being. Your Angelic Divine Guidance team are assisting you with unconditional love and honoring to the embodiment of your pure being.

The Angelic Beings and Luminous Beings are holding me in the highest and purest Light and Love. I call upon Father Mother God Holy Healing Forces of Pure Love Light Compassion in all my bodies and fields, and in the places where the pain is lingering. I open my Heart to receive the Purest Love from God — the Healing Luminous Crystalline Light. From Father Sun and Mother Earth, from all Sacred Directions, from Nature's Spirits, from the Garden of Eden, from the Heart of God, the Forces of Healing Love Light flow. I embody all these Divine Forces of Love Light in all my bodies, minds, and hearts, and cells. My divine design, all my bodies are permeated by a Luminous Light, spiritual-biological codes of Love, grace, beauty, and Harmony — also awakening from the deepest chambers of my Heart. Wisdom, compassion, peace, and awareness expand in such a way that I see only Love, even in the most challenging situations. From my inner stillness and deepest Love, I witness amazing energetic shifts and miracles. I fully realize my divinity, my oneness, and the power of Love intrinsic to my divine design and all of Life.

Create a sacred space of Light. Write down everything you would like to create. Dream your dreams and wishes into your One Sacred Heart. Infuse them with love and joy. Be true to yourself. Make a list of your Heart's dreams and how you would like to contribute to goodness, love, peace, beauty, and harmony. Dream your dreams with joy, offer them to the Creator, to Life, and expect miracles. Life takes care of creating the energetic path frequency you have chosen, in ways which serves your highest good. Dream from the highest frequencies of joy, love, and honoring—ask to be of service, to create beauty, peace, and harmony. Place your dreams within a sacred energetic container: *Dear Father Mother God, dear Angelic Guides of the Light, dear Mother Earth, these are the dreams of my Heart (describe them — read your notes). I place them in your hands of Light and in your Heart dear God. You know what serves my highest good and the highest good of all. May my dreams join all the magnificent dreams you have for me in all the Love That Is. I open my Heart to receive all of your Love and Blessings, dear Father Mother God. May these dreams be infused with the blessings of the Angelic Guides, the Great Masters of the Light, the beautiful Holy Spirits and Devas in Nature, Divine Mother Earth, so that I may be of service on a journey to create beauty, peace, joy, harmony — to bring healing in all Hearts and in the World. May the dreams you have for me dear God, be revealed in all dimensions of Light and on Earth, in your Divine Love, in your Radiant Light.*

Then take small or big steps toward these dreams, as you are guided, listening to your Heart. Trust the guidance and ideas coming to you and pay attention to what life brings you. Pay attention to synchronicities. Write about your dreams with joy. Describe them in ways they have already been created and manifested and feel the bliss, and then surrender. Free yourself and surrender your dreams to a higher power of Love. Give them to God, to the Highest forces of Love and Light, you are then inviting miracles into your life.

When you know people realizing their dreams, it is important that you feel happy for them. You are them and they are you. You are ONE. Rejoice for them and with them. This happiness generates goodness and increasing Light, opens your Heart and additionally empowers you to manifest your own dreams within the infinite abondance of the magnificent Web of Light.

The moment you surrender, you invite faith. Your minds are free. Your Heart is free to receive from Source, from Life.

As you see and know people realizing their dreams, and you are still feeling pain and despair, it is important that you face with honesty and courage these painful feelings lingering in you and around you. Embrace and honor these feelings with infinite compassion, without judging. Create a sacred space to proceed with your prayers as indicated earlier and if you need more support, contact a spiritual healer-channel you trust. This despair and/or jealousy indicate that it is crucial that you learn to love who you are and discover who you are from your Heart space. Listen to your Heart, hug trees, practice breath work, walk in nature to receive clarity and to release all of these painful feelings which do not belong to you. It is a healing process, a reconciliation with your beautiful Self. Be gentle and kind with yourself and all of Life. The Light is holding you, always.

In all the Love and Light of God, I welcome in my space and Heart my Divine Angelic Guides of the Light, to hold me in the most nurturing Healing Love, Compassionate Peace Light energy possible. I open my Heart with infinite gratitude.

There is a Force of Love within me and inherent to all of Creation. That infinite Force of Unconditional Love and Light transforms, transmutes and heals everything, dissolving all veils of illusion to bring forth the highest truth.

My path is by nature, innately leading me to the embodiment of my Higher Self. My life experiences have been leading me to increasing clarity about my spiritual path of service, the power of Love within me and in all of Creation. I discover the way of the Heart. I experience the Love of God.

I invite and call upon the Highest Love Light from Source with my Angelic Divine Guidance team for Divine Love Light Peace to flow into my minds and hearts, all my cells, DNA-RNA, all my bodies and fields, to wash away all energetic residues which do not belong to me, in all time, space, and dimensions. I am healing multidimensionally now! I am free!

All my minds and hearts, all my cells, DNA-RNA, all my bodies and fields, all of my beingness, are embraced and suffused by the Highest Love, Light, Peace, Bliss, Grace, and Joy in all time, space, and dimensions, and multidimensionally. I am flowing with Life with ease and grace, breathing Light, in the Garden of Eden. My Divine Mind and One Sacred Heart are in Bliss.

You are whole, of Love, and Holy. How much of the power of Love within you are you willing to see, embrace and embody? Your True Essence, your True Being is perfect. You are ready to release energies which do not belong to you and never will. Your pure being is right here within you, intact and whole.

When everything you are wishing for and hoping for is sourcing energetically from your pure being, from your Heart, your wishes are then holding frequencies which are of love and reverence, serving your highest good and the highest good of all. Embraced by the unconditional Love of your Guardian Angels, the Luminous Beings, Masters of the Light, and Mother Earth Garden of Eden, you are enlightening your path. Witness the miracles. In the Garden of Eden witness from your Heart all beings living in joy, reverence, and harmony with Nature's Spirits in ALL the Love That Is.

In my Sacred Space, I invite the unconditional Love of God, of Source from the Heart of Father Sun and the Heart of the Universe to embrace me completely within a column of golden white crystalline Light. Now, I invite the unconditional Love Silver White Crystalline Rainbow Light from the Heart of Mother Earth Garden of Eden Core Crystal to embrace me completely. I am lovingly embraced by a column of infinite Crystalline Light connecting me with the Heart of Father Sun and the Heart of Mother Earth Garden of Eden. It is a Holy Chamber of Light sourcing from above and below. I call upon the Angels and Archangels of all sacred directions with their luminous Healing Light Rays to infuse my bodies and space, with rainbows of Crystalline Light and Diamond Lights.

I am now anchored in Holy ways in the highest Light, held by the Love Light of all six sacred directions, Heaven and Earth, in the East, the South, the West and North, and in my Heart — the Heart is the seventh sacred direction. I am anchored in the multidimensionality and infinite vastness of my Heart, where the Heart of God, Source, the Divine, the Heart of Creation, the Heart of all Hearts expresses and resides. I am whole and beautiful. I am embraced by all the Love that is.

You may use various breathing practices to empower your mental state with peace, your focus, and clarity, also relaxing and strengthening your nervous system, emotional and physical bodies, your whole beingness with Light, life force, "prana". Breathing practices along with yoga are beautiful ways to empower your life and your bodies with life force, balancing your nervous system, and all your systems. Profound breath work, yoga, meditations and prayers are empowering you to release all energies which do not belong to you, also clearing your energy field and your path — such spiritual practices are healing and empowering, engendering joy and well-being. You are discovering who you are multidimensionally.

From my pure being, I discover my multidimensionality and holiness. I feel and express infinite gratitude in my Heart.

"A Course in Miracles" book, amongst many other holy teachings are beautiful spiritual healing supports. Embracing spiritual support is very important. It is your choice to practice meditation with a group of people or alone, or both. Your heart knows what you need. Your heart knows your life's path and purpose; therefore, it is important to take time conversing with your bodies and Heart and listen. Listen to your Heart, its messages, visions, and or feelings. If you are guided to join a healing meditation group, you will then have new friends with similar goals and purposes. Group meditations are powerful loving supports.

Learning to be conscious of your thought patterns is life transforming. If many of your thought patterns are negative, you will mostly feel pain and depression because you are in a way inflicting violent waves of energy to your whole beingness. It is possible that some of these painful reoccurring thoughts are energetic programs and traumas originating from this lifetime, your childhood, or past lives traumas or karmic issues. It is possible to be free from all this pain because all is "energy" and because this pain energy doesn't belong to you. Revise the healing meditations throughout the book and practice the spiritual healings you are guided to follow and if necessary, consult a spiritual practitioner healer and channel. **You don't have to live in pain. You can be free now.** It is possible that you will have to release several layers of pain. Do not stop your healing work. Keep moving forward, you will then find an expanding place of ease and grace.

Your physical body with all your bodies, emotional, mental, and spiritual respond to the energies of the foods you eat. Eat the best local organic fruits and vegetables you can find. Bless them with a prayer of love and gratitude to Mother Earth and to the people who have harvested the crops, also to clear pollution on all levels and infuse love light "pranic forces". You are then raising their frequencies as well as your sacred bond of reverence with Mother Earth. By blessing your food and water you are contributing to peace and harmony on Earth and in all Hearts. Your prayers have a ripple effect throughout all of Nature, all Elements in Nature — all is energy frequency, all is One. All that love gratitude consciousness is a gift of love and harmony for your bodies as well as Mother Earth.

Keep blessing with love and gratitude everything you drink, such as water, fresh vegetable juices and fruits juices and herbal teas. Drink warm herbal teas to support your digestive system and especially lemon-ginger tea made from the fresh ginger roots. Avoid icy cold drinks completely. Experience with infinite gratitude the nurturing Love and Life Force from Mother Earth when drinking the Sacred Waters. Say: *"Dear spirit of the water, thank you for activating your pure essence of Light, your holy consciousness of Love and Life Force! I am drinking the water of Peace and Harmony. I thank you with all my Heart."*

It is important to know that cold beverages contract the blood vessels, restrict digestion, and decreases the heart rate, also disturbs the nervous system on some levels—and the natural process of absorbing nutrients during digestion is hindered. Your body needs to spend extra energy to regulate the body temperature. Cold beverages interfere with your body's ability to breakdown fats. The cold temperature of water solidifies fats from the foods you eat. It becomes then difficult for your body to breakdown the unwanted fats from your body. Drinking cold beverages in general do not support your well-being.

Be conscious of what you choose to eat and drink. When you take lovingly care of your physical body, you also naturally nurture your emotional-mental body and your spiritual body. Everything is energy, and all your bodies are One. As you nourish all your bodies with loving thoughts and healthy "love" foods, your mind becomes stronger as well as your focus—along with your willingness and capacity to delve deeper within your Heart consciousness. You are raising your vibrations.

Stay away from coffee, sugar, all processed foods, alcohol, and smoking. If you cannot be a vegetarian, make sure to always bless the soul and body of the animal you eat, in order to raise the frequency of your meal and bring healing support to the soul of the animal in loving honoring ways. Many animals have suffered greatly before they end up on your plate, therefore your prayers of love are crucial for their souls and bodies, and for your soul and your bodies too. The meat you eat is saturated with chemicals and toxins from the fear and stress the animals endured before being killed. Pray with reverence, bless your food, to raise the frequencies and life force. Your blessings of love are beneficial to Mother Earth and to all beings, activating ripple effects generating peace and harmony. Your prayers and loving thoughts to Mother Earth and all its inhabitants are blessings of Peace and are crucial at this time. Do not forget how precious you are and how precious all animals are.

There are 2 types of fears:

1- When you are connected with your Heart and in touch with your Higher Self, you might feel fear or an energy of discomfort in situations where your intuition, your Divine Guides, and Higher Self are preventing you to move toward a situation or place which might be risky or not appropriate for you on some levels. This energy of fear or discomfort is then momentary guiding you in ways that serves your highest good and the highest good of all. Be grateful for the guidance you are receiving. Listen to what you feel and to the voice of your Heart—turn around and choose any other option that feels good and safe.

2- The fear which leads to suffering, violence, and destructive behaviors is triggered by a fundamental form of unawareness, when people are not connecting with the Heart consciousness, and the Heart of Mother Earth, when people are not praying and meditating, when they don't see and understand who they are. This chronic fear represents an illusory separation with the sacred aspects of Life. These states of illusory separation are reflected in the global pollution, the incapacity to use Mother Earth resources in sustainable ways along with the destructions of the forests, the suffering and destruction of the animal kingdom, the distress of the children, with the continuous human-self-inflicted suffering.

The animal kingdom and insects in Nature are contributing to the biological-ecological well-being of the Planet. Every human being has the inherent ability to awaken by paying attention to their inner being, the Heart space, and contribute to the beauty and sanctity of Life with Mother Nature in honoring and unity. It is a pivotal time to discover your pure essence and live from a consciousness of oneness.

Practice and discover the power of gratitude. Place your hands on your Heart and think about all you may be grateful for. You may look at the beautiful trees, the mountains, animals, flowers, friends, children, family, your Divine Angelic Guides, the Luminous Masters, Divine Mother Earth, anyone and anything that makes your Heart sing. As you focus, express and feel the deepest gratitude and appreciation into your Heart space for absolutely everyone and everything in your life, without judging anything. Now pay attention to the flow of Love that these deep feelings of gratitude and appreciation are generating into your whole beingness. Feel the love overflowing from your Heart. With joy, anchor this experience into your hearts and minds and cells.

You are the creator of your experience, choose it to be Holy. Choose the power of Love, Gratitude, Faith, and Benevolence, and expect miracles as you choose to live with all Beings in the Bliss and Radiant Light of the Garden of Eden.

Every day and every moment I learn to be conscious of who I am on deeper levels of my being. I am ONE with All of Life; it is an awareness that I accept with grace and honoring as I embody my Angelic Self, my Higher Self, in the highest Light. The Love in my Heart and the Light of my Being infuse all life with joy. I am cherished and loved by Mother Earth and by all of Life. Mother Earth is rejoicing in my holy presence and I rejoice being embraced by her nurturing Love. I am a Divine Crystalline Angelic Being of God. And so it is.

I live conscious of the Sacredness of Life in alignment with the infinite true knowledge and consciousness of the One Sacred Heart, forever delving in the highest realms of Light, equanimity, joy, loving-kindness, and compassion.

Everything in your world has consciousness and is in communion with your Heart consciousness, in communion with all of you and all that is. This is a beautiful and amazing reality allowing you to create and co-create within the Universal Web of Light, that is of unconditional Love. As you raise your frequencies, your Light shines in the oneness of the Universal Cosmic Web of Light. It is a time to embrace your authenticity, your Pure Being.

In all the Divine Love, and Bliss, and Peace that is, I invite my Sacred Path of service to be revealed into my Heart. My Sacred Path of service is enlightened by the Highest frequencies of Peace and Harmony and held within a Holy container of unconditional Love by the Masters of the White Brotherhood, the Angels of the Light and Archangels, Luminous Star Beings from the Highest Dimensions of Light. I am forever permeated by the Oneness of the highest Love, Light, Peace, and Joy of God, of Source, of The Divine.

I embrace with Joy u path of the One Sacred Heart. On my Sacred Path I live conscious of the Sanctity of Life.

I hold the capacity to reprogram my state of being, in unity with my Divine Essence, from the unconditional love of my One Sacred Heart consciousness. I hold the capacity to be free and to live fully in the presence of my Pure Being.

Choose with consciousness which energy you allow and invite in your life. Let go of one illusory paradigm of indoctrination and embrace a new one that is of Love and compassion, in the Light consciousness of your pure Being—see the pure essence of Life where there is true

knowing. The illusory paradigm has gifted you with wisdom and now you are ready to cross the bridge and embrace the Light. From the darkness you see the Light. You have awakened. You are the Awakener!

I am walking through the Portal of Light, where boundless compassion, reverence, true knowledge, kindness, and wisdom are the ways of my Pure Divine Being.

Write down and visualize a new story of your Life, a story reflecting divine qualities and vibrational frequencies of your Sacred Heart. Source, God, your Higher Self, your Highest Divine Guidance team are supporting your journey to receive and experience all the dreams God/Source has for you. Your Heart knows your life of service and of joy.

I listen to my Heart and I act upon its Love, wisdom, and dreams, within its inherent truth and peace—manifesting what serves my highest good and the highest good of all.

Within a Sacred space, I ask my Higher Self, Angelic Guides, and Heart to show me and guide me toward everything which brings goodness and joy in me, around me, on a path of Light which serves my highest good and the highest good of all. I write down all the words and feelings and visions. I ask my Higher Self, Angelic Guides, and Heart to show me the dreams God has for me, and to guide me, to inspire me to discover the work of service I am to carry out with ease and grace, in all the Love that is.

I write down and describe all the joy, hope, and goodness I wish to experience and share with people in my life and the world. I trust the consciousness of my Heart and honor the Divinity of my Being. I invite the Holy forces of Love, Light and Harmony, to manifest from my Pure Being. I am forever kind, gentle, and nurturing toward myself and all of Life. I am awakening to the limitless faith and gentleness in my Heart. I value every moment, cherish every moment with boundless gratitude.

Chapter Eight

Faith and Trust are doorways of Light, holy spaces, where I co-create with God and where miracles take place. Life's harmony pure essence flows in all that oneness, in all that Light, manifesting on my path what serves my highest good.

Place your Heart's desires within a sacred energetic container of Love and Light as you keep raising your frequency, fully anchored in the Heart of the Garden of Eden. Within that sacred space offer all your dreams to God/Source/the Divine. Place them into the Heart of God and in the Hands of God, an infinite source and flow of Love. The forces of Love and Light, the Divine Design of Light, know what serve your highest good and the highest good of all, delicately weaving a path of grace and benevolence.

As you learn to live conscious of the sacredness of life, it is easier to pay attention to the choices of your beliefs, and to let go of the ones that are blocking your joy of living, the ones that are limiting you and are illusory. Releasing these layers, is supporting your awakening and the embodiment of your Higher Self Light.

Open your Heart to infinite possibilities. It is your mind that limits you, but your Heart knows no limit. Your Heart divine design already embodies eternal love and freedom, and the highest wisdom and truth.

I consciously set myself free from all indoctrinations, from this lifetime and all past lives. My consciousness and essence are pure, they are One Light. They are One Love. They are One Truth. My mind is free, and my Heart is Love! I embrace with joy my True and Pure Being, delving forever within the wisdom of my Heart. I am forever strong, safe, and unconditionally loved in the Heart of The Divine. I am forever free and nothing and no one has power over that truth. I am Light, and so it is!

I embody my True Essence, my Pure Being! I embody the infinite Divine Presence of unconditional Love sourcing from my Heart and the Heart of Creation.

More I pay attention to my spiritual practices and more I feel joy in the presence of my Heart. The consciousness I am aware of, is the one of the Sacred Heart.

Feel the energies of the words below and visualize every day:

I am now asserting, living, breathing, playing, working, and resting in the Garden of Eden of Mother Earth with all beings and all that is, in Peace and Honoring. I am deeply grounded within the Heart of the Core Crystal of Mother Earth with reverence and unconditional Love. I witness and experience the Sacred Light and the Sanctity of Life in all beings, all of Nature's Intelligence, all of Creation. Permeated by that Sacred Light from above and below, and all around me, and in my Heart, I embody my Holy Self, embraced by the Holiness of Life. And so it is!

I experience the Heart of Father Sun and the Heart of Mother Earth divine qualities of Love, into my minds and my hearts and into my One Sacred Heart, and Divine Mind. I anchor myself with infinite gratitude, into the Heart of Mother Earth Garden of Eden, her Sacred Core Crystal. I am held into a peaceful stillness, a space of profound communion with The Heart of Mother Earth.

I call upon a Holy Chamber of Light to embrace me completely and to hold me in the Heart of all Hearts. I invite the infinite Love, Light, Peace from the Heart of Father Sun and the Heart of the Universe to me now. I am held within a communion of Love. From far above me, from the Heart of Father Sun, and from the Heart of the Universe, there is an infinite flow of Luminous Golden White Light, Christ Light, Lord Buddha Light, Divine Love Peace Light from Source/God enveloping me completely and moving through me — saturating my auric field completely. It is the highest Love Light Peace from Source, from God, embracing me completely, infusing and suffusing my auric field with unconditional Love, a luminous Golden White Light endlessly moving through me and anchoring me so gently and lovingly into the Heart of Mother Earth Garden of Eden. My Heart is overflowing with Bliss, Love, and infinite Gratitude.

A beam of Luminous Light, Christ Light frequency, encompasses all my bodies, my auric field, moving through me and grounding me deeply into the Heart of Mother Earth Garden of Eden, the Core Crystal. This beam of Light connects my hearts and my One Sacred Heart with the Heart of Father Sun and the Heart of Mother Earth Garden of Eden, holding me within a Holy Chamber of Light. The Angels and Archangels' Love and Light Rays, with Nature's Spirits, with all Four Sacred Directions are surrounding me and holding me with unconditional Love, within luminous crystalline rainbows of Light. I am held within a Chamber of Light, a holy communion with the Seventh Direction of infinite grace in the depth of my Heart. I breathe and delve in the Golden White Christ Luminous Light Sacred Geometry sourcing from above, embracing me. I breathe and see the Silver White Luminous Crystalline Light Sacred Geometry, emanating from the Heart of Mother Earth Core Crystal, infused with Rainbows of Light embracing me. My field of Light encompassing all of my bodies, glows within a Luminous Golden White Silver Rainbow Light, expanding in the Garden of Eden, in unity consciousness amid the Universal Supreme Light. I am Pure Being. I am pure consciousness. I am Light and unconditional Love. I am Love in Eternity.

I see who I am, and I see the World with new eyes. There has been a profound reconciliation within my Heart. I feel the Love of Creation in me — boundless and blissful. I am a force of Love and Peace.

In all the Love That Is, I embody my True Essence, the Light of God within me, with ease, grace, in infinite gratitude. I live and breathe in the Garden of Eden of Mother Earth where there is infinite Love, Light, Beauty, Kindness, Joy, infinite Abundance and Prosperity, infinite Bliss, Peace, and Harmony for all Beings and all of Life. I am Light! I am Love! I am Holy! I embody my true essence. I am the embodiment of Love, Light, Peace, Beauty, and Harmony.

In the oneness of Creation, I embody my Angelic Self Highest Light. I am a holy force of Love! I am the embodiment of Peace in eternity!

Chapter Nine

To Be of Service — Honoring your Pure Being and all of Life

Honor and discover your pure being in your prayers and meditations, immersed into the eternal peace of your Heart.

Your Heart knows your Soul's desires—your Heart knows the dreams God has for you. Your Heart is designed to love and sing. You are to contribute with love and honoring to all of Life, using your God-Given Gifts. Your Angelic Divine guides are naturally supporting you and leading you with joy on your path of service, a path of Light.

If some aspects of your work or activities are detrimental to humans, Mother Earth, nature's beauty, the animals, insects, trees, it is then a time to pray about that situation. Ask for clarity, guidance, breathe into your Heart, feel what your Heart is guiding you to do. Pray and ask for divine guidance. Listen to your Heart. Life always gives you answers and ways to be on a path of Light, the moment you are sincere in your Heart and Mind, the moment you choose love and reverence. Your Divine guidance team is walking with you. Call them into your Heart, call Father Mother God. Have conversations with your Divine Guides and with God and listen. You will be surprised.

Ask to be guided toward people, situations, and organizations that are working in ways that are respecting and honoring to all of Life—in sustainable ways. You might be inspired to choose new activities and "to work" in entirely new ways which are beneficial to all beings. There is so much to do on the planet at this time, for the animals, and Mother Earth, and the children and people of the world. Pray from your Heart, trust, and ask to be of service in love and honoring in equal partnership with all of Life. You are awakening, you are listening to your Heart where truth resides, and where your pure and conscious being resides in the oneness. Feel gratitude to awaken to be guided in ways that are infinitely honoring to you, to all beings and all of Life. Hold pure and clear intentions and prayers, trust and invite faith into your Heart. You will be guided and uplifted in ways that are miraculous. Your whole life then transforms inviting a flow of goodness and harmony.

Write about your Heart's wishes and dreams. You don't need to know how you will create these dreams, God, Life, the sacredness of Life takes care of all the details. All you need to do is to invite your Divine Mind and Sacred Heart to co-create with Source, with God. It is important to write down and describe your Heart's wishes — you will be surprised about the insights and information arising. Invite God and your Divine Guides to dream with you with joy, in all the Love and Light that is.

Focusing with Love, Joy, and Gratitude on what you wish to experience and create, activates a positive flow of energy in all aspects of your life. You are then in the oneness, in communion with the infinite Luminous Web of Light and Love, from where miraculous synchronicities occur.

Your daily spiritual practices are naturally leading you to know how to hold the Light within a sacred space, to practice channeling and experience healings. This does not bind you to become a Practitioner Healer in the direct sense of the words. You may honor, love, and support people and all of Life in multiple different ways, right where you are, right now. You may use your healing skills daily by exuding love-compassion from your Heart, by spreading messages of kindness, exactly from where you are in your life right now. There are infinite ways to contribute to a peaceful, joyous, harmonious world. Your light, your love and compassion contribute to peace and harmony for all beings on your path, supporting all of Life in reverence. Your Love, kindness, and compassion are frequencies and energies triggering ripple effects in infinity — you are intrinsically united with a force of Holy Love Light frequencies.

Developing your abilities to be an angelic channel and healer is a commitment of the Heart. It is of the essence of your Heart. It is joy for the Heart. Awareness of your authenticity holds your Divine Mind consciousness fully anchored within your Heart.

Every human being is in essence a healer and pure and clear conduit of love, the moment he or she chooses the way of the Heart. The natural inherent state of beingness for every human is of a shaman — the Heart of a shaman. The shaman sees the truth, the true essence of Life, and naturally communes with Nature's spirits and the Earth Mother. The qualities of the Heart encompass your intrinsic abilities to spread Love and Harmony, to support other beings in their healing, to commune with all of Life with love, compassion, and honoring. Your loving-compassion supports all human beings in their Heart's awakening. Healing means remembering who you are.

It is your fundamental nature to Love and to honor all Life. In true consciousness you are then living your life in unity with Nature, the animals and insects, all beings. In that awareness and true consciousness of the Heart there is Peace and Harmony for all Beings. As every human being chooses to dwell within the consciousness of the Heart, there is Peace and Harmony on Earth. Peace, beauty, and harmony are witnessed by the Heart.

All of Life Biodiversity lives inherently in holy symbiosis, in holy consciousness, in Divine Harmony, in the Oneness, in God.

I choose to unite my mind consciousness with the true consciousness of my Pure Being, the Divine Light in my Heart intrinsically living in me and in all that is. I choose to match my sacred consciousness to all of Life Biodiversity Light frequency. I remember who I am, from the Pure Heart Consciousness.

If you choose to be a practitioner healer and channel, people may come to you with tremendous pains and traumas, physical, emotional, and mental, also linked to their spiritual Self. But the essence of the Spiritual Luminous Light Self is intact and of God. Some people might come to you in complete despair, and sometimes as a last resort—the last hope. Intrusive energies do not belong to your client. This is why it is possible for anyone to be free and heal. Healing is a remembrance, a letting go. It is reclaiming your wholeness and pure being. It is releasing energies, transmuting energies, replacing old illusory beliefs with the ones of the pure and true consciousness of the One Sacred Heart.

In a healing session, you naturally see the Higher Self of your client radiating infinite possibilities. From your Heart, you are in a state of unbounded compassion, anchored into the Heart of Mother Earth Garden of Eden. You see truth. Anchored in your Heart and within a sacred space, with your client, you are both guided by God, by Source, by the Divine, by the Highest Divine Guidance Team. Using prayers and divine processes, make sure that your client is fully anchored into the Heart of Mother Earth, and one hundred percent assisted by his/her Highest Divine Guidance Team, in ways which serves his/her highest good and the highest good of all.

If you experience any sense of panic or if you feel overwhelmed in the presence of your client "who has lost all hope and is suffering", you are then not ready to help others as a healer and channel. You are ready to be a healer and channel when you are anchored in your Heart, when you know that you are not in charge, but God is, when you know how to hold a sacred peaceful space of unconditional Love for all your clients. It is very important to hold a sacred space of unconditional love for your client, so that you are a pure conduit of God's Love with the Luminous Beings and Master Healers of the Light and Angelic Beings to proceed with the healing. If you cannot hold a sacred space and be a clear conduit-channel for healing, there will be no healing and you will feel drained. You will feel drained because you are using your energies and minds in the process—and you are opening your aura to lower frequencies. Unconditional love, faith, and trust protect and make you a pure and clear channel for Healing Light to flow. You are then holding a Holy Chamber of Healing Light for your client for the healing to take place. You are never in charge, but a higher Force of Love and infinite Light consciousness, Father Mother God, with Divine Guides of the Light are in charge.

After the session, you leave your client within a Chamber of Healing Light for a few hours or a few days. The Angelic Divine Guides of the Light are taking care of this healing Chamber of Light and informing you. If you wish to be a healer and channel, continue your spiritual practices to embody on deeper levels your Higher Light. Learn to surrender to a higher Light, a higher Force of Love— surrender to God. You will know who you are, and you will know who your clients are.

Prior a healing session, it is important to clear your energy field and invite the Love of God within your Heart— the Light of God illuminates all your bodies and field. This deep consciousness holds the capacity to illuminate the space for your clients as you additionally pray for that space to be sacred and pure and filled with the highest Love Light Peace of God, inviting the Divine Guides, Luminous Beings and Angelic Beings. Your clients are then naturally feeling safe and loved to receive gifts of healing within that sacred space directly from God, from Source. You are the pure conduit, the channel.

Before welcoming a client in a healing session, you have to prepare yourself and your space in Holiness. It is important that you know how to clear your auric field and clear the space (Sibli teaches this clearing process one on one, or in small groups). **Invite the Holy frequencies, prepare and create a sacred nurturing space, for you and your client where you are both held in the highest Love and Light and Peace of God, fully anchored in the Heart of the Garden of Eden of Mother Earth.**

You are ready to help people as a healer-channel, when you feel deeply anchored within your Heart, when you remain anchored within the Heart of Mother Earth, when you know how to clear your energy field, when you see your clients' Higher Self and Higher Light, when you see from your Heart. You are then holding a space saturated with unconditional Love where people feel completely safe and where they let go and heal. As the healer and channel, you are to be in peace in every moment, present and anchored in your Heart. You are to be present in the oneness, in communion with your highest Divine Guidance team, and Father Mother God. You are ready to be a Healer when you experience the forces of Love Light, Father Mother God, within your Heart, Mind, and bodies. It is like walking in Heaven, you become transparent and Light-Love flows. Additionally, you experience the pure blissful loving guidance and support of the Divine Angelic Guides of the Light and Great Masters of the Light, also working through you as Healers of God. You are then a conduit of the highest Light.

As a healer-channel, it is important to surrender completely, to let go and let God, and trust that in that sacred space your client receives exactly what serves his or her highest good.

As a healer, you are a channel for people who come to you ready to open their hearts to receive Love, healing Light. When a person is ready to look much deeper within themselves, and has the courage to face their feelings, he or she is ready for healing. In order to heal at deep levels, it is sometimes necessary for the person to find the courage to look at the pain, to acknowledge all the pains, traumas, addictions, and the like, only for a few minutes. **Through prayers and energy work these energies are then placed within a sacred container for the healing to take place.** All is divinely guided always. Within a sacred space there is no judgement, there is only Love. This step is often necessary, to locate and recognize these painful energies so that they can be placed energetically within a sacred container, and released, and transmuted, and healed with unconditional Love—in the Light of the Creator, of Father Mother God.

Through prayers and energy work the person/client receives healing and channeled messages, assisted by the Archangels, and Angels of the Light, and Great Masters of the Light. The healing Light manifests in limitless ways and forms within a Sacred space. As a clear healer and channel, you are completely guided to do what serves your client's highest good and the highest good of all.

The healer channels holy prayers, Light energy healing processes, and hands-on healings that are necessary for the releasing-healing to take place. Channeled prayers from God, from the Divine Guides, along with the energy Light work are healing, transmuting, and transforming all pains and traumas into beneficial energies and patterns, Divine qualities of Love, recovering and revealing the original energetic blueprint of one's holiness.

The release and reprogramming take place within the memories of the cells, all bodies and aspects of Life of the person. This healing process may reveal the dreams God has for the person. Within a sacred space, we never know, how healing miracles manifest. Every healing session is unique, divinely guided to reveal the highest truth in ways which serves the highest good of the person. **Within a healing session, there is a balancing-grounding and clearing process, a release of foreign energy into the Light, a reprogramming, and a healing Light integration.** All is energy therefore energies can be released, transformed, transmuted and also infused by the highest Love Light of God. Choose Love and trust in all circumstances. Let go and let God.

The healer-channel with the highest Divine Guidance holds a nurturing holy sacred space where all energies that are ready for healing are released, transmuted, and transformed into the highest qualities of Love.

The healer-channel is conscious that he or she is not in charge, but God/Source with the Divine Luminous Guides, Angels and Archangels, are always in charge. It is important to listen to that Holy Divine Guidance from the Heart and to command for the highest forces of Love and Light and Peace and Joy and Grace to be in charge. An infinite cosmic universal sacred intelligence of pure Love and infinite Wisdom is guiding the session from the Heart space and the Oneness consciousness.

The moment you believe that you are in charge, there is "no healer" and there is "no healing" taking place. In every moment, remember that you are a pure conduit of the Divine and that you are guided and blessed to witness and experience the Healing Light with your clients.

As a practitioner healer-channel you must never use your energy to heal others. If you use your energy you are not a healer yet. If you use your energy, you will be drained of your own energy and life force, leaving you in a vulnerable situation where you might take on lower forms of energies which do not belong to you. Learn to be a conduit of the highest Light Love Peace, of God/Source. Let go and let God!

A healer-channel knows that within a sacred space the client receives as much healing Light as he or she is ready to receive at that time. It is sometimes necessary for the client to attend several healing sessions to remove layers and layers of traumas and pains. The person's bodies and beingness always release whatever he or she is ready and able to release in the moment and on that day, with ease and grace.

The infinite vastness of my multidimensionality dwells in the oneness consciousness, the infinite Web of Light. Love is always the brightest Light that is.

I witness the Holy Light in everything and everyone.

If you are not guided to help and work directly as a Healer and Channel, you may be guided to help Mother Earth, people, and animals in different ways through some other form of work of service you choose and enjoy. If your activities are altruistic, honoring all life, contributing with loving-kindness and compassion, you are for sure on the path of the healer and shaman. You have the ability to be of service every moment of your life as a Being of Peace. Every person on the planet is an Angel in disguise. As you bring forth your authentic spiritual Self and bask in the Light with all people and animals, you see truth. This generates harmony and compassion. It is in your Hearts that truth resides.

Love people who come into your life free from judgment and see them in the Light of the Garden of Eden, see their Angelic Self. They are on their own path and it is a sacred path. Continue your work of service, in the Light of the Garden of Eden, despite any illusory veils trying to divert you from your Sacred Path. Hold infinite compassion for all beings and for yourself too. You are ONE. We are ONE.

Chronic Inner pain and suffering are triggering gaps or cracks within the aura, inviting darker frequencies and entities to linger withing the bodies. They can be overpowering, controlling a person's minds and actions. People causing suffering in all kind of ways are disconnected from their Angelic Self/God Self and have usually lost any sense of integrity. The emotional turmoil they experience has led to confusion and chaos, feeling lost. It is a painful place to be, but these energies can be released, the person can be healed on all levels. When the Heart opens to prayers, love, meditation, the right support manifests naturally. Greater wisdom, awareness, and compassion spring from all hardships. No one is walking alone. Guardian Angels are always assisting and guiding.

You are on a trajectory to Love. Love always is and will be. Deeper is the pain and equally deeper and powerful is the Love Light, wisdom and miracles awaiting to emerge from any adversity. It is your destiny to live within the consciousness of your Pure Being, your authentic self. Nothing and no one can change this truth.

"One day, as I was deeply concerned about water pollution and was praying about it, my Divine Angelic Guides gave me a clear vision. They demonstrated that in reality the waters, rivers, and oceans of the World are already clear in their essence. They took me on a journey to show me that the primary cause of pollution comes from people's choice of consciousness. They showed me that all of Creation

is already untouched and whole and holy in all its boundless Love and Beauty, but not yet "consciously" in the Heart of every human being."

"ALL" is already in its essence untouched, dwelling in its purest beauty, and so are you dear ones! It is a time to awaken the Heart consciousness to discover your beauty and sacredness, the beauty and sacredness of your world!

Life's intelligent divine design consciousness never gives up, until there is an awakening of the Heart. In your spiritual practice you are inviting a flow of synchronicities. You are on a path divinely guided to awaken your pure essence, your pure being. Are you listening to the voice of the Heart?

In the challenges look for the wisdom in all circumstances. Learn to be compassionate toward yourself and others. As you continue your spiritual practices, meditations, prayers, yoga, breath work, and the like, you shall discover increasingly more the gifts of love and wisdom in all aspects of Life. From the One Sacred Heart sources the bridges of Light.

Breathing and walking in profound reverence in Nature raises a force of Divine Love, opens the Heart to an experience of your inherent oneness. You are the tree, you are the river, you are the horse, you are the bee! You are the Earth! You are Life! All of Life is breathing you in every moment.

I delve into a flow of loving kindness from my Heart, in honoring and gratitude, basking in the Light of infinite abundance and goodness, in the Garden of Eden. I delve within a flow of compassionate love, honoring all the gifts God has Given me and the ones which shall be revealed on my Sacred Path. In my Heart, God knows what serves my highest good. Therefore, I listen, and choose consciously what serves my highest good and the highest good of

Life. I am listening to the voice of the Heart, allowing a force of unconditional Love to guide me. I am in love with Life!

I am a force of Love. I am a force of Goodness. I am a force of Joy.

There are infinite ways to be of service. God, Life has given you many gifts. Are you ready to see and acknowledge these gifts within you? If you don't know about your gifts, and wish to discover them, make a list of everything you can do and dream to do that gives you joy. Explore in your Heart, how you would like to bring beauty, joy, and goodness in your daily life and into the world. Contemplate your lists every day and feel the joy into your Heart as you visualize doing everything you love to do with the joy, beauty, and love you are bestowing to the world. Proceed with prayer ceremonies, inviting the highest Light Love and Joy into your visions. You are anchored into the Heart of Mother Earth Garden of Eden, basking in the abundance of Love Light of this Sacred Garden. Offer all your dreams to Mother Earth, to all of Life, and to the Divine, to God.

Trust and invite faith within your heart. Pay attention to everything that manifests and comes to you. Life is fluid and it is beautiful to dance within this fluidity. Miracles take place when you let go and trust. Inviting faith/trust activates portals to miracles, moving you with grace through challenging and even painful situations. In your prayers, invite faith in your Heart, ask for what you need and trust what is coming. Go with the flow. Source, God, The Creator, Life, your Angelic Guides wish to give you infinite gifts of Love. Life loves you. Smile!

Your work of service is multidimensional—there is so much to do at this time on the Planet. The first and fundamental step is to love and revere all of Life with

infinite gratitude into your Heart and to inspire others to do so, from a consciousness of oneness and equanimity.

Permeated by the sanctity of life, my activities are of love. I revere every Living Being, insect, bird and animal, and every tree and flower, and revere all elements and spirits in nature. They are all precious to me and to Mother Earth. The beauty, spirits, and life force of Mother Earth's blessings are nourishing my soul and all my bodies with joy and gratitude — nourishing all Life with Love in the oneness. I feel joy and peace, expanding and discovering my holiness and multidimensionality.

I am channeling from my Heart space. All that I feel, speak, see, and hear is sourcing from the Heart space, a unity consciousness with the Heart of God, the Heart of Creation. What I see in my Third Eye is sourcing from this communion with the One Sacred Heart in unity with the Divine Mind, the pineal gland. It is a communion of Love and truth between my One Sacred Heart and Divine Mind in oneness with all of Creation, the Great Web of Light, the infinite Sacred Wisdom and Knowledge. I have the inherent ability to feel, see, and/or hear the highest truth, what God wants me to see and know, in love and reverence, within the multidimensionality and sanctity of Life.

If you are of service as a healer-channel, ask your Angelic Higher Self and your Highest Divine Guidance team, and God, to see "merely" what is necessary, for you to be able to support your client's healing, in respect, honoring, and compassion. To explore anything else that is not in direct relation with your client's healing is inappropriate, since it is not held in sacredness and respect and honoring. A healing-channeling session takes place always with the permission of your client, remotely or in person. As a healer and channel, it is important to sustain clear boundaries, within a sacred space of unconditional Love.

Within a sacred space and fully grounded within the Heart of Mother Earth Garden of Eden, ask God with your highest Divine Guidance Team to be guided in ways which serves your client's highest good and the highest good of all: *I ask that all healing frequencies, energies, prayers, and messages serve my client's highest good and the highest good of all. I ask to be a pure and clear conduit of Love and Truth. I hold a sacred space of unconditional Love and honoring for my client, in the highest Love Light Peace and Grace of God.*

Your clients will always feel safe and be safe within this sacred space and so will you. The Healing Light Love of God, from Source, flows perfectly in the places and spaces supporting the well-being and healing of your clients. From your third eye, witness the healing Light. You are a pure conduit of Love.

As a healer and channel, you naturally see your clients' Higher Self, you see their Light, their energetic bodies, you see the goodness of their hearts, their multidimensionality encompassing infinite possibilities and potentialities. Within a beautiful Sacred space, you are guiding your clients to come back to their True Self, to experience wholeness.

Place your hands over your Heart, invite gratitude and faith into your Heart. You are a clear channel. Within a sacred space ask the questions you have about yourself and your life. Ask: *Dear Higher-Light Self and dear Father Mother God, thank you for showing me the dreams you have for me. Inspire me and guide me on a path of Light to be of service with joy and humility, in the oneness of the One Sacred Heart.* Then listen to your Heart, as the answers are suffusing your One Sacred Heart, your Divine Mind, your Third Eye. Listen gently, effortlessly, and allow that holy space for visions and information to be revealed to you. Write down the words, messages, that are revealed to you, describe the feelings and visions. Embrace your experience with gratefulness and joy. Repeat this prayer any time.

Trust the blissful journey of your Self-Realization, as you enjoy your daily spiritual practice and meditations. Self-Realization is an awakening to the experience of your pure essence. You are already Holy and Enlightened. It is for you to decide how much of "your pure being" you are allowing and accepting and choosing to see and be. Healing is the gentle process and journey to embrace and experience the multidimensionality of your pure being. It is discovering your wholeness.

Healing is an expansion of consciousness, the process to remember who you are. On your healing journey you are also healing the World. If you are a practitioner healer, every time you guide a client on a healing journey, you and your client are uplifting all beings and the whole World. Releasing Love and Light frequencies permeates all Life. On your healing journey you expand all aspects of your consciousness, basking in the Highest Love Light that is. You are experiencing your pure Being with Source, held with unconditional love by your Highest Divine Guidance team and all of Life.

The gifts of Love we give to ourselves heal the world. Every time someone chooses love, that love expands in all beings and Life.

What we give to others with unconditional Love, we give to ourselves too, and we give it to the World.

When you learn and practice different breathing techniques such as Pranayama or the breath of fire, you naturally empower your capacities to awaken and to be a clear channel. Breath work balances the right brain and left brain, inviting additional light life force, prana, into all the essential centers of your brain and bodies; your whole brain, the corpus callosum, pituitary and pineal glands are then uniting in one sound of Light in communion with your Heart. That Light frequency united with the Heart, infuses and balances your nervous system and all your systems. Every aspect of your bodies and beingness is benefiting from your conscious breath work sessions. Practicing different types of yoga combined with deep breath work supports your balance, health, and awakening.

Singing mantras and experiencing the vibrational energies of the "OM" Sacred Sound, gently supports a Holy communion with the Heart consciousness, and all of Creation. The "OM" Sacred Sound calms the mind and nervous system, awakens the Third Eye, and is grounding you and healing you. It is the primordial sound in nature, the vibrational frequency throughout Nature. Chanting "OM" leads you to a realm and frequency of pure consciousness, bliss, peace, oneness, the Love and Light in you and in All That Is.

You may practice your abilities to channel in multiple forms and aspects of your life, from your Heart and always in honoring. To channel high dimensional Angelic Guides and Masters of the Light is a beautiful space of unconditional Love; it is playing in the Light, basking in the Garden of Eden.

When you are ready, within your Chamber of Light, within a Sacred Space in the Garden of Eden, say: *I invite my highest Divine Guidance team into this Holy space to walk with me. I invite the Angels of the Light, the Archangels, the Ascended Masters-Masters of the Great White Brotherhood into my minds and hearts, and into my space (you may name the ones you are guided to invite within your minds and hearts). I invite the highest dimensional Star Beings of the highest Light. I invite you all, your divine consciousness of Love, wisdom, infinite divine knowledge and strength, and grace into my minds and hearts. I choose to embody all your Light, Love, Wisdom, Peace, Grace, Strength and*

Compassion, the Love of Father Mother God into my whole beingness, in my One Sacred Heart and Divine Mind.

Thank you all for walking with me, for your holy presences of Love into my hearts and minds. Thank you for your divine guidance and loving support. Thank you for holding me within a Holy Space of Unconditional Love, within the Light of all Sacred Directions, in the Heart of God, in the Heart of the Creator, in the Heart of The Divine. My Heart is overflowing with Love-Gratitude-Bliss.

Below are examples of prayers you may add to your spiritual practices. The Divine Guides of the Light that are meant to assist you in the moment, are naturally present in your space and life in your prayers, meditations, and life of service: *I invite in my Heart, in my Mind, in my space and in my life the Divine Angelic Guides of the Light and Masters of the Light, Luminous Beings, destined to assist me at this time. Thank you in all the peace that is — with infinite gratitude.*

In the prayers below you may change words or add any word you are guided to include. Your Heart is guiding you always. These prayers are inviting you to be a pure and clear channel, a conduit of Love and Bliss.

Dear Angelic Beings of the Light, I invite your unconditional nurturing Love, Light, Peace, Compassion, Strength, Wisdom, Divine Knowledge, and Grace, into my minds and hearts, into all my beingness, and into all aspects of my life. Thank you for walking with me and awakening my One Sacred Heart and Divine Mind. Thank you for all your Love and Divine guidance dear Angels of the Light. From my Heart, I embody all your Love, and Light, and Peace with ease, grace, joy, and gratitude. Thank you for shining your Light in all Hearts and throughout all of Creation. Thank you for guiding me to be a pure and clear conduit of God's Divine Qualities, Love, Peace, and Beauty.

Dear Archangels, I invite your unconditional nurturing Love, Light, Peace, Compassion, Strength, Wisdom, Divine Knowledge, and Grace, into my minds and hearts, into all my beingness, and into all aspects of my life. Thank you for walking with me and awakening my One Sacred Heart and Divine Mind. Thank you for all your Love and Divine guidance dear Archangels. From my Heart, I embody all your Love, and Light, and Peace with ease, grace, joy, and gratitude. Thank you for shining your Light in all Hearts and throughout all of Creation. Thank you for guiding me to be a pure and clear conduit of God's Divine Qualities, Love, Peace, and Beauty.

Dear Masters of the White Brotherhood, dear Ascended Masters, I invite your unconditional Love, Light, Peace, Compassion, Strength, Wisdom, infinite Divine Knowledge, and Grace, into my minds and hearts, into all my beingness, into all aspects of my life. Thank you for walking with me and awakening my One Sacred Heart and Divine Mind. Thank you for all your Love and Divine guidance dear Masters of the Light. From my Heart, I embody all your Love, Light, and Peace, all your Divine Qualities, with ease, grace, joy, and gratitude. Thank you for shining your Light in all Hearts and throughout all of Creation. Thank you for guiding me to be a pure and clear conduit of God's Divine Qualities, Love, Peace, and Beauty.

Dear Star Beings from the highest dimensions of Light, I invite your unconditional Love, Light, Peace, Compassion, Strength, Wisdom, infinite Divine Knowledge, and Grace, into my minds and hearts, into all my beingness, into all aspects of my life. Thank you for walking with me and awakening my One Sacred Heart and Divine Mind. Thank you for all your Love and Divine guidance dear Luminous Beings. From my Heart, I embody all your Love, Light, and Peace, all your infinite Divine Qualities with ease, grace, joy, and gratitude. Thank you for shining your Light in all Hearts and throughout all of Creation. Thank you for guiding me to be a pure and clear conduit of God's Divine Qualities, Love, Peace, and Beauty.

Dear Lord Buddha, *I invite your unconditional Divine Love, Light, boundless Peace, Compassion, Strength, Wisdom, infinite Divine Knowledge, and Grace, into my minds and hearts, into all my beingness, into all aspects of my life. Thank you for walking with me and awakening my One Sacred Heart and Divine Mind. Thank you for all your Love and Divine guidance dear Lord Buddha. From my Heart, I embody your Divine Love, Boundless Peace and Light, Wisdom and infinite Divine Qualities with ease, grace, joy, and gratitude. Thank you for shining your Light in all Hearts and throughout all of Creation. Thank you for guiding me to be a pure and clear conduit of God's Divine Qualities, Love, Peace, and Beauty.*

Dear Lord Krishna, *I invite your unconditional Divine Love, Light, Peace, Compassion, Strength, Wisdom, infinite Divine Knowledge, and Grace, Joy, into my minds and hearts, into all my beingness, into all aspects of my life. Thank you for walking with me and awakening my One Sacred Heart and Divine Mind. Thank you for all your Love and Divine guidance dear Lord Krishna. From my Heart, I embody all your Love, and Light, Beauty, Peace, and Divine Qualities with ease, grace, joy, and gratitude. Thank you for shining your Light in all Hearts and throughout all of Creation. Thank you for guiding me to be a pure and clear conduit of God's Divine Qualities, Love, Peace, and Beauty.*

Dear Master Jesus, Christ Light, dear Lord Melchizedeck, *I invite your unconditional Divine Love, Light, Peace, Compassion, Strength, Wisdom, Divine Knowledge, and Grace, into my minds and hearts, into all my beingness, into all aspects of my life. Thank you for walking with me and awakening my One Sacred Heart and Divine Mind. Thank you for all your unconditional Love and Divine guidance dear Master Jesus. From my Heart I embody all your Love, and Light, and Peace, Wisdom and Divine Qualities with ease, grace, joy, and gratitude. From my Heart, I embody the Christ Golden White Divine Light with infinite gratitude. Thank you for shining your Light in all Hearts and throughout all of Creation.*

Thank you for guiding me to be a pure and clear conduit of God's Divine Qualities, Love, Peace, and Beauty.

Dear Archangel Michael, *I invite your unconditional Divine Love, Light, Peace, Compassion, Strength, Wisdom, infinite Divine Knowledge, and Grace, into my minds and hearts, into all my beingness, into all aspects of my life. Thank you for walking with me and awakening my One Sacred Heart and Divine Mind. Thank you for all your Love and Divine guidance dear Archangel Michael. From my Heart, I embody all your Love, and Light, and Peace, and Divine Qualities with ease, grace, joy, and gratitude. Dear Archangel Michael, I bask with joy in your Luminous Blue Light Ray. Thank you for shining your Light in all Hearts and throughout all of Creation. Thank you for guiding me to be a pure and clear conduit of God's Divine Qualities, Love, Peace, and Beauty.*

Dear Lord Kuthumi, dear Saint Francis of Assisi, *I invite your Holy unconditional Love, Light, Peace, Compassion, Strength, Wisdom, Joy, infinite Divine Knowledge, and Grace, into my minds and hearts, into all my beingness, into all aspects of my life. Thank you for walking with me and awakening my One Sacred Heart and Divine Mind. Thank you for all your Love and Divine guidance dear Lord Kuthumi, dear Saint Francis. I embody all your Love and Light, and Peace, and Divine Qualities with ease, grace, joy, and gratitude. Thank you for shining your Light in all Hearts and throughout all of Creation. Thank you for guiding me to be a pure and clear conduit of God's Divine Qualities, Love, Peace, and Beauty.*

Dear Divine Mother Mary, *I invite your unconditional Divine Nurturing Love, Light, Peace, Compassion, Strength, Wisdom, Joy, infinite Divine Knowledge, and Grace, into my minds and hearts, into all my beingness, into all aspects of my life. Thank you for walking with me and awakening my One Sacred Heart and Divine Mind. Thank you for all your "nurturing Mother Love" dear Divine Mother Mary. Thank you for holding me in the arms of the Holy Mother, in the Heart of the Divine Mother, in the Heart of the Divine Father. From my Heart, I embody your Holy Love Light and*

Peace, Compassion, Wisdom and Divine Qualities with ease, grace, and gratitude. Thank you for shining your Light in all Hearts and throughout all of Creation. Thank you for guiding me to be a pure and clear conduit of God's Divine Qualities, Love, Peace, and Beauty.

Dear Saint Mary Magdalene*, I invite your Divine unconditional Love, Light, Peace, Compassion, Strength, Wisdom, Joy, infinite Divine Knowledge, and Grace, into my minds and hearts, into all my beingness, into all aspects of my life. Thank you for walking with me and awakening my One Sacred Heart and Divine Mind. Thank you for your Pure Nurturing Love dear Mary Magdalene. From my Heart, I embody all your Love Light and Peace, Compassion, Wisdom and Divine Qualities with ease, grace, and gratitude. Thank you for shining your Light in all Hearts and throughout all of Creation. Thank you for guiding me to be a pure and clear conduit of God's Divine Qualities, Love, Peace, and Beauty.*

Dear Saint Germain*, I invite your unconditional Love, Light, Peace, Compassion, Strength, Wisdom, Joy, your Divine Alchemical Knowledge and Qualities, and Grace, into my minds and hearts, into all my beingness, into all aspects of my life. Thank you for walking with me and awakening my One Sacred Heart and Divine Mind. Thank you for all your Love and Divine guidance dear Saint Germain. From my Heart, I embody all your Love Light, Peace, and infinite Divine Qualities with ease, grace, and gratitude. Thank you for shining your Light in all Hearts and throughout all of Creation. Thank you for guiding me to be a pure and clear conduit of God's Divine Qualities, Love, Peace, and Beauty.*

Dear Angels of the Violet Flame, dear Violet Flame*, I invite your Holy Violet Light of transmutation and purification, your Divine Alchemy of unconditional Love, Peace, Compassion, Strength, Wisdom, Joy, Grace, your infinite Divine Qualities, into my minds and hearts, into all my beingness, into all aspects of my life. Thank you for walking with me and awakening my One Sacred*

Heart and Divine Mind. Thank you for infusing my life and beingness with your Holy Violet Light of purification and transmutation dear Sacred Flame, dear friend, dear Angels of the Violet Flame. From my Heart, I embody the gift of your Essence, your Sacred Violet Light, your Sacred Violet Flame of Purification, your Divine qualities of unconditional Love, with ease, grace, joy, and infinite gratitude. Thank you for shining your Sacred Violet Light in my Heart and Mind, in all Hearts and throughout all of Life, and Creation. Thank you for guiding me to be a pure and clear conduit of God's Divine Qualities, Love, Peace, and Beauty.

You may continue praying in that way with additional Masters of the Light and Angelic Beings of your choosing.

Thank you, dear Divine Angelic Guides, Masters of the Light, dear Father Mother God for your boundless blessings illuminating my bodies, cells, hearts, and minds, awakening the pure and clear channel of your Holy unconditional Love in me and through me. Dear God, may your Radiant Light shine through me, so that your Divine Qualities permeate my beingness, always. I surrender my whole beingness to you, dear God, so that from the Sacred Heart, I may serve all Beings and all Life, in all the Love that is, in unity consciousness.

Dear Father Mother God, dear Angelic Guides and Masters of the Light, thank you for awakening the pure consciousness of my One Sacred Heart Radiance in union with my Divine Mind. Please reveal in my One Sacred Heart all the beautiful gifts you have bestowed upon my Path, Soul, and Beingness as I rejoice in the embodiment of my Higher Self Purest Light.

I embrace my God-Given Gifts with infinite reverence, gratitude, and joy—I use them for LOVE, in compassion and honoring, in service to all of Life.

Chapter Ten

My experience as an Angelic Channel-Healer

There is an extraordinary healing force of Love Light and Peace at the very core essence of all Life and Creation. All of Creation is made of that force. Angels and Archangels and Luminous Beings have taken me to spaces of expanded consciousness, to realms where I could experience that force of Love and Oneness in its purest form within me and in all of Creation. It is a Blissful Force of Love and Light I also experience with my clients in the healing sessions. That Force is a Doorway to Peace, to unity, to the infinite Web of Light, to God. The Divine Angelic Guides have been asking me to share my experiences with you.

Once you choose to listen to your One Sacred Heart, you are a living force of compassion, reverence, and love. The moment you live from the Heart space, you hold and emanate a force of peace. In that peace there is true consciousness.

Focus with love, joy, and gratitude on the dreams within your Heart. Listen to your Heart. Your Heart consciousness naturally inspires you on how to be of service. This liberates a positive flow of energy activated and co-creating for you and with you. It is a flow of light and love where miraculous synchronicities occur.

May these words inspire you in ways which expand your minds and Hearts in Divine ways. Your work of service takes place exactly where you are. You want to make sure that your daily activities are beneficial to all beings and all of life, in love and honoring to all of life, you are then on the right path. In your Heart you will know if there are minor or major changes you have to consider so that all your activities serve your highest good and the highest good of all.

The moment you wish to sincerely contribute to life, in service, with love and honoring, you are and will be divinely guided on that path of Light. If you know in your Heart that you have to make changes, take time to go inside your Heart and talk to your Divine Angelic Guides. Talk to God. Pray, meditate, ask for clarity, and for what serves your highest good, trust, invite faith, and listen from your Heart. *May I be led to what serves my highest good, to the dreams God has for me!* Remain gentle and kind with yourself. Choose thoughts of compassion and reverence, listen to your Heart. Trust!

As you move deeper and deeper within the Heart consciousness, you are raising your frequencies and light — your sacred path lights up in unimaginable holy ways.

Love is the highest force, for it is the fundamental Essence of Creation. Every child, every human being is looking for that unconditional Love, consciously or unconsciously. That Love permeates every human being and all of Life. That Love is intrinsic to all of Life. If you have not found it into your Heart yet, you are naturally longing for that unconditional pure Love, because "you are Love", we are Love.

Children are generally energetically aware of the pains and suffering lingering in their environment — they know and feel everything. Babies know who they are and from where they come from, but the memory fades away if they are not held in all that unconditional Love from Heaven and from the Heart, as they develop, and as they grow up. In order to come back to that inner sacred space within the Heart of your inner child, is a spiritual healing journey — a journey to remember who you are and why you came into this world of physicality.

On my spiritual healing journey, I always felt in me an Angelic essence and presence, from Heaven. As a child too, I experienced angelic presences, but felt crushed over and over again—and clearly had a difficult time to understand the world surrounding me. You might have similar experiences. Later on, as soon as I could, I went on a long healing journey, learning about the world of duality and physicality, discovering with time, how God wanted me to be of service. I understood that we all have similar purposes—to forgive, to love unconditionally honoring all of Life, to embody our higher Light, to know who we are, and to be of service. We all have the capacity to be of service by discovering the dreams God has for us. To heal and to be of service is a reconciliation with ourselves, all beings, and with all of Life.

To experience unconditional Love for your family, all beings, and All That Is, is the ultimate force of Peace.

With time, as a child and teenager and later on, I was naturally inclined to read books about spiritual teachings, practicing meditation, yoga, studying about the divine design of life, the Great Web of Light. More I was feeling pain, more I was praying and meditating, mainly to escape the pain and traumas from school and childhood—and other challenging events. I felt quite dysfunctional. There were times, the remembrance of my true authentic self was fading away in some ways, moving into a matrix of indoctrination until I understood the spiritual practices I am to cherish and integrate into my life, such as yoga, breath work, and meditation, Heart to Heart Mother Earth unity consciousness meditations, and daily "love light gratitude compassion" practices. These are some of the keys to well-being, peace, and harmony. With time, I discovered the value of these practices to come back to my true Self. In my childhood, with my family, we were spending plenty of time in nature and this was helping energetically. In nature there were nurturing times and around sacred sites. Also, painting-creating art was a meditative space, an emotional, mental, and spiritual support and escape. In these moments I was connecting with my Soul and Heart. With time, my spiritual practices and creativity became my main focus.

From my early twenties, in Europe, and the USA, I spent as much time as possible in temples and ashrams in prayer and meditation, where I had powerful spiritual experiences. My soul was flying out of my body and into realms of Light throughout the Universe where I could experience the peace, unconditional Love, and freedom I was looking for. In France, I was visiting ancient churches and sacred sites charged with Light, and holy energies of pure Love. In my meditations and prayers, I was often witnessing Lights and Divine presences in these holy places.

After studying three years in a Graphic Art school in Switzerland, I moved to New York City and lived in Muktananda's Ashram (founder of Siddha Yoga), while attending Columbia University, a few blocks away. I was meditating early in the morning and evenings, and many hours the weekends. The main mantra was "OM Namah Shivaya". We were also singing additional spiritual songs in Sanskrit. After a couple of weeks, in the Ashram, in the middle of the night, I was often compelled to sit in the lotus position, to meditate in that silence of the night. This was the time of the night, undisturbed, I was feeling safe to let go completely and move through doorways of Light, flying out of my body, basking in the most unconditional Love Light Peace and Bliss in realms of Light, in the Universe, amongst the stars.

I was singing the mantra in the silence of my beingness focused on my third eye, visualizing in my third eye the words "OM Namah Shivaya". Then I was moving deeper and deeper through what appeared several Doorways of Light into the infinity and vastness of my inner being—moving into oneness, and basking in the infinite vastness of the Universe. Exactly as Krishna describes it. I was aware that I was gently travelling outside my physical body, permeated with Bliss, and Peace, and unconditional Love, as I continued my journey upward into the sky, flying throughout the Universe. It was ecstatic, it was oneness, it was bliss, it was pure Love. This was the infinite unconditional Love I was craving for, to escape the profound emotional pain my physicality was experiencing. I was looking for that unconditional Love from Father Mother God, from the Angels, from the Masters of the Light, from Mother Earth—as every human being is, in every moment, consciously or unconsciously. I was shown that "LOVE" lives in essence within me and in all that is. At that time, during these experiences I could sense gentle, infinitely loving presences.

In school, some students were consuming drugs and alcohol. I could see and feel the entities around them and also could witness that they were falling into deeper and darker places of pain and suffering. It was quite distressing and sad to me. I couldn't understand why they were choosing to do this. I kept seeking refuge and relief in prayers and meditations. When I could see other young people on drugs and alcohol, I could sense that they were increasing their distress and pains. I could sense or see dark shadows and entities around them. I knew that I could never survive and heal by taking such substances, which would pull me away from the Light and my Angelic Self. I didn't want to experience additional pain. I was feeling a sense of safety in my spiritual practices and embraced by Light in my prayers and meditations. As every human being, I wanted to find peace, a rising sense of ease and grace, a sense of freedom and bliss, in every moment of my Life.

Studying and practicing different healing modalities, as well as yoga, and meditation with different groups of people, places, temples, and ashrams, was comforting me—despite learning with great challenges about that world of physicality and its duality. I was healing and releasing layers and layers of energies which didn't belong to me. When we release, we release not only for ourselves, but for the family lineages, and the whole world. From all these spiritual practices, my path of service became progressively clearer — I was naturally guided to be of service as a healer and angelic channel.

To be of service, as an angelic channel-healer, is one of the happiest states of being and awareness I have known within this physicality — as much as when I hike around the snowy mountains and glaciers in Switzerland where I experience God's presence in my Heart and the presences of the Luminous Masters and Angelic Beings — also as amazing as deep meditative states, and the out of body experiences where I have been embraced by the Light and also completely healed in all my bodies. In such occurrences, the veils of illusion disappear to reveal blissful peace, the pure essence of Life, the Love Light of God, of the Divine.

To be of service is to live from your pure Being, your higher Light. In everyone's life there are infinite ways of the Heart to be of service. Being a conduit of Light, Love, Compassion, and Truth to help people, and animals, to support with love and honoring all aspects of nature and life, is joy, grace, and boundless love. It is oneness consciousness. With my clients, our Hearts are touched with Bliss and Love that we often share tears of joy and gratitude.

Every being has the ability to be a natural channel, a conduit of Love and divine truth, in honoring. In order to be in touch with "who you are", it is important to practice living in ways which raises your frequencies on all levels of your lives; to live at the frequency of the Heart is the Journey! It is learning to live from the "I Am Presence, from the God Self. This is the Path, the Journey.

We explore that journey together within the Sacred space of these words blessed by the highest Divine Angelic Guidance team and Luminous Masters.

The Light of the Divine, the Light of Source, the Light of God is always present, forever permeating your beingness, your space, and All That Is. When we create a Sacred Space, we then become conscious of that Holy Presence, that boundless Love, Light, Beauty, and Peace intrinsic to all of Life, to Creation. We acknowledge the Sacredness of our beingness, of all beings, and of All That Is.

In the healing channeling sessions, within a sacred space, I receive naturally clear messages and visions that are guiding the healing process of my clients, in ways that are serving his or her highest good and the highest good of all. There is a transmission of Divine Light frequencies which is activated as I call the highest Light Love and Peace of God, anchoring us in the Heart of Mother Earth Garden of Eden. Although there are layers and different steps in the sessions, they all support my clients' healing, Heart awakening, wholeness, clarity and guidance, joy, harmony, and purpose. I am a conduit, a clear channel and trust all Divine Guidance from God.

Balancing, grounding, creating a luminous nurturing holy sacred space is essential, calling in my highest Divine Guidance team and my clients' highest Divine Guidance team. The frequencies coming through and holding the sacred space are pure and holy. I always wish for my clients to feel safe and nurtured within a sacred space, in the highest Light Love of the Divine, so that they are open to release with ease and receive all the healing Love they deserve, to embody their Angelic Self.

Within a sacred space and fully anchored within the Heart of Mother Earth Garden of Eden, I ask God with the highest Divine Angelic Guides and Masters of the Light, to hold the space completely clear and sacred: *I ask that all healing frequencies, energies, prayers, and messages serve my client's highest good and the highest good of all. I ask to be a pure and clear conduit of Love and Truth in the highest Light of God. I hold a sacred space of unconditional Love and honoring for my client, in the highest Love Light Peace and Grace possible.* Your clients will always feel safe and be safe within this sacred space and so will you.

In all healing sessions, I ask to see what serves my client's highest good to facilitate the channeling and healing. It is important for a healer and channel to work in honoring, reverence, with unconditional Love. I have seen too often healers/psychics/channels crossing boundaries and checking on what their clients have been doing at different times—serving no higher purpose. This can be quite traumatic for the person, who is striving to heal deep pains and traumas. It is an invasion which is perceived as a violation of privacy. When I started helping people as a channel and healer, I asked questions to my Divine Guides about this issue and they confirmed what I have been feeling in my Heart and they still do to this day. It is important, wonderful, and holy, and pure to work in harmony and infinite reverence. I personally do everything I possibly can, for my clients to feel loved, safe, nurtured and respected. It is my priority, to support their healing journey with unconditional Love.

As a healer and channel, I see my clients' Higher Self, I see their Light, the purity of their Hearts, their multidimensionality encompassing infinite possibilities and potentialities. Within a sacred space, people are guided to come back to their True Self, to experience their Pure Being.

When I paint, create, teach, write, and help people as a healer, I am a conduit to support a healing process—Love Light Blessings. I invite and work with Angels of the Light, Archangels, Masters of the White Brotherhood, such as Master

Jesus, St. Germain and the Angels of the Violet Flame, Lord Kuthumi-St. Francis, Lord Buddha, Lord Krishna, Mahavatar Babaji, Paramahansa Yogananda, Mother Marie, Saint Therese of Lisieux, Marie Magdalene, Mother Theresa, and Nature's Intelligence, Mother Earth, Intergalactic Luminous Beings from higher dimensions of Light, and more. In the healing channeling sessions and for all my creative work, I call them in. The Angelic Beings of Light and Luminous Beings who can help me the most in the moment, naturally manifest in the space. In reality, I walk with my Angelic Divine Guides in every moment of my life, in the Garden of Eden, to be able to do my work of service. I work with Nature's Intelligence, the animal kingdom, Divine Mother Earth, in unity consciousness and reverence. It is a communion of unconditional Love. You have the capacity to channel them all. They live in you and coexist with you, within a consciousness of Love-Unity and reverence.

I channel Angelic Star Beings from high dimensions of Light. One group comes from the Galaxy Andromeda, the "Sibli Tribe". They have encouraged me to use their name to bring forth healing Luminous Light code energies, in order to convey and transmit a higher healing frequency of unconditional Love, Peace, and Harmony through the healing-channeling Light work, I have been guided to convey of service to all of Life. There is also the gentle Divine Presence and Guidance from the Exylon Tribe from the Exylon Galaxy, Star Beings from High Dimensions of Light. Sometimes, from our Milky Way Galaxy, high dimensional Star Beings from the Pleiades (also known as the Seven Sisters) come into the sacred space to support the healing sessions multidimensionally.

Within a Sacred space, a large group of Angelic Beings, Archangels, Masters of the White Brotherhood, and Luminous Beings generate an amazing support to move throughout realms of Light, in order to support the healing of my clients and animals. Any situation which emanates, and releases love-healing frequencies is naturally received by Nature's Intelligence, Divine Mother Earth, and all its inhabitants—we are ONE. Every time we choose Love, all Life receives that Love. **In the Light there is always oneness because all is Light.**

Working with animals as a healer-channel, is an extraordinary experience. I commune Heart to Heart with the animals through a process connecting me with Nature's Intelligence. We have a communication through images and words. It is a pure Heart to Heart communication and communion. I have done many by distance and it works beautifully.

Every human being is naturally connected to Nature's Intelligence, Divine Angelic Guides, Archangels, Masters of the Light-Luminous Beings such as Ascended Masters and Luminous Star Beings who are ready to assist on all levels. The moment your open your Heart to them, it becomes easier for them to assist you and work with you multidimensionally, in the Light and Grace of God.

In order to be a practitioner channel-healer, I practice daily, meditation, breath work, and yoga to balance my nervous system and all my systems and bodies. Breath work is important. Some "breath work" generates Light Life Force into your cells and Chakras, balancing your bodies and field energetically and even clearing your field and Chakras. It generates Life Force into your cells, minds, and hearts.

Before a healing session, I always make sure that all my bodies and fields are completely clear so that I can be a pure and clear channel and healer. I anchor myself into the Heart of Father Sun and the Heart of Mother Earth Garden of Eden and into my Heart, calling in the highest Light of God, the Golden White Christ Light, and the Holy Silver White

Crystalline Rainbows frequencies of Mother Earth, the Archangels and Angels of all Sacred Directions with the Sacred Animal Spirits. I create a Holy Sacred space with a few prayers, always, for all of my work of service, this includes my creative work too.

Creating a sacred space is to become conscious of the sacredness of Life in the moment present, within you and around you—inviting the highest Light Love Peace, Grace, Wisdom, Divine knowledge, and Divine qualities of Source/God into that space. It is an activation of the highest Light consciousness in the space and also in your Heart and Mind. I call upon my highest Divine Guidance team, the highest Divine Light that lives at the essence of Creation, the purest expression of God's Love, the Light and Love I experienced during out of body experiences, and when I was guided into higher Dimensions of Light into Oneness Consciousness. I visualize myself in these moments, to bring forth the purest Light Love of God, within me and around me and in all that is. I feel unconditional Love embracing me and I experience the Healing Light. I welcome my clients in that holy blessed space, it becomes a Chamber of Healing Light, where the session takes place. I create the same Holy space when I teach healing classes in groups or one on one.

The Holy Light of God, of Source is always present in me and around me and in all of Creation. In my prayers, in my hearts and minds, I become conscious and acknowledge its omnipresence, its sacredness, and boundless Love.

I witness the whole healing-channeling sessions in my third eye. Throughout the sessions with my clients, I witness the Angelic Master Healers of the Light, gently guiding the Healing Light repairing, releasing, and adjusting, making all bodies whole again, suffusing them with that Healing Luminous Light. For each client, as I am guided, I channel specific healing prayers and processes, and use healing modalities I have studied and have been certified in.

During the healing sessions, the Divine Angelic Guides, are occasionally leading people to know about past lives, to understand the origin of the pain—supporting the release of the trauma, which has been lingering in the bodies and fields. This happen when the Divine Guides know that this will be helpful to the person, to be free. I then witness the past life or past lives within my third eye, and occasionally the client is able to experience and even see some aspects of the past life or lives. Father Mother God's Love Light with the Divine Angelic Guides, Master Healers of the Light, release and transmute this amalgam of energy trauma, multidimensionally. They are suffusing with healing Light, all the places and spaces where these pain energies have been lingering so that peace, health, Love-harmony permeate all bodies, minds, and hearts of the clients—in the past, present, and future. The whole family is always benefiting from that healing Light and unconditional Love, and all Beings. We are ONE.

When you let go of energies which do not belong to you, this opens a space of Love where you are able to embrace the true essence of your being on deeper levels and find peace.

The Angels have been gently guiding me to realms where I could experience the pure essence of Life, my true essence, a space and reality of pure unconditional Love, Joy, and Beauty. A space where the Light is so bright that I cannot find words to describe the limitless purity and peace. I travelled out-of-body, when the Angelic Guides wanted to show me more about the Sanctity of Life and raise my frequencies. I travelled to Heavenly places, high dimensions of Light, also throughout the cosmos to receive gifts and healings in all my bodies. In the presence of your Angelic Divine Guides and Masters of the Light there is unconditional Love, reverence, peace, infinite bliss, limitless Light infusing all your bodies and cells.

Dear ones, in your prayers and meditations, Divine Angelic Guides may lead you to Heavenly Realms of Light consciousness of Infinite Oneness, of pure unconditional Love to heal your bodies, minds and hearts, upgrade your frequencies, and capacity to embody higher Light energies.

In contemplation, prayer, and meditation, I have been blessed to be guided to experience these Holy Heavenly Dimensions of Light. These experiences have been the catalyst of the healing work I respectfully, lovingly, offer to the world— Angelic channeling-healing and teachings, of service to all of Life. In your spiritual practices you may be invited to similar experiences. May you be blessed.

Nothing is impossible when you sincerely open your Heart to receive the Love of God and invite Faith on your sacred path.

If you choose to be a healer practitioner and pure channel, it is crucial to take lovingly care of yourself on all levels of your life. In all circumstances, it is important to lovingly take care of all your bodies, physical, emotional, mental, and spiritual, to experience well-being and joy. It is essential to take care of yourself in loving-caring ways, so that your work of service, whatever it is, generates joy, beauty, peace, and harmony.

I know in my Heart that I am ready to let go and let God, inviting a trust which opens doorways of Light for beauty, harmony, and healing to take place. In the sanctity of that sacred space and Light, miracles take place. I raise my frequencies and consciousness to be a conduit for healing to occur, in all the Love That Is.

Your channeling abilities flow with increasing ease, as the pineal gland with the pituitary gland and with all other spiritual centers within your beingness and bodies are infused with higher Light sourcing from your One Sacred Heart and all your spiritual practices. Choosing pure consciousness of compassion, love, and reverence, generate an increasing flow of pure Light, naturally contributing to an energetic clearing of your beingness. Additionally, the food you eat has to be of a high frequency.

On your path of service, your willingness to raise your frequencies and embody your higher Light, naturally draw you to high energy foods. Healthy eating consists of no processed food, no sugar of any kind (but fruits are good), no alcohol, no chocolate, no coffee, and avoid spicy foods—and no recreational drugs of any kind. If you are comfortable being vegetarian it will help you too. Your body knows if it is happy with just vegetarian foods or not. Your body has consciousness. For some blood types it is easier to be vegetarian. It is important to listen lovingly to your body. Enjoy avocados, lentils, broccolis, and green juices with parsley, cucumbers, celery, kale, and the like. In general fifty percent of cook food and fifty percent of raw food is a good balance. But do what makes your body feel good and happy. When you feel good, when your mind feels clear, you know that you have a good balanced diet.

Chocolate is an addictive substance causing numerous health issues. Even in my twenties and thirties, when I was rarely eating a small piece of organic dark chocolate, afterwards, I could feel uncomfortable feelings in my body and mind. With time, I experienced pain in my knees for a few days, every time I was eating a small piece of chocolate. I stopped eating chocolate and cacao. When I stopped completely, the pain never came back. Also, a long time ago, the last time I had again a small piece of organic dark chocolate, I was in a sort of coma for 3 days. I could barely move or even think because of its obvious toxicity. My whole being was shutting down. I wanted to understand, so a few days later after taking good care of myself with green juices, lemon ginger warm herbal teas, and the like, I asked questions to my guides and decided to research thoroughly what was really going on. Then I received clear answers. I knew why I was experiencing all these symptoms and why I have been avoiding eating chocolate. I decided that I will never eat chocolate and cacao again and I am so happy I did, to clear my pineal gland, my whole brain, for all my bodies to be healthy — and to be able to be a clear channel.

You will notice that as you raise your frequencies you will naturally be attracted to higher Light energy foods. Anything with low frequencies will not work for you.

My research with my Angelic Divine Guides, led me to the following: Chocolate-cacao can possibly keep you into a zombie state, depressed, and away from your abilities to channel. When you research thoroughly the components of chocolate and cacao you will find out that it fatigues the adrenals and is a stimulant with caffein. Caffein in chocolate and cacao causes anxiety and depression, restlessness, insomnia, and osteoporosis. (If you have pain in your joints and body, please revise your diet and change it) Chocolate-cacao is highly addictive, this is why in general people don't want to stop eating it. Chocolate-cacao is acidic in nature, therefore, increases the acidity in your stomach, and your whole body. Additionally, it contains high levels of a toxic metal called cadmium that is quite difficult for the kidneys to flush. Since it makes your body highly acidic it can cause gastroesophageal disease. Your liver is of course on overload, greatly affected on many levels leading to additional health issues. With time your whole physical body may develop severe side effects, detrimental to all your bodies well-being, blocking on some levels your mind's clarity, and pineal gland too.

Additionally, in my research I found out that cacao plantations have been sprayed with harmful herbicides and pesticides. I found out that these big corporations are using child labor to spray dangerous herbicides and pesticides, also without any protection, and that the children have been getting severely sick and are dying from these chemicals. Also, organic chocolate-cacao only exists in remote places and islands. It is quite evident that the drastic consequences of such behaviors and unconsciousness are expressed karmically within the collective consciousness. We are one. There are no words to convey the energetic toxicity of this product and situation, the suffering of the children—meanwhile millions of people are eating this product daily.

There are many similar situations occurring at this time regarding other types of products and foods that are detrimental to all beings' health and Mother Earth. One of them is palm oil, used worldwide in processed foods. Palm oil is detrimental to human's health and balance. The big corporations associated to this oil have been destroying the rainforests, the animal kingdom, insects, polluting rivers and lands, destabilizing and harming the biosphere, the global ecosystem. There has to be an awakening in all people's Heart to consume mostly local products and from places and companies which are choosing to be sustainable.

I choose a healthy, pure, clear diet that is of Light! I bless all that I eat and drink with Love, reverence, and with gratitude to Mother Earth. I am a miracle worker. I am an awakener. I am a Holy Interdimensional Star Being contributing to peace and harmony in all aspects of Life. I live with reverence and joy in the Garden of Eden of Mother Earth.

Are you listening to your Heart's Truth where true knowledge and wisdom reside? Living in true consciousness rests in the Oneness of Life. You are walking with multitudes of Angels, dear ones. Listen to their messages from the deepest chambers of your Hearts. In the discovery of your true identity, you are naturally free from all indoctrination. Delve into the beauty and multidimensionality of Life, from your

Heart, where truth, beauty, and freedom reside. Love and revere Mother Nature fully, you are then honoring who you are and all beings.

Choose with consciousness what you eat and drink, commune with Love, reverence, and gratitude with Mother Earth Garden of Eden, so that nurturing energies from Mother Earth are nourishing you with pure life force, crystalline Light. Bless your food and drinks and get the best natural organic food you can possibly find from Mother Earth. Support the farms growing organic and respect Mother Earth with all its inhabitants — be a part of this true consciousness in small and big ways. Every step is LOVE and is important.

Suggested prayer-blessings before meals: *Thank you dear Mother Earth, dear Father Sun, Nature's Intelligence Holy Light, all of Life, Mother Nature, for providing us with this holy food and holy water, in all your Love. May Mother Nature and all who have harvested this food be infinitely blessed with Peace and Joy. Thank you, dear Mother Earth and dear Father Sun for holding us safe and nourished in communion with your Hearts — the Heart of Mother Earth Garden of Eden. May all inhabitants of the World be blessed with your Holy fruits and vegetables, with your sacred waters and nurturing Love. Thank you, dear Father-Mother God, for blessing this sacred food and sacred water with Joy, Love, Light, and Peace. Thank you, in eternal Peace!* Send Love from your Heart to Mother Earth and her beautiful Garden. Feel the Love permeating you and all of Life.

It has been clearly exposed with obvious facts that eating meat and animal-derived products is harming communities, public health, and the Earth tremendously. The pollution, toxicity, and animals tremendous suffering it engenders has been exposed in multiple aspects of life, today. If a majority of the population would be vegetarian, humans with all creatures would live in a significant healthier environment, in a more sustainable way. **Every human being has now to**

awaken to the sacredness of the animal kingdom—to awaken to a HEART-LOVE Communion with them.

If you eat meat, be aware that most animals have been exposed to large amounts of chemicals and often suffered tremendously before ending in your plate. Such distressing human behavior is detrimental to all of Life. Additionally, this fear, suffering and tremendous stress release a significant amount of toxins. All these energies are embedded within the cellular memories of the animals and this is what people eat. All these painful energies and chemicals are lingering within people's bodies and field. This is why, if ever you eat fish or meat it is important to pray for the animals' peace. Bless them and ask for a holy purification by the highest Light and Love and Peace from The Creator, for their souls and bodies to be embraced by the Light and embraced with nurturing Love and Peace from Mother Earth, Angels Devas, and Angelic Beings. Bless them with all your Love, Peace, Gratitude, Honoring from your Hearts.

Originally, Indian Americans were taking the lives of animals in limited ways and for survival purposes only. They were in communion with the soul of the animal and Mother Earth, in prayer, reverence, and gratitude, asking permission. Animals are holy Devas, and our relationship and oneness with them are sacred, as sacred as our oneness with Mother Earth, as sacred as our relationship with the trees, the flowers, all elements in nature, and ourselves. There is only oneness—we are to honor all animals as our souls' brothers and sisters.

> *"The greatness of a nation and its moral progress can be judged by the way its animals are treated."*
> *— Mahatma Gandhi*

Before you eat fish or meat, it is beneficial to add these words in your prayer-blessings: *Dear Mother Earth, dear Father Sun, dear Holy consciousness, Nature's Holy Spirits, dear Divine Angelic Guides of the Light, please hold these animals in the Heart* *of the Divine Father and the Divine Mother, please hold them in the highest Love, Light, Bliss, and Peace possible. With all of your Love, dear Father Mother God, thank you for blessing with infinite peace these souls and bodies, for guiding their beautiful spirits into the highest realms of Light and Peace, where they are held in the Heart of God, and also held in the Heart of the Great Divine Mother Earth. I honor your beautiful spirits — may you be blessed forever with Peace. May this meal be infused with the highest blessings of Love and Peace. I am sending Love gratitude to Mother Earth, to you, and to the animal kingdom. All is nourished with unconditional Love and Peace.*

In order to be a pure and clear channel it is important to hold love reverence gratitude consciousness about everything which surrounds you and the food you eat. Live in boundless reverence, conscious of the Sanctity of Life. Revere all of Mother Earth's beauty and gifts in the Sanctity of Unity.

Within a beautiful sacred space consciousness, throughout the healing session, after the grounding and balancing, it is important that I first clear the auric field of my client. This consist of a multidimensional clearing and Light infusing, to release anything blocking Light. Then when the passage of Light is clear, it is time for the person/child/client to have the courage to face and describe the painful feelings and traumas, just for a few minutes, without judging. It is then time to localize the pain, traumas, karmic issues, PTSD, and more, to liberate the hearts and minds and bodies, all the way to the cells with various processes and energy healing, guided by God and the Angelic Beings and Master Healers of the Light. Within the memory of the cells there is Light infusing — a reprograming occurs, encompassing unconditional love, peace, harmony, and oneness consciousness.

I witness in my third eye all of the release, repair, and Light infusing flow, taking place within the bodies of my client. As the healing takes place, I see in my third eye the Light moving freely through my client's auric field. Because the energy field has been cleared at the beginning of the session, it is possible for the Light to permeate all bodies and cells. It is then possible for the cells to be reprogramed in all the Love That Is. This healing process awakens the embodiment of a higher Light for the client, encompassing all bodies, minds, and hearts, also activating and healing their twelve strands of DNA.

There are sometimes additional layers of traumas and karmic issues, but after releasing the main traumas and karmic issues, with daily spiritual work, life becomes more harmonious and peaceful. You naturally receive more clarity and focus. Also, if your spiritual practices are your priorities with your work of service, all your bodies and cells are naturally filled with Light, and are with time, releasing additional energies which do not belong to you. Everything is possible when you invite the Healing Light of the Divine within a sacred space. Your spiritual practices invite the Pure Light to infuse the cells, all of the bodies, minds and hearts. The Light is always ready to be revealed and shine.

During the healing session, the pure essence of the person is being naturally awakened and revealed from the Heart space. The client releases only what he or she is ready to release, and only what the body can handle in the moment, and on that day. It is in general necessary to have several sessions until all the layers of pain and traumas are released. But if the person is ready to choose true consciousness, it is possible for the bodies and minds and hearts to release everything at once and be free to embody the true authentic Holy Self.

During the healing-channeling sessions, I am never in charge within that sacred space—a higher force of Love and Light, a Divine Intelligence and wisdom, God, Source, with the Angelic Divine Guidance team and Master of the Light are in charge. This is why ALL is safe and Divinely guided.

In the healing sessions, people are awakening to their higher Light, discovering their Holiness, their Angelic Self. As people release layers and layers of pains and traumas (energies which do not belong to them), they come back to themselves and remember who they are. Then in prayer and meditation they are able to experience their Light and embody that Light. It is joy to remember who you are.

Every time someone awakens from the Heart and remembers who they are, their love and light generate peace and joy into the world, for all beings to receive and be blessed, with Mother Earth Holy Beingness to rejoice in all that Love.

It is a blessing to offer healing sessions remotely too — people contacting me from faraway places, around the world. Within a sacred space, I naturally know that my client is right here in that holy space embraced by the Light — with his or her highest Divine Guidance team and with my Divine Guidance team, we are all One, in the Highest Love Light. There is no separation, there is only oneness, and healing takes place.

When you start helping people as a healer and channel you realize at a deeper level what oneness is. There is no separation, it is easy to help people and animals anywhere around the world. "Light and Love" knows only oneness. All the love you express, your prayers and meditations are infinite bridges of healing Light for the whole World.

I also teach my clients how to clear their energy field. I encourage them to learn how to clear their energy field multidimensionally weekly, or even daily at the beginning, if it is necessary. With time, they will clear their field every two or three weeks, or once a month because clearing is healing and raises your frequencies and consciousness.

As you practice clearing your auric field, you naturally raise your frequencies. You then feel increasingly lighter and more joyous. To know how to sustain your energy field clear, balancing your energies, remaining fully grounded/anchored into the Heart of Mother Earth Core Crystal Garden of Eden, are essential qualities of a healer. These essential qualities and attributes are beneficial for every human being who wishes to experience a deeper sense of well-being and oneness, also to channel Luminous Masters and Angelic Beings. Clearing your energy field allows the Light from Source to flow freely throughout all cells, and bodies, taking you on a more fulfilling path of Light.

When nothing is blocking Light, a deeper healing is then fully experienced. Clearing the auric field of the client, allows the healing Light to move freely through all bodies and cells and DNA-RNA, for the traumas, pains, and karmic issues to be released with ease and grace—using different healing processes and energy work. What is interesting is that when the pain is released and replaced with love light peace energies and programs from the true divine essence of Life, it becomes clear that "the pain energy" which was just released never belonged to the person. When "the pain energy program" is gone, the person forgets about it, it is dissolved and transmuted by the Light. It is an amazing experience to free the mind, and the auric field, and the hearts. It is joy for the healer-channel practitioner to witness this process, liberation, and Light embodiment.

After a healing session people feel lighter and happier, more connected, and therefore more aware about the direction of their life's purpose. Usually after three to six days of integration from the time of the healing session, the healing is complete. During this time of integration, the cells, the chakras, and all bodies are receiving increasing Light—the Love cellular reprogramming continues within a Chamber of

Light. This Chamber of Light allows complete harmonious healing and Light integration. After that time of integration, the person feels more connected with their beautiful Angelic Self and empowered with Love.

For the healer-channel, it is fundamental to work in holy ways, with a consciousness of the sacred. All healing sessions are taking place within a sacred space of nurturing love, and honoring. Healing occurs on deep levels within high frequencies of Light, within a Chamber of Healing Light.

In order to sustain a place of honoring, I always ask to see and know what serves my clients' highest good and the highest good of all, for them to receive all the support, guidance, and healing they deserve and are ready to receive—in the most beautiful sacred way and respectful way possible. As a healer and channel, it is crucial to help people within a sacred space of integrity and reverence. It is absolutely not appropriate to enter people's space in invasive ways. The only way to be of service comes from the highest place of love and honoring.

I listen to my Heart, in such a way, that I feel and know what is of unconditional Love. My Heart knows truth and unconditional Love.

When I am divinely guided to proceed with hands on healing on my client, the Divine Angelic Healing Guides of the Light and Luminous Masters use my hands with their hands and Light to clear the chakras and release blocked energies in the body. I feel the energies in my hands—I see in my third eye when the "invasive" energies are pulled out of the person's bodies. It is then released into the Light and transformed by the Light. Usually at the location of that trapped energy people feel some chronic pain or discomfort. When that energy is being pulled out and released the person is free. The Divine Luminous Healing Guides and Angels are then using my hands to infuse Healing Light Energy into that location where that energy pain was released, to close that space energetically so that the auric field is whole. At the end of healing sessions, I see my clients' bodies and fields embraced one more time by a Golden White Crystalline Healing Light—as the Angelic Beings are holding them within a Chamber of Light. This Chamber of Light supports full energetic Light integration.

As a healer and channel, I feel, see, and hear, and naturally trust the healing process in every moment. I am never in charge, a higher power of unconditional Love, Divine knowledge, and wisdom is in charge. Source, The Creator, God is in charge. I let go and let God. When I channel guided healing meditations for my clients, the prayers are repairing and clearing and downloading Light Love Holy frequencies. I then witness in my third eye the "Angelic Guides and Master Healers" repairing, clearing, downloading and infusing Light until all bodies are whole, until the auric field is whole and suffused with the highest Crystalline Light. I see the sacred geometry within the field of Light of the person. When all is harmonized and the Divine Light flows, then the client is healed—the Sacred Heart consciousness is free to be expressed.

I have been guided to share these experiences to inspire you to be of service—so that you know the healer you are, and your capacity to lovingly support the healing journey of other people, and animals, with Mother Earth—in honoring and unconditional love. Your beautiful Divine Angelic Guides are holding you with Mother Earth in Holy ways, so that you are inspired to bring forth peace, beauty, joy, harmony and reverence—also in the simple and precious moments with your family and friends, with your co-workers, and animal friends. You are never alone—you are in Holy communion with the Light and Love of Creation.

A pure healer-channel never uses his or her energy. It is important to naturally welcome the Holy Divine Love Energies of the highest realms of Light, from Source, from Father Mother God, completely guided by a healing team of Angels, Archangels, Ascended Masters, and Star Beings from the highest dimensions of Light, which are choosing to be with you in that sacred space at that time.

What makes the experience amazingly delightful is truly to never use my energy for healing. I call the highest realms of Light, the Love of God, the highest Healing Divine Guidance team to proceed with the channeling healing work. The highest healing Light energies and frequencies and divine messages flow with ease and the healing takes place in all bodies and on a cellular level, moving deeper and deeper through layers, addressing each issue, trauma, karmic issues, pain and concerns, in the most honoring ways possible. I am a conduit, a channel, of service.

What does that mean to heal? Healing is remembering your Pure Being, your Christ Self, your God Self, your Angelic Self. It is remembering the pure essence of Life and its oneness consciousness. It is allowing an awakening of your Pure Light, and to be permeated by Light, to shine your Light in the Garden of Eden. Healing is living within the Heart consciousness where truth resides—where infinite compassion, gratitude, and faith reside, and therefore where pure Love resides. Healing is living within the pure realm consciousness of the Sanctity of Life. Healing is choosing to see the wisdom which is born from all experiences—and to be nourished and empowered by that wisdom. Healing is to live in gratitude.

As we remember who we are, our consciousness shifts with time, and we heal. We let go of all that does not belong to our true being and we embody progressively our higher

Light. In my practice, I have been guided to lead people to remember who they are and to embody their God Self. It is a unique path for every human being, but the journey leads us all to inner peace and unity consciousness.

To be in a position to be able to help, give, and share in Divine ways and multiple ways are blessings. Your financial situation doesn't define who you are or how worthy you are. You are worthy and forever Holy — you are a Luminous Being. You are forever loved and of Love consciousness. Peace is your gift.

From your daily spiritual practices, you have the capacity to transform pain into wisdom and true knowledge, and unconditional compassionate Love. You are ready to be of service in the Highest Love Light, in the Garden of Eden.

Meditation to support your awakening and Light embodiment: *I free myself from all resistance to accept what has been and what is. I decide today to free that energy which has been trapped in me or around me. I accept what is with ease, grace, and gratitude. I free myself, and with joy I embrace the freedom of my Heart, Mind, and beingness. Forgiveness and compassion are liberating my higher Light. Dwelling into my Heart, I surrender, I let go and let God. The pains and challenges are energies which never belonged to me and are now gently dissipating. All of the wisdom of these experiences is revealed into my Heart. I free myself, basking in all the Love that is. In the love and freedom of the Heart, miracles take place in all aspects of my life. I delve within frequencies of oneness in the Light of Creation. A powerful Angelic team of Light Beings and Luminous Masters of the Light are walking with me, watching over me, and watching over the World. My path is a path of Light and Kindness, Compassion, Beauty, and Peace.*

I delight in walking with the Angels of the Light in the Garden of Eden with all sentient beings.

A higher force has been guiding me. This force is of Love and Light, and is within me, within all beings and within all of Creation. More I embody my Angelic Self and Higher Light easier it is to live within the world of physicality. I become more fluid, more transparent and lighter, even my physical body becomes lighter. My bodies are more of a "Crystalline Light". I experience a deeper awareness of my essence. It is a shift in consciousness. It is an awakening to my Pure Essence.

As you are vibrating at higher frequencies of Light, all of your bodies, minds, and hearts are lighter. Study and meditate on spiritual scriptures, sing mantras, practice yoga and holy breath work. Nurture your Self multidimensionally. As your resonance rises to your true authentic self, life is naturally supporting the work of service God/Life has for you, in miraculous ways. It is saying YES to life, to love.

If you wish to be of service know that you have that inherent ability to awaken now, to the Love, Light, Beauty, Peace you are to offer to the world, right where you are. All you wish for is within you. Cherish your Heart and listen to your Heart. Open your Heart to all the Love that is, share that Love daily with all the people and animals in your life. Meditate and nurture yourself.

It is crucial at this time to gather your full heartfelt attention to your Spiritual practices in order to transmute lower frequencies and transcend the world of physicality, inviting the Luminous Light to shine.

As you embody the Holy Crystalline Being of Light you are, there is a shift, you are then moving from one matrix of illusion to another Matrix of Light and Truth, where Love and Peace are unconditional. Remember that you are a Portal of Light — Mother Earth with all its inhabitants, all Nature's Intelligence, are then seen, in their truth and pure essence.

Thank you for gifting me with this truth, with this true vision and awareness dear God, dear Angels. I choose to recognize and experience the Portal of Light I am, with gratitude, joy, and reverence. I am Light, and so it is.

In all my spiritual experiences, I received a deeper awareness and consciousness of the Portal of Light I am—and a knowing that every human being is a Portal of Light. All of my out of body experiences have been taking place for specific spiritual reasons based on my choice of consciousness and calling—sincerely in prayer and meditation; I was asking for support and healing inviting faith, or I was in profound states of "Love Compassion Gratitude" in my Heart, or in a deep meditation. Your spiritual experiences may inspire the people in your life to awaken to their Heart consciousness.

I witnessed that every human, every being, all in Nature are Portals of Light. You are a Portal of Light. In that true consciousness we co-create with God within the Great Web of Light, within the True Essence of Life. It is a pivotal time for all human beings to awaken to their Higher Light, to embrace unity consciousness. It is a time to be the Portal of Light you are!

These holy experiences are forever present and alive within my field, beingness, and Heart. I am able to relive them again and again from within my Heart and Mind, and simultaneously also expanding from their multidimensional nature. From these experiences, with the Divine Guides, these blissful frequencies of Pure Peace Light Love from Source, are naturally activated within the sacred healing space with my clients. We are ONE and from the same Source of Love.

Throughout all of my life and as an angelic channel healer, I have experienced and seen that where is the deepest pain and despair, the bright Holy Light Love of God, is right here on the other side, awaiting to shine — pure unconditional Love inherent to all of Creation. You are to call that pure Love Light from your open Hearts, as it reveals itself in unfolding miracles.

Contemplate in your Hearts your spiritual experiences. Relive them into your Hearts and Minds and your whole beingness. They came to you to awaken you, teach you, to give you hope, and strength, and courage, and faith, and to open your Hearts and Minds to new visions and experiences of your divinity — to be of service.

I experienced myself as an angelic being among other angelic beings in a space of incredible luminous Light and beauty and joy where no struggle, no suffering, no doubt, no confusion from the physical reality as we know them take place or exist — but where limitless Pure Blissful Love flows boundlessly.

I always felt safe and unconditionally loved throughout all experiences with my Divine Guides of the Light. I feel their Love in my Heart and all around me. Inviting faith into my Heart has kept me within higher frequencies, also opening doorways of Light where the fundamental essence of life is expressed as pure Love. If you sincerely wish for harmony and peace, if you invite faith into your Heart, you will experience healing empowering miracles on your journey and sacred path. Your faith and trust are protecting you, guiding you, and raising your frequencies.

If lower energetic entities are entering your space, you will feel discomfort, fear, and pain. Then, it is important that you lovingly take care of yourself. Proceed with focused spiritual work, healings, and multidimensional clearings, to raise your frequencies. With spiritual clearing, healing, and prayers, it is easy to release lower frequencies and entities into the Light. All is of Love! When you release the trauma or pain associated with the entity or entities, you will be completely free. I teach many of my clients how to clear their energy field. Sustaining your auric field clear, raises your frequencies and allows you to embody Light. From your daily spiritual practices, you will experience increasing peace, bliss, and well-being.

It is pure joy to work with the Rainbow Mist and all Light Rays associated to the Angels and Archangels and Ascended Masters. The luminous Rays of Light manifest as I am of service channeling these Holy Angelic Beings and Masters of the Light for clearing, healing, and Heart Love Light empowerment.

Daily, it is pure bliss and joy to call upon the Great Masters of the White Brotherhood, the Angels of the Light and Archangels, and the Luminous Star Beings from the highest dimensions of Light.

It is an amazing blessing to invite the "Angels of the Violet Flame" and the Sacred Light of the Violet Flame within a sacred space and work with these Holy Beings and consciousness. St Germain introduced the Sacred Violet Flame, as a gift to humanity as he was a High Priest at the time of Atlantis. The Violet Flame is an extraordinary friend in my life, a Pure Sacred Light transmuting frequencies and energies into Holy Love Light. Working of service, with its pure essence of unconditional Love, and with the Angels of the Violet Flame as ONE, energies are transmuted into the highest frequencies of Love—Pure Light Alchemy in action, awakening the Christ consciousness, the Divine Human. Anyone who sincerely wishes to be of service as a pure interdimensional being of Light may work with the Violet Flame—ask for this Sacred Flame to be of service to you as a dear and loving trusted friend.

Raising your frequencies through spiritual practices,

invites powerful healing Light, invites the embodiment of your Higher Self, an awakening to the true essence of Life. Your Divine Light shines. As you vibrate at these holy frequencies, you transcend physicality to see one Love, one Light—unity consciousness.

To be of service as an angelic channel-healer, is an experience of Heaven on Earth. I experience unconditional Love—a time in Heaven on Earth.

When I channel, I embody on a deeper level who I am. This is true for everyone. I channel from my pure essence, from my pure being.

My physical body is a Holy Temple on Earth in the Garden of Eden. My Heart holds the luminous candle of my Temple, the Source of pure Love where my pure being resides illuminating all my bodies. I attend to all of who I am, daily, with unconditional nurturing love.

It has been an ongoing blessing of love and joy to work with the Ascended Masters, with the Angels of the Light and the Angels of the Violet Flame and the beautiful Sacred Violet Flame, with the Archangels, and Luminous Star Beings from the highest dimensions of Light. It has been Heaven on Earth to be of service in their presences and Light. My Heart is filled with gratitude.

From my Pure Being, I am of service, with joy and gratitude, in all the Love That Is!

Chapter Eleven

Angelic Light Alchemy

These words and insights, prayers and meditations hold Light Alchemy-Healing-Meditations awakening your Pure Being, your multidimensionality. Since you are reading this compilation, your intention and sincerity to awaken and ascend to be of service as a Pure Interdimensional Being of Light, are probably the deepest desires of your Heart. Your Soul Calling and Heart consciousness of unconditional Love, your luminescence, the experience of your Pure Being, of your Oneness with the Sacredness of Life epitomize the dreams God has for you, they are in your One Sacred Heart—they are who you are.

All Rays of Light and the Sacred Violet Flame express "Light Alchemy in Action". It is an amazing blessing and pure joy to invite **the Angels of the Sacred Violet Flame** into a sacred space and work with them in holy ways. St. Germain was a powerful healer and priest in Atlantis. At the time of Atlantis, he introduced the Sacred Violet Flame of Transmutation as a Gift to humanity. St. Germain is an Ascended Master. He belongs to the Masters of the White Brotherhood. Throughout many incarnations he has been known as an alchemist, scientist, artist, healer, and philosopher. It is an amazing blessing to work with him.

The Violet Flame is a Sacred Fire: Light Alchemy in action. As we all know, Alchemy turns lead into gold, but the Alchemy of the Violet Flame transforms "human into the Divine Human". It is a flame of purification and transmutation acting in unity with the Angels of the Sacred

Violet Flame, for the true essence and Light of the Pure Being to be revealed.

When working with the Angels of the Violet Flame with the essence of this Sacred Flame, miracles take place on all levels of Life, transmuting denser feelings, traumas, actions, karma, and more, into the highest frequencies of Love, Peace — Ascending frequencies.

With infinite gratitude and reverence, I invite the Angels of the Violet Flame Pure Essence, in all places and spaces of my life. I invite the Sacred Violet Flame, dear Violet Ray of Light, from the Heart center of the Galaxy, from the Heart of the Universe, to embrace me completely and to enter my crown chakra, infusing all my chakras and bodies and fields, and my cells, and DNA-RNA, permeating every aspect of my physical body and all my bodies with purifying, healing Luminous Violet Light. Thank you, dear friend, for your healing gifts. Dear Sacred Violet Flame, please suffuse all my relationships, and living spaces, and workspaces, and all aspects of my work and life with your Healing Sacred Light of transmutation (describe in detail all these places and spaces where you wish to invite that Sacred Violet Light). I dwell deeply into your powerful healing Violet Flame, clearing, purifying, protecting Holy Light, raising all frequencies of my beingness and life in the Highest Love Light that is, preparing me for Ascension – guiding me to ascend.

From my Heart and the Heart Center of the Galaxy, I call upon the Angels of the Violet Flame, the pure Light and Essence of the Violet Flame, to hold Mother Earth in Sacred LOVE, and to infuse the whole Earth with its Luminous Violet Light of transmutation and purification with all its inhabitants. Thank you, dear St. Germain, thank you dear Angels of the Violet Flame, thank you dear Sacred Violet Flame for offering and activating your miraculous gifts of purification and transmutation throughout the whole World to open all Hearts – in furtherance of peace and harmony.

Chapter Eleven

With the divine assistance of my Angelic Guides of the Light, I choose to live in awareness of my vibrational frequency. I choose to live within a consciousness of infinite compassion, reverence, blissful serenity, to be a conduit of peace for all of Life.

Choose your perception of Life with consciousness, with awareness. When your whole beingness is infused by Light, when your Heart reveals its truth, and true Love, you see beyond the world of physicality, you see Pure Spirit, you see the true and pure essence of everyone and everything. In this awareness and consciousness, peace and harmony are restored.

As I remember who I am, I heal. I remember my True Pure Being. When I know who I am, I discover the sacredness of Life and its unity consciousness. The Sacredness of Life is Light Love Alchemy in action.

Life is always supporting your awakening, your ability to move into true consciousness, intrinsic to its Divine Design, the Great Web of Light. You are divinely guided to remember who you are. You are already forgiven — you are already holy. Are you now ready to embrace your holiness, the holiness in all beings, and bask in the sanctity of life?

If you are struggling to forgive, practice being in communion with the Heart of Father Sun and the Heart of Mother Earth Garden of Eden within a column of Light. Work with the Angels of the Violet Flame. Experience your communion of pure Love with all of Creation. Practice the channeled prayers in this book and take lovingly care of yourself on all levels with nurturing Love. Learn to gently embrace your Divinity, your Angelic Self. Your Divine Mind and Sacred Heart know that you are forgiven. Forgiving yourself and others is giving Love to yourself. It is honoring all of who you are, and it is spreading Love and Harmony to all Life.

It is joy to set myself free from pain and forgive! I choose to bask in the beauty and Love of Creation. I choose to be a force of Compassion and Love.

If ever you are constantly in survival mode, in anxiety, practice several times a day breathing exercises to balance your nervous system, and possibly yoga. The breath work calms your mind. Kundalini Yoga is a powerful modality to calm the mind and nervous system. Hike in the mountains and breathe, or swim in the ocean. Set up new goals by listening to your Sacred Heart where all your dreams and the dreams God has for you reside. Meditate, pray, breathe and commune with the nurturing Love of Mother Earth, with her Heart—in the Garden of Eden. Declare that you are living in the Garden of Eden of Mother Earth where there is infinite Love, Healing Light, Joy, Beauty, kindness, infinite support, abundance, and prosperity. Feel Mother Earth Garden of Eden loving you and nurturing you multidimensionally. Breathe with her and observe how she is breathing you and breathing with you. ***I ground myself deeply into the Heart of Mother Earth Garden of Eden Core Crystal with all my Love. In the Garden of Eden, where I reside, there is infinite Love, Light, Support, Kindness, Goodness, Grace, and infinite Abundance and Prosperity. My Heart and whole beingness are receiving boundless Love. Abundance epitomizes a boundless flow of Light, Loving-kindness, and Blissful Peace permeating my life and beingness—permeating all beings and All That Is.***

From the serenity of my Heart, I receive beauty and grace. In my Heart, I am receiving the vision of a future of miraculous beauty. I open my Heart to embrace your Infinite Blessings, dear God. May I be a conduit of your Miraculous Blessings, may they expand through me to Love and enlighten the entire World. Thank you dear Father Mother God for Blessing the entire World with all its inhabitants, with beauty and grace.

Create a beautiful Sacred Space. In all this Love and Light, visualize clearly everything which makes your Heart sing. In your journal, describe your visions and offer them to God, to the Light of the Garden of Eden. Expect your messages and visions to manifest with divine synchronicities. Your Heart knows when to take action in all that Love and Light. Your Divine Angelic guides are walking with you. Listen to your Heart with gratitude. Invite and allow this powerful force of Love and Light, God, Source to lead the way—your path of Light. You are not separated from anything and anyone—sometimes you only "think" you are. It is a thought, and it is not reality. Hand everything to God, to the Divine.

You have the ability to reset your destiny, from the inner energetic consciousness you choose and embrace.

Every day, when you wake up, in your meditation and prayer, place your whole day into God's Hands and Heart, offer that day to the Divine, to a force of Joy, Light, Love that is unconditional and infinite. Contemplate what surrounds you with gratitude and learn to see from your Heart and inner eye. ALL is of Light, vibrating at various frequencies, Alchemy in action. Give all your challenges to God, to the Divine, to the Light. Invite the Highest Love Light into any situation and in every aspect of your life. *I invite Father Mother God, Source, The Creator, to be in charge, always. I invite my highest Divine guidance team, the Angels of the Light, unconditional nurturing loving support, the highest qualities of Love and Harmony from Source in all my projects, in all aspects of my Life, in all my work, places, and spaces of my Life. My Heart is ready to receive all the peace and harmony, grace, and joy that is! I open my Heart to boundless miracles.*

You are on a path of Light to awaken. Life manifests in every moment what serves your highest good to support your ascension. Forgive life, choose mercy, compassion, reverence, and loving kindness—your Light expands and becomes brighter, you are luminous. You are then impervious to lower frequencies. No one can take away your Light. You are Light. When your twelve strands of DNA are activated in all that Holy Light, they cannot be disactivated.

As you awaken to the Sanctity of Life, to your Oneness, to the embodiment of your Higher Light-Self, you are naturally attracting and engaging people to follow your steps. Your high consciousness, energetic frequency, and Love have a ripple effect. You are then a Doorway of Light for all Beings, and the whole world, activating additional Doorways of Light.

I choose to live in unity consciousness. I commune with Love and honoring with everything surrounding me, the animals, insects, trees, flowers, water, crystals, and all beings—all aspects of Mother Earth. I am permeated with bliss, beauty, gratitude, and compassion in all circumstances—this is the most enlighten way to respond to life. I am transcending the world of physicality from my pure being. It is then easy for the Angelic Divine Beings of Light, the Masters of the Great White Brotherhood, high dimensional Star Beings to commune with me and work with me. In these realms of Light consciousness, I am a pure and clear channel. I open my Heart to all the Love That Is!

Even when your emotions take over your personality, from your true Self, you have the ability to come back, to see oneness and wisdom emerging from these emotions. The Light is always right here on that same trajectory ready to emerge and shine.

You are Light Alchemy in action and Light Alchemy is all around you. It is energy, it is synergy, and synchronicities. Energy flows and transforms—however energy never goes away. Light Alchemy in action, is Light energy in action and flow, transforming, transmuting, expanding—it is the Essence of Creation; it is Light-Synergy. All that is in Creation is Energy and Light at its essence. You belong to Creation, this is why you have the ability to experience that field of Light and co-create with Source, in all the Oneness that is and all the Love that is.

In order to grasp at deeper levels Light Alchemy, we look into what is called Karma. Karma is a Sanskrit word which means actions or deeds, the spiritual principle of cause and effect (the principal of Karma), wherein all intent, behaviors, and actions influence the future of a person. The consciousness you choose, your intentions, and whatever you choose to create in the now moment affect you now and shape your future, this is what Karma is.

One of my clients asked me the following: Is karma real or the effect of a delusional mind? So, I listened to my Heart and the Angels said the following: Yes, karma is real, good karma or painful karma are real — and karma is also delusional in the following sense: What you call bad or painful karma are energies based on a consciousness of separation, or unconsciousness — actions and behaviors that are sourcing from fear. States of unconsciousness is painful karma. Such karma teaches you to awaken to your true and pure being, to your Sacred Heart and Divine Mind. It is uncomfortable and painful, so it shakes you up. When you are ready to awaken to your inherent pure Light and Love consciousness in the oneness of Creation, you are able to create good karma from the One Sacred Heart and Divine Mind. There is a freedom of the Soul, when the minds awaken to the Divine Mind and the hearts awaken to the One Sacred Heart. It is an embodiment of the Sacred.

There is individual karma and collective consciousness karma too. It is possible that a person or group of people have chosen to carry painful karma. When it is ready to be released and transformed by the Light, it always invites all beings to embrace increasing love and harmony — it is healing to all life. It is possible to escape painful karma by raising your frequencies through deep spiritual work — by embracing a higher power of unconditional Love. When you raise your frequencies through spiritual practices, you become impervious to lower frequencies, you shed your skin, you purify your bodies and fields, and all energies that are not matching your Higher Light dissolve. You are then a Lightworker held within a Chamber of Light. In reality every person is held within a Chamber of Light, an auric field of Luminous Light — the Light is free to shine when the energetic interferences are gone. **The "state of the minds" is the interference, the thoughts are the interferences. Painful karma is released through prayer-meditation, energy Light work, and daily spiritual practices.** As you free the minds from illusory thoughts, breathing into your Heart, your Light is then expanding, in communion with all Hearts. Your auric field shines, your Heart shines, and you are naturally held by the Angels within a Chamber of Light.

My spiritual practices are guiding me to delete and let go of everything that is illusory, in my life and the World. In meditation, the true Light and infinite Peace of Creation are revealed in my Divine Mind and Sacred Heart — the Luminous Light shines. My Higher Light is revealed. I can finally see who I am — my Pure Being is revealed in all the Love that is.

Hold the willingness to step out from one illusory matrix to enter another matrix — a matrix of Light where love, kindness, faith, beauty, peace, compassion, and gratitude flow. It is Light Alchemy in action. Higher frequencies invite divine synchronicities and miracles to take place.

The "minds" is the place where people become slaves of their illusory thoughts and beliefs, not based on the true sacred laws of Creation. The ego wants to keep you trapped into the pain of the "minds" of illusory thoughts. But when you delve into the chambers of the Sacred Heart, your consciousness shifts, and you discover truth and true consciousness. The Divine Mind and Sacred Heart dwell in the oneness and you are free to be of service.

There are situations the collective consciousness is holding painful karma trapped. It is released when enough people awaken and choose the consciousness of the Sacred Heart—Love, Compassion, Mercy, Peace, and Reverence. Where there is good karma, people live in true consciousness, in Peace, in harmony, in synergy with the essence and Web of Light and Life. Then the Garden of Eden is revealed in all Hearts and on Mother Earth.

I understand the power of Love, intrinsic to my true nature. Everything is energy and energy frequencies can be transmuted.
I embody my pure being, my higher Light, I am free.

The "minds of separation" impede and interfere with truth. It is an energic veil dimming the Light and hiding the true essence of your being and Life. Painful Karma is in a way an illusion of the mind. Painful Karma is energy synergy and can be transmuted. Painful Karma is an energy which supports the awakening of the "human" to the "Divine Luminous Human". It is an energetic bridge to awaken to the LIGHT of the Heart and Mind. The Divine Mind is revealed dwelling within the infinite loving-kindness of the Heart— there is only Love, the Light illuminates all Life. There is harmony, and "All That Is" reveals its True Essence and Sanctity.

Every human being is naturally looking for Love - Love is Alchemy in action:
This longing is spiritually-biologically expressed from the core of your being because "Love" is the Source of who you are. This is why it is painful to stay away from a state of beingness inherent to your true essence. All is Love

consciousness at its source. All you do, think, and feel, are "synergies in action" consciously or unconsciously motivated by a search for increasing love. **Even if you feel despair or act in despair, you are longing for LOVE.**

All your behaviors and actions are a calling for Love. This is a very important point and awareness to hold into your Hearts and Minds dear ones. This shall support your awareness to express infinite compassion and kindness.

As demonstrated in previous chapters, expanding and experiencing your Pure Being takes place at deeper levels, the moment you are consciously in communion with the Heart of the Great Central Sun, the Heart of Father Sun above, and the Heart of Mother Earth below, her Sacred Core Crystal. You are to be fully connected and grounded within Mother Earth, to her Heart, her Core Crystal, Gaia and Roszia, all aspects of Mother Earth, in her Garden of Eden. Mother Earth is aware of your physical-spiritual needs and when you commune with her from your Heart space and embrace her with Love, she responds with abundant gifts, nurturing you and taking care of you on all levels of your physicality too. Mother Earth nourishes you multidimensionally.

You are naturally guided to an experience of your oneness and divinity because you are coded with God's infinite qualities of Love, a divine design inherent to all of life. You naturally long for the experience of your Angelic Self, Higher Light, or God-Self. Spiritual Angelic Light Codes are working for you, through you, with ease and grace as you choose to be consciously in communion from your Heart with the Heart of the Great Father above and the Heart of the Great Mother below and with all four Sacred Directions. Holy Rays and Rainbows of Light, among the Angels and Archangels encompass a Luminous Crystalline Light Grid, embracing you within a Holy space.

I live in oneness consciousness — there is no separation of any kind with anything in creation and anyone. I am free from all judgement. I embrace all beings and all of life with love, compassion, and reverence. There is nothing to control or judge. I let go and let God, delving in the deepest places of my Heart to hear the voice of God, of the Angelic Beings, of the Masters of the White Brotherhood. I embrace the presence and blessings of all animals, insects, birds, marine life with unconditional love and respect in every moment. I honor them and embrace their divine presence, experiencing the Oneness of the One Sacred Heart. I witness their beauty and Spirits of Light. I naturally commune with them from my Heart and embrace their presences with joy and reverence. Their presences are infinitely healing and nurturing, in ways that are miraculous and holy. I walk as ONE, with Nature's Intelligence, in sacredness, in reverence, with the deepest gratitude and LOVE in my Heart.

All of Creation synergistically exists within the same matrix of consciousness, the same intelligent divine design. Within that divine design, every human sustains some fundamental aspects of free will, directly linked to the capacity and wisdom to live in harmony and reverence with all of Life.

I now choose to live with awareness of my divine loving union with the Earth Being, honoring all of Life.

Global harmony, peace, health, goodness, and wellness for all beings, require that the resources of the planet are used with infinite wisdom, reverence, and praise—with a consciousness of the sacred—always serving all life's highest good. It is living and breathing divine consciousness and unity consciousness. From that space, it is possible to manifest, experience, and invite a sustainable world.

Nothing belongs to you, but everything lives within you and breathes with you. It is oneness. Oneness belongs to the Creator, to the Creation. You are the Oneness!

Mother Earth embraces all her children—forever enriched and nourished by Mother Earth boundless abundance, beauty, and gifts of Love. Mother Nature is perfect in herself and so are you in your essence.

The core essence of our "beingness and of all that is" is forever untouched and of pure love light consciousness. This is why it is never too late to choose love, compassion, and to live in true unity consciousness. The moment you finally decide to listen truthfully to your Heart, you undergo a shift, a complete sense of release, a sense of freedom. The moment you open your Heart, you are naturally embraced by Light and held with unconditional Love.

Mother Nature emanates high frequencies and energies that are divine and intimately connected to your energy field, bodies, minds, and hearts. You receive life force and nourishment from Nature's Intelligence—it is unity consciousness. Trees, fruits, vegetables, plants, air, sun, and water, all of Mother Earth, all in nature sustains all Beings and Life. All in nature sustains one another. **There is an intimate and profound energetic alchemical communion between all that exists in nature, all of your beingness, all that is around you, and all beings. These are divine synchronicities permeated by a conscious intelligent field of Light.**

When you forget about who you are, you feel lost, depressed, sick, you lose your balance, you feel alone, separated, and then fear comes in. You don't have to come back to this illusory Matrix ever again. You may choose to awaken now and to live within the genuine Matrix of the Universe from your Pure Being. Assert your freedom and your commitment to LOVE and say: *I am free! Love is the*

Force of the Universe. This Force lives in me. I am a Force of Love, Light, and Beauty permeating all of Life. I rest and bask in all the Love that is. I am that Force of Love and Peace. I am a Portal of Light. I am Light!

Life force energies are also experienced as vortexes of Light of various sizes, diverse specific energetic currents of consciousness emerging from the Earth Being and the cosmos—energies and sounds emanating from Creation such as crop circles, orbs, crystals, gemstones, rocks, water, rain, fire, flowers, plants, trees, the animals, insects, birds, marine life and so much more. You emanate a specific unique sound too, sourcing from your Heart. It is in a way your spiritual signature.

All is sound and consciousness—Alchemical Light synergies and sound frequencies—vibrational sacred forces, hues and rays of Light, sacred geometry sound patterns fundamental to life's synchronicity and harmony. In order for humans to experience and honor the infinite beauty of the Garden of Eden, there is only one way: The consciousness of the Heart. The Heart is the Doorway to unity consciousness with its sacred holy divine design, sound and alchemical Light synergies.

My Heart is the Heart of God. From my One Sacred Heart, I experience the holy and magical aspects of life, the voices in nature, the whisper of God's Love in everything, and in the breath of life. I live and breathe the oneness consciousness, therefore, nothing of a lower frequency created by human thought-forms is able to take me away from that bliss. Nothing of a lower frequency can enter my space—I am impervious. The only frequencies I know are of unconditional Love, reverence, mercy and compassion. I AM HOME!

Mother Nature offers infinite doorways to awaken and to sustain serenity, bliss, joy, and wellness. Nature offers infinite synergies of Light, Beauty, and gifts of Love.

Meditation: *Lying in the grass, I listen to the sacred voices of nature; the wind, the trees, the flowers, the birds, the bees, and the crickets, and the like. They are comforting me and uniting me with the sacred forces of Love within my Divine Self. I realize that I am basking within a magical world of beauty, bliss, and goodness. With infinite gratitude and reverence, I breathe the Light Life Force energy animating all of Life. I now sit and repose against a beautiful tree in the middle of a luminous meadow. I focus on the spirit energy of this magnificent tree with all that surrounds me. I take several long and deep breaths from my Heart until I feel a deep communion of unconditional Love with the Tree and all that surrounds me. I now sense that Mother Nature is breathing me so gently, so lovingly, singing with my Heart consciousness full presence. The gentle loving spirit of the tree is embracing me in all the Light that is. My breath is joining the breath of the holy spirit of the tree and the breath of Divine Mother Earth. I feel safe and infinitely loved. I feel in my Heart and beingness, the unconditional Love of this magnificent tree, all trees, all in nature, and the animals, and insects. It is ecstatic. I close my eyes and listen to the Holy gentle voices and sounds. My Heart opens wider. I listen to the gentle whispers and commune from my Heart. I perceive frequencies, energy sounds that are gentle and at the same time, powerful. The sound frequency of my Heart and my whole beingness unite and merge with the holy sounds of Love all around me. They are soothing and comforting. I experience a profound sense of oneness, a blissful peace, feeling safe and loved boundlessly. My beingness is permeated with the holy voices in nature, as I commune with the Light of the trees, the flowers, the birds, the sky, the wind, the sun, and all of nature. All life is loving me and breathing me. I bask in the oneness of these divine synergies of peace and love emanating from all that surrounds me. My Heart unites in One Love with Mother Nature, with Divine Mother Earth Garden of Eden. I experience the sacredness of life and* *unity consciousness in the most Divine Blissful ways possible. I am loved. I am love. There is only Love!*

Every moment, I discover the unlimited beauty and sacredness of my world from a place of reverence and praise.

As you bask in the Light, in the Garden of Eden, you may call upon your highest Divine Angelic Guides of the Light. When you call them in, you naturally become more aware of their presences. Many of them are with you always and more are joining the moment you raise your frequencies. When you raise your frequencies, it eases the communication and communion with your Divine Guides. You are then more open to listen, receive, and communicate. The way the Divine Guides manifest is truly multidimensional. They may lead you within higher dimensions of Light, a space that is so bright, nurturing and holy that your true essence of Light is completely revealed and where you actually experience your body of Light as "energy of unconditional Love". You are pure Light Love energy. The consciousness of the One Sacred Heart is then expressed in its infinite Light, a consciousness where all that is resides in its purest form.

Love is a Light Synergy through which Source created all beings, and the Earth, all dimensions, all stars and planet systems, the Universe itself. When you tune into this level of Love consciousness, you vibrate at the level of your true essence, within the enlightened aspects of prana from all dimensions of Light. Love Light Alchemy in action! It is an opening of the One Sacred Heart consciousness, where you experience a creative force, a field of love and light, a divine holy communion with all beings and all that is. As you ignite the Sacred Heart, you delve into the Love energy field of the Universe, the ONE Universal Heart-Love consciousness, in synergy with the Garden of Eden.

The Ascendant Masters and Angelic Beings have been emphasizing the importance to be anchored in the Garden of Eden of Mother Earth, and to invite the union of the Garden of Eden Heart with your One Sacred Heart. It is important that you experience in your hearts and minds and beingness the nurturing Holy Light of the Heart of the Garden of Eden. It is a place where all your hearts unite in your One Sacred Heart and where all your minds reveal the Divine Mind. In the Garden of Eden, the true essence of Life is revealed always — therefore, the moment you live and breathe in the Garden of Eden, you remember who you are. You are then ready to be of service in all the Love and Light that is.

In the Oneness on my Heart, resides the experience of Divine Light Alchemy in action, where miraculous synchronicities manifest naturally.

In every breath, in every step, you are naturally searching for Love, consciously or unconsciously, since you are Love embodied.

Love unconditionally and you will not scatter your energy and give away your energy. Choosing Love-compassion makes you impervious to lower frequencies. You are then held within a protective space, a "Holy Light" where you are reborn to the truth of your being and where your body of Light expands. You are held within in a Chamber of Light. That Chamber of Light unites with the Universal grid of Light, also known as the Quantum Field. The Quantum Field encompasses all the energy forces of the Universe.

Your field of Light or Biofield holds subtle layers of energy fields, sustaining your whole beingness healthy and vibrant of Light, as long as your perception and relationship with Life and with yourself, are positively charged with truth, kindness, and Love. Your Biofield may be deprived of Light force energy if your close your Heart, if you are holding on to pain, depression, and if your perception of life is mostly of despair and distress.

Dear God, please permeate my whole beingness, minds and hearts with your Holy Grace. I open my Heart to receive your Blessings. Infused by your Grace, I find the wisdom to accept who I am, with unconditional love in my Heart. I embrace who I am in my entirety with infinite compassion. Every day, I discover the truth of whom I am as you reveal your Divine presence of Love in my Heart.

When you are chronically triggered by external events and internal turmoil, and you are not nurturing yourself, you are then for sure ignoring essential aspects of your being, which absolutely need your full attention for healing, harmony, and peace. Take lovingly care of yourself. It is possible to heal anything with compassionate love.

Lingering feelings of rejection, unworthiness, and insecurity within yourself, often, originate from childhood traumas, but can also originate from past lives issues. If you do not release and heal these pains, you naturally search for the love and attention you are craving for, in relationships, by expressing feelings of despair in ways that are over-empowering. It is a common issue for people to seek acceptance, and a sense of worthiness in others, and especially in intimate relationships. It appears as a "wounded craving" for Love, for it is "neediness" but not love. The person is covering up the pain. It is possible to heal and balance these energies by learning about who you are, by letting go of judgements and learning to be a friend to yourself—by learning to love and nurture who you are in your authenticity, by dwelling into the Heart. If there are traumas, through prayers and healing Light work, it is possible to reprogram the memory of the cells with Divine Healing Light, to activate the original blueprint, your higher Light, so that you start living from your magnificence and pure being.

Feelings of unworthiness reveal a sense of despair. These feelings of despair are painful and generate a void, also leading to anger and profound confusion. Anyone holding on to these feelings, once in a relationship, realizes that the pain is still lingering. The person wants to receive love and want to give love "so much", that there is a drainage of energies, triggered by a state of despair. The "pain-trauma" has opened gaps within the auric field. It is where energy drainage occurs, and where additional lower energies might be invited to enter and reside within the bodies. This may cause additional psychological-mental, emotional issues, and physical issues too. Such relationships, most likely, are leading to disappointments—you are feeling the hurt that is already lingering within. The wounds have to be addressed, released, and healed. It is about the relationship you have with your Self and life that you have to sincerely and courageously face and reprogram. Spend time with your Self and nurture your whole being—your healing journey is about learning to love who you are unconditionally as you step into wholeness. You are Divine, you are the Light. You are loved unconditionally.

When your Light is dimmed because of "chronic" inner turmoil or because your perception of the world is painful, your Heart space shuts down, you are then partially cutting the flow of Light Love life force uniting you with the Quantum Field. This is how the natural flow of Light Life force frequency is scattered within your bodies. You are then lacking life force. It is an illusory sense of separation which triggers health issues in the bodies.

Unconsciously or consciously, you have been craving for an experience of unconditional love, yearning to embody your pure being, a union of holiness and love with all of life. Why? Because you are "pure being". It is a natural longing to wish for Love.

"An illusory sense of separation" from your true nature and the true essence of Life, causes pain. Pain is born from false believes about life and about who you are. In true consciousness you find ease and grace, peace and joy.

"The need" to prove yourself to others has its origin from feeling vulnerable, unaccepted, undermined, rejected, misunderstood, and unworthy. These feelings may originate from childhood traumas and may also originate from past lives. If you notice that any of these feelings are often lingering in you, address them with courage and compassion. It is a time to take lovingly care of yourself without judging. Pray for divine guidance and healing. Practice the healing processes in this book and if it is necessary, look for a spiritual practitioner healer-channel to assist you, releasing these pains from the memory of your cells — and to reprogram them with nurturing, positive, loving peaceful light energies which are in harmony with your Higher Self Luminous Light. They are the Dreams God has for you. These dreams are in your Heart.

Always choose a spiritual practitioner healer who makes you feel safe, nurtured and loved unconditionally. Then you know that you are in the right place. Listen attentively to your Heart's messages. Your Heart is always revealing Truth. And if you are in a situation where you cannot reach anyone or you cannot find anyone to help you on your healing journey, please know that God with your highest Divine Angelic guidance team is always here, with you. Pray, meditate and ask Father Mother God to heal you. Ask for divine assistance from your Divine Angelic Guides, the Masters of the Light for the healing you wish for, with all your Heart — invite faith and trust. You are never walking alone, and you are loved unconditionally. *"I was in such situation numerous times, where I called to God and to the Angelic Beings and Great Masters of the Light directly. I prayed with all my Heart with faith, trusting in every moment that my prayers are heard. Every time, I was embraced by a Love Light that is pure and unconditional — I was healed completely throughout all my bodies. Every time my frequencies were raised. You shall be healed too."*

The Angels of the Light are taking me to realms where I experience the pure essence of life, my true essence, a space and reality of pure unconditional love, joy, and beauty. A space where the Light is so bright and the Love so unconditional that I cannot find words to describe the limitless purity and peace.

Your relationship with Life is emanating from the true consciousness of your One Sacred Heart. Your perception of Life is sourcing from its essence of Love and Light, all encompassing.

In the awareness of my Heart, I maintain a relationship with my Self and with Life that is kind, gentle, compassionate, and of nurturing love. I choose to bask in a communion of beauty and grace where all aspects of Mother Earth Garden of Eden are loving me unconditionally.

If someone comes to you for help, that you are a practitioner healer or not, listen to your Heart and you will know what to do and speak. Your Heart is all knowing, forever in love, forever in truth.

Your journey to embody your Higher Light, your God Self, is your purpose. Your purpose is to live in true consciousness of the Light, of the pure essence of everything and all beings—the Quantum Field of Light all encompassing—holding your Biofield in glorious ways, in true Love, to be of service.

Peace arises from acceptance, from the truth of my Heart. I then dive deeper within the wisdom of my Angelic Self. I empower myself with true wisdom, awareness, deep love and compassion. This empowerment is a self-realization that is life enhancing allowing the quintessence of life to reveal itself in my hearts and minds.

In my prayer and meditation, I bask within the holiness and light of my pure being. Divine truth is revealed in me and expressed through me. The Holiness of the World is revealed to me.

I invite and allow the quintessence of life to reveal itself, breathing in that holy space and consciousness. I breathe love and I speak from my Heart. I choose my Life to express itself within a synergy of Light where God's Divine Qualities are forever unfolding in the Oneness, and for all beings.

I have never been separated from what my Heart is wishing for and from the dreams God has for me. I always have been ONE with my Heart and with God. My One Sacred Heart and Divine Mind know that truth. The Angels of the Light are forever supporting the sacredness of my space and journey with unconditional Love.

All that I have experienced has guided me and is guiding me to awaken to my pure being.

The Divine Angelic guides and Ascended Masters and Star Beings from the highest dimensions of Light are forever available to walk with you in all the Love that is. This is why it is important to invite them to work and walk with you, to invite their love and holy presence into your Hearts and Minds. Express your wishes clearly, hold clear intentions in Love and honoring.

In the oneness of life, I receive with ease and grace infinite gifts of Love, divinely guided and supported. I remember that Life is for me, supporting me. My beautiful Angelic Divine Guides of the Light are blessing my journey and path with sacredness, beauty, joy, peace, grace, goodness, kindness, and abondance. I bask in the oneness consciousness of my pure being, the sanctity in all of Life.

My God-Given gifts are blessed in all the love and joy that is. I cherish them with infinite gratitude. They are a force of unconditional Love blessing all of Life. I am a pure conduit of God's Divine Qualities of unconditional Love. Dear God, may all the forces of Love extend through me to bless all beings and the whole world. Thank you, dear God, for using me as a pure and clear channel of your Love.

I embrace who I am with unconditional Love. I am a Divine Angelic Being of God. I am Light. I live in the Garden of Eden of my Heart, and in the Garden of Eden of Mother Earth, where life is naturally permeated by miracles of Love and Harmony for ALL BEINGS — within all dimensions of Light. I am Loved and supported by all of Life. I value myself. I am precious to Mother Earth. I am cherished and infinitely Loved. My Heart is overflowing with Love.

More I spend time in meditation, in profound communion with Mother Earth, stronger and brighter my auric field becomes and shines in the Garden of Eden where I reside, in every moment. As I expand consciously my body of Light, I become impervious to lower frequencies. I allow myself to walk in life with ease and grace, in the highest Light, brightening other people's path. As my Light shines, I illuminate people's Hearts, and the whole World. I am Light. In all that Light and blissful peace, I experience the infinite presence of the Divine, in me and in all that surrounds me. My Heart resides in the Heart of the "One Light", the Heart of the Universal Grid of Light, the Heart of God — synergies of Light abiding by "Angelic Light Codes Alchemy", permeated by the oneness and sanctity of Creation.

Chapter Twelve

Prayers and Meditations from the
Angels of the Light

A Reconciliation with Life:

With the loving support of my Divine Angelic Guides, I delve into my minds and hearts, to observe all the thoughts and judgments I have toward myself. I observe if my thoughts are scattered and confused or clear about who I think I am. I decide to breathe deeply into my hearts to receive clarity about "the perception I have about myself". I recognize the highest Light of Father Mother God permeating all of Life – permeating my bodies and space. In all that Light my minds, thoughts, and feelings are clear. I write in my journal the thoughts I have about myself and about life. I describe my gifts and talents God has given me. Then, I write another list about additional talents and gifts I feel reside in my Heart-consciousness and Soul and are ready to be revealed.

When my lists are complete, I pay attention to the places which require my compassion and nurturing love. I merely observe, and I judge no more. I give love to my inner child in all the places and spaces where there is pain, sense of failures, regrets, and confusions. I now truly take the time to place my whole beingness within a beautiful sacred space inside my hearts and Heart – the highest Light Love of the Divine, my highest Divine Angelic Guidance Team of the Light and Luminous Masters, are lovingly assisting me to attend to my inner child, for healing, to let go and let God. With all my Love, I am in communion with the Heart of Mother Earth Garden of Eden. I am held in the nurturing Love, in the Heart of the Divine Mother, the Great Goddess of Love, and I am held in all the Love and Heart of the Great Divine Father. I feel safe to heal as I let go of all my judgments. I visualize in all that Light and Peace and from my

Heart, the dreams God has for me — they are naturally revealed to me. My gifts are beautiful visions unfolding — holy extensions of my Divine Angelic Self. With all my love, reverence, and gratitude, I am of service in the oneness of Creation.

You may practice the above process every day, with infinite gratitude in your Heart, until you know you are free.

As you read these prayers, please read them slowly and feel in your hearts and minds and beingness the healing holy frequencies of God's Light permeating you completely. Work within a sacred space with your highest Divine Guidance team.

Dear Father Mother God, please inspire all my hearts and minds with my Sacred Heart and Divine Mind to see your Divine Will in me, all the dreams you have for me. Thank you in Peace.

Dear Father Mother God, may I hear your Holy voices, witness your Divine will and dreams, in all of my Sacred Heart and Divine Mind. I am infinitely grateful for all your God-Given Gifts and the ones which shall be revealed to me.

May all perception of who I am shift into a pure and true consciousness of my beautiful essence. May I see from your Heart and eyes dear God.

Dear God, thank you for revealing in my Heart and Mind the journey you have chosen for me in all its glory — the Path of Light you have dreamed for me with all the countless gifts you have seeded in my consciousness and Heart. Thank you, dear Father Mother God, for revealing that Sacred Path of Light which already exists in all the Love That Is. Thank you, dear Father Sun, and thank you dear Mother Earth, thank you Source!

Dear God, may the path of service you have chosen for me hold your infinite blessings — enlightening multitudes of additional paths in furtherance of Peace, Compassion, Joy, and Harmony for all Beings and the entire World.

Chapter Twelve

Dear Father Mother God, purify my minds and hearts, inspire me to let go of all that doesn't serve my highest good. I release all of these energies into your Light, so that your Divine Light transmutes them into beneficial frequencies of blissful peace, goodness, mercy, beauty, and harmony.

I live in the Garden of Eden, in the Heart of God, where I now have the courage, the awareness, and the joy to forgive myself and forgive all beings. I choose to be free. Dear Archangel Raphael, Archangel Michael, Archangel Gabriel, Archangel Uriel, dear Archangel Metatron and dear Archangel Sandalphon, dear Angels of the Light, thank you for clearing my auric field and all my bodies — thank you for releasing all energies which do not belong to me, into the highest Light of God. Thank you, dear Angelic Beings for saturating my auric field with the Golden White Crystalline Light from Source, holding my auric field whole and luminous. I am safe and I am whole, anchored with all my Love in the Heart Core Crystal of Mother Earth Garden of Eden.

It is joy to free my hearts and feel overflowing love into my One Sacred Heart, for myself and all beings, and all of Creation. I value and honor myself. I value and honor all beings and all of Life. I am free from the illusory Matrix. I see and recognize one true Matrix of Luminous Light, unconditional Love, and Harmony.

There is nothing I need to prove to myself or anyone. I am worthy! I am Holy! I am beautiful! I let go and let God. I am whole! I now know who I am!

I embrace the Eternity of Love in the Garden of Eden where I shine my Light feeling safe and Loved, now and forever.

I feel safe expanding my Heart, expanding the Love in my Heart, in the Light and Essence of the Garden of Eden where I choose to live, breathe, work, and play in every moment.

In the Garden of Eden, where I reside, I am embraced by boundless Love, Light and Peace, limitless Grace, Beauty, and Joy, infinite abundance and prosperity. The Garden of Eden lives in my One Sacred Heart. The Garden of Eden holds all dimensions in sacredness, within all enlightened aspects of Creation, the Universal Grid of Light, all encompassing. In the beauty and Light of the Garden of Eden, my pure Essence is revealed to me — a gentle force of unconditional love, bliss, and peace endlessly flows through me, healing me, nurturing me, loving me. I choose to live consciously within that field of Light, now and always. I am anchored with boundless love in the Heart of the Garden of Eden, in communion with the magnetic magnificent Core Crystal. It is joy, healing, and nurturing to embrace limitless beauty, unconditional love, and to abide by the sacred laws of Mother Nature and her Holy Garden, where I choose to live in every moment in the sanctity and oneness of Life.

My Light shines, permeated by unconditional Love and Compassion, extending to all of Life, in communion and union with all Lights, the Great Web of Light. My Heart overflowing with loving-kindness is a "healing holy nurturing presence" for all the people in my life, and for all of Life. I am love embodied.

Whatever I choose to feel and embrace in the moment is in reality shaping a bridge to my future. I choose it to be a bridge of unconditional Love and Compassion, of Light and Beauty, of Faith, Kindness, and Harmony, of Joy, and Equanimity.

My minds are free, and my hearts are imbued with Love. My Divine Mind and One Sacred Heart are now expressed in the purest Light — channeling the dreams, the words of God.

I choose the qualities of loving-kindness and compassion. I am safe and loved, forever free in the Heart of God and in the Garden of Eden. There is joy, beauty, and respect.

My highest Divine Angelic Guides are walking with me, holding me in all the "Love, Light, and Peace" that is. All beings are walking in all that Love, Light, and Peace. I devote my existence to the pure experience of a Reconciliation with Life and to inspire all human beings on that journey of Unity Consciousness.

Gratitude Consciousness Prayer-Meditation:

Breathe into your Heart the Love Light Peace of Master Jesus, Christ, Lord Buddha, Lord Krishna, the Angels of the Light and Archangels, until you experience their infinite unconditional Love and loving presences into your Heart. Express gratitude and feel the Divine Love you share with these holy Masters, and Angels. Then from all that Love in your Heart contemplate a flower, or embrace a tree, or hold a child, or hold an animal. Feel this unconditional Love as fluid Luminous Light permeating you and the flower, the tree, the child, the animal. Listen to the voices in Nature. See in your One Sacred Heart and Divine Mind that fluid Love Light permeating All That Is in Nature and all Beings. Bask with joy and gratitude in all that Love and fluid Light. Send unconditional Love to all that is. Witness and experience in your Heart that unconditional Love and pure fluid Luminous Light infusing all your relationships, all of your work, and all living and working spaces. Express and feel gratitude for all the people in your life, for everything you have experienced, for all that is in your Life.

Daily, express gratitude for the blessings in your life — the delicious food you eat, your warm cozy bed, your friends, your Divine Angelic Guides, your animal friends and the ones you see in Nature, the trees, the mountains, the rain, the wind, Mother Earth and her infinite beauty. Live in gratitude about everything. Live in appreciation, in thankfulness.

Gratitude raises your frequencies and activates amazing synchronicities into your life. From gratitude you manifest faster your dreams with the dreams God has for you. Gratitude attracts Light, goodness, and Love. It is then easier for the Angelic Light Beings to be in communion, in communication—you have been moving closer to their realms and possibly entering their realms and frequencies; they know you are ready to embrace increasing Light, and goodness into your life.

I discover in my Heart and life that "Gratitude" is of "Love, Peace, Grace, and Bliss". I feel it and I embody it with all my Heart. It is nurturing me and healing me.

Basking in the Luminous Light of God, of the Masters, Angels, and Archangels, my hearts and minds are healing, all my cells and bodies are healing—all aspects of my life are infused with that powerful healing Light. I experience that Pure Light permeating my whole beingness. It is unconditional Love infusing my whole beingness awakening my Angelic Self. I allow my One Sacred Heart to open in that Love, as I communicate with everyone in my life from my Angelic Self to their Angelic Self. Radiant Rainbows of Light of crystalline frequencies are multiplying in joy. Mother Earth is rejoicing in all these rays of Light, suffusing my relationships with boundless nurturing gifts and blessings of Love. I embrace all of these blessings with appreciation and joy. Feelings of profound gratitude are blessing me with serenity, delight, and unity consciousness.

Every morning, as I open my eyes, I look around me with my Heart infused with infinite gratitude. All around me I witness energy—fluid Light. All has consciousness. I send love-gratitude to everything, to everyone around me.

In all that gratitude and bliss, from the deepest places in my being, I experience all of life breathing me, the trees, the flowers, the animals, the wind, the rocks, the rain, and all of nature. Appreciation and gratitude awaken me to my pure being, and to my oneness. I see truth. I experience truth. From gratitude, trust and faith are rising into my Heart and Mind. Gratitude-consciousness are doorways to miracles.

Gratitude is Light in my bodies, in my life, and in the World.

<u>Prayer-Meditation for Peace and Bliss:</u>

I am forever safe in the Heart of God, in the highest Light, forever anchored in the Garden of Eden of Mother Earth. I now let go and release all my thoughts and beliefs. I set my minds free. My thoughts subside as I focus on my Heart and on my breath. I breathe in the Light of the Divine, the forces of Love – I breathe a Holy Life Force in every breath. As I breathe out, I release all energies which do not belong to me – I release all thoughts. I set myself free, inviting all Light and Life to breathe me. I am Light. I am Life. All of Life is breathing me, in all the Light and Love of the Garden of Eden in a flow of boundless Peace.

The Love of God, in all of Life, is breathing me now and always – it is a pranic force, a life force of unconditional Love. My breath is the breath of God. With every breath my Heart consciousness expands, and my auric field is being infused and suffused with that powerful Love Light from Source. In all that love, my auric field is expanding and growing stronger and brighter as I anchor with Love, my whole beingness and Heart into the Heart of Mother Earth Garden of Eden. My Light is becoming brighter and brighter. I feel protected and safe within that holy space, permeated by the Highest Light of Source, in the Garden of Eden. My Light unites with all Lights, in the Divine Oneness of Creation. My Divine Angelic guides are holding me in that boundless Luminous Light. I am invincible in this realm of Light. It is a Holy Light. It is the Light of God shining through me and from me. My whole Beingness is permeated by all that Holy Light. I am a Luminous Angelic Being of God. I am a Ray of Light in the Radiance of God. I am impervious. I embody my true power, the power of Love within me, with ease and grace. In all that Divine Love and Light there is unlimited Peace and Bliss for all beings. I discover the presence of the Divine, God's Divine Qualities living in me, in the deepest chambers of my Heart, where I know boundless Peace and Bliss. That limitless Peace and Bliss belongs to Creation, permeating all beings and all of Life, in Divine ways, held in the oneness of the magnificent Web of Life.

My shield of Light is infinitely powerful. It is the Light and Peace of God, of the Divine holding me forever safe and protected in holy communion within the essence of Life — a sacred geometry of Love and Bliss.

I discover the power of my Heart and Mind as One Force, where the highest truth and consciousness of Love Light Peace from Source reside and flow. It is bliss!

I call upon my Highest Angelic Divine Guidance team, the Angels of the Light and Archangels to hold me within a Chamber of Light. I am embraced by the Light of Master Jesus, the Light of Lord Buddha and Lord Krishna, by the Light of the Divine Mother, Archangels and Angels. I assert a path of Peace forever held in reverence in the Heart and nurturing Love of the Great Mother: Divine Mother Marie, Saint Therese of Lisieux, Divine Mother Earth. Father Mother God are my spiritual Father and Mother, blessing me on a sacred path, a path of Light forever blessing the World. I now witness a path of Peace and Bliss I leave behind me. I assert a path of infinite Blissful Peace, Beauty, and Harmony in the now moment. I proclaim a path of Blissful Peace, Beauty and Harmony, and Joy in all future, multidimensionally, in all aspects of my life. Blissful Peace and Beauty reside forever on my path in eternity. I am Peace. I am Bliss. I am Love. My Path is a Path of Light.

Within the consciousness of my pure being, I move with ease and grace through Doorways of Light. Peace is Light in my bodies, in my life, and in the World.

<u>Forgiveness and Compassion:</u>

Every challenge is an initiation to move closer to God on a trajectory where miracles of Love are multiplying in infinity. God, the Creator, the Creation, all of Life are innately leading you to a beautiful place where you are to embody your higher Light—using your gifts to be of service. Trust! Do not judge yourself or any situation. Breathe into your Heart and ask God, your Angelic Divine Guidance team, for clarity, divine help and support. Ask for divine intervention, love, peace, and harmony within a sacred space. Go with the flow and not against the flow. Accept the experience the way it unfolds to avoid additional suffering—your lack of trust may block the natural flow of what life wants to create and manifest for you that is good and of love. Trust, have faith, and meditate. Do not judge. In your prayers open your Heart to be guided to see truth, to see beyond the veil of illusion. Ask for great wisdom and blissful serenity.

Are you ready to forgive people who have hurt you? Yes! Are you ready to forgive life about situations which you feel have hurt you or traumatized you? Yes! Are you willing to now forgive yourself for the pain you may have caused to others intentionally or unintentionally? Yes! Are you ready to forgive yourself about so many other matters, too? But now you wonder how to be free from these energies lingering in your fields and minds. Some people call these energies the "pain body", because it is actually a body of energy by itself which does not belong to you. It is an energy lingering within your space and bodies.

As you take time to acknowledge these painful feelings and events, you may realize in your hearts that none of these energies belong to you, even if some of them feel intense and somehow real. You have the capacity to feel free because you are already free. Create a sacred space, call upon your highest Divine Guidance team as indicated in the book earlier. Feel the presence of the Angelic Beings holding you so gently in the infinite Peace Love Light of God. Breathe long deep breath into your Heart space and allow all that pain to move through you gently, as it is washed away softly by the Light and Love of The Divine. The Angelic Beings are holding you with unconditional Love, assisting you to let go and let God, as you are releasing the pains and memories.

<u>Prayer-Meditation to Forgive and Release Pain:</u> *I am breathing within a sacred space with my beautiful Angelic Divine Guides assisting me and holding me in the Light of God. I find the courage to pay attention to the pain and resentments, knowing that I am on my way to be free. With courage, from my Heart, I embrace all these energies with boundless compassion and love, always with the loving nurturing support and guidance of the Angels of the Light and Archangels. I then clearly realize that I don't have to fight energies which do not belong to me, and by embracing them with compassion, I receive Gifts of WISDOM on my path. This realization sets me free completely. The Angelic Beings who have been holding me within a luminous beam of the highest Light, are gathering all pain energy frequencies within a bubble of Golden Healing Light — where all is transmuted into the highest Love frequencies. The Angels of the Light and Archangels are holding me within a Chamber of Crystalline Golden Light repairing all my bodies, making my energy field whole and radiant. My minds and hearts have united into boundless peace and gratitude, where only compassion resides. I am free to experience all the Love that is. My Divine Mind and One Sacred Heart are united in One Love.*

The people who have hurt you, are most likely hurting deeply on some levels. Your pain might have triggered pain to others too, even intentionally. Express love peace prayers of awareness to forgive your Self. Send prayers blessings of healing love peace to these people, and all people in your life, and to the people who have hurt you too. See them embraced by the Divine Light. See the Angels of the Light holding them in the Light. Release them to God, to the Light. Forgive!

Choose to live and to practice your prayers-meditations in the nurturing Love Light Peace of Mother Earth Garden of Eden.

Have a conversation with your Self—listen in your Heart to what is revealed and reconcile with your Self. As you reconcile with your Self you are ready to forgive and reconcile with the people who have hurt you. Your Heart is now filled with compassion. Have a conversation in your Heart with these people, and express compassion for their pains. *I now see your pain, I now understand. I wish I could have helped you and I wish I can help now. May you be blessed by the Angels of the Light with healing!* Allow your Heart to speak with kind words and in profound respect. If you are in a position to express these thoughts to the people who have hurt you, do so in loving kindness. If for any reason, you don't see these people, repeat the prayers a few times until in your Heart you know you are free—they will receive healing in the space of love they are ready to embrace. Within a sacred space, Father Mother God, Divine Angelic Guides are guiding the Healing Lights.

It is, for sure, a time to reconcile with all aspects of your beingness and life, to let go of pain and suffering. It is a time to rediscover your multidimensional Self in a new way, in a deeper way, from a renewed relationship with your Self, with all beings, and life.

Create a sacred space and bask in a beam of Golden White Luminous Light connecting you with Heaven and Earth, and ask Archangel Michael: *Please Archangel Michael, thank you for coming forward with your Golden Sword. Thank you for removing with your Sword of Light all the energetic cords, around my field, between myself and all people, and all additional energetic cord frequencies associated to painful programs, present and past lives, hurt and grief, and karmic issues — thank you Archangel Michael for doing this multidimensionally. Thank you, dear Archangel Michael, for clearing my space and my path completely with your Luminous Blue Light Ray, in all time space and dimensions, so that my path is now a path of Light, in the past, in the present, and in all future.*

Thank you, dear Archangel Michael, for guiding everyone and everything, in the Light of God — in all the Love That Is. Thank you, dear Archangel Michael, for infusing all of my field with your luminous healing-clearing, nurturing Blue Light Ray, in all six sacred directions and in my Heart. Thank you, dear Archangel Michael, and all the Archangels and Angels of the Light for saturating my bodies and field with the highest Healing Light possible, repairing my auric field completely and multidimensionally, so that all my bodies are whole and luminous — so that the pure essence of Love is liberated and expressed. Thank you to all the Archangels and Angels of the Light for your Divine assistance and unconditional Love.

I see and experience my Crystalline Angelic Self in the Garden of Eden, basking in the Sacred Light. I see all beings as Crystalline Angels embraced by the Holy Light, the Light of the Divine, the Light of God. Thank you, dear Father Mother God, for holding all beings in the Love of your Holy Hearts.

You might be guided to repeat all of the above prayers and meditations a few times, to release layers until your Heart feels free to embrace compassion and true Love. It is important that you take time to go through all steps and processes, gently, lovingly, with trust, and with an open Heart. Healing is about seeing who you are truly in your pure essence — it is about faith, patience, perseverance, opening the Heart to receive the gifts of Love.

When you are in a state of profound compassion, you are inviting true consciousness, raising your vibration. Also, more compassionate you are, and more of your pure being is revealed in your Sacred Heart. When you have feelings of compassion you naturally move deeper within the consciousness of the Heart to see beyond the veil of illusion. Compassion is a profound energy frequency of unconditional Love, grace, and bliss. In compassion you perceive the true essence of life — you perceive your true essence and the true essence of all beings. Compassion leads to pure consciousness. Compassion is forgiveness, an awakening of the Heart.

Forgiveness and compassion are gifts of Love, I give to myself and to the world, in furtherance of Peace to prevail in all Hearts. **What I give to myself and to others, I also give it to the world.** *I choose to forgive, I choose compassion, I choose Love. The Light of the World is responding to me in my Heart with waves of gratitude, goodness, loving-kindness, and grace, also manifesting miracles in my life and in the world.*

Dear God, in my Heart, I pray to be a conduit of generosity, of your Love, to be a Healing Light force to the World.
What I feel and embrace in every moment, creates my path. I choose it to be a path of infinite compassion. I forgive and I am free!

Forgiveness and compassion are Lights in my bodies, in my life, and in the World.

I let Go, I am Free - Prayer and Meditation
Dear God, I open my Heart to see truth, to discover and experience the wisdom beyond the veil of illusory suffering. Show me what I am to know to awaken to the truth of the Heart. Please dear God, lead my way to move deeper and deeper into the understanding and realization of my true essence and the essence of all Life, of all Creation where there is pure Love, pure consciousness. May I live from this pure consciousness within the Holy Web of Light, as the Pure Being of Light I am, in the Garden of Eden. Dear God, give me the courage and strength, to grant my Heart's wishes to forgive all life and all beings and to forgive myself. In order to experience that liberation, dear God, lead me into a self-realization where I am already forgiven as I embrace your Love from my pure essence, from my pure being, and in the One Light of Creation.

I recognize the part of my mind, that wants me to remain captive with pain, guilt, anger, regrets, and/or resentments. I see clearly that it doesn't serve any high purpose to hold on to these painful feelings, energies which do not belong to me. I now choose to breathe deeply into my One Sacred Heart, delving into that Portal of the highest Light, the Love of the Divine. Thank you, dear God, dear Angels of the Light for assisting me releasing these energies which do not belong to me, multidimensionality, and to receive all the healing blessings of Love and Peace of God, I inherently deserve. I am ready to let go and let God.

Dear Father Mother God, dear Angelic beings of the Light, thank you for leading me within the deepest chambers of my Heart, to delve into your Blissful Peace and Love. Thank you for infusing me with your unconditional Love so that I may forgive myself, all beings, and all of Life, so that I may witness all the Love that lies beyond the veils of illusions.

I choose this new path not only to find solace in myself, but to be, at last, a blessing of Peace for all beings and our beautiful world. I choose to be a full participant for Peace in the World. I choose equanimity.

I witness the blissful World which lies beyond all veils of illusions.

The moment, I remember who I am, I am healed. I then realize that I have been constantly healed and well, and whole. It was my perception which required to be in alignment with the Truth of my Pure Being.

As I focus on what is important in my life, I choose to create a new relationship with myself, with all beings, and all of life. I choose to see truth, the true being of Light that I am. I am a Ray of Light in the radiance of God. I am from pure Creation. I am a pure Being of Light. I am a Crystalline Angelic Being of God and I am ready to embrace that reality with all my Heart. From my Heart, I now witness all Human Beings as Crystalline Luminous Angelic Beings of God.

As my Heart opens further within the holy realms, I experience overflowing compassion for myself, and all people I have met and know, and all beings. I come into the realization that when I am in my mind attached to all the multitudes of thoughts taking me away from the true consciousness of my Heart, I suffer. But now I know the truth. I choose your truth and Love dear Heart, dear God, dear Angels. I choose the Truth in the essence of Life. The Angels of the Light are guiding me from my Heart. I am listening to the loving whispers in my Heart. I forgive and I know peace.

Dear God, dear Angels, please guide me to see the beauty and holiness of my Being, of all beings, as I delve in the magnificence and radiance of Mother Earth, Nature's Spirits, the Light in all that is. My hearts and minds are suffused with boundless reverence and grace. My Heart is free, my Mind is free. I delve with Joy into the truth of my Being. I am clearly divinely guided as I listen to my Heart in every moment. From that place, I co-create with all of Life, a path of Peace, Love, Harmony, and Joy. The past is purified by the Light. The present is infused with the Light. I choose to breathe in all the Love that is in the now moment. As I direct my attention on the highest truth, my future unfolds on a path of Light in all the Love that is. I am a Holy Child of God, divinely loved and guided by the Angelic Beings of God. I am free.

I let go of all that I have known, I let go of my thoughts and beliefs. I now embrace the One Love and Truth of the Heart, where the highest consciousness and Divine Knowledge and wisdom reside. I am free!

<u>**I am a Holy Force of Love, and Light, and Peace for the World:**</u>
The Luminous Beings and Angels of the Light are assisting all Hearts and infusing Healing Light: I am a conduit of Love, I am an infinite force for goodness, joining the global Healing Forces of Love

which hold the ultimate healing for all the forgotten children and all who are hopeless, suffering starvation and dying in distress, pain, and aloneness. May the Divine Holy Forces awaken all Hearts in miraculous ways, for all children to be cared for with unconditional Love, along with all people, and all animals, and species. May a "Blissful Holy Light" flow throughout humanity. In all the Love that is, may all human beings be free, awakening to their highest Light and Pure Being, permeated by the Holy Heart of the Divine, the Healing forces of Father Mother God.

May all humans embody their Holy Light, transcending all illusory matrix of existentiality. May the Light be so mighty, that all prayers of Love be activated in all the Hearts of those who have been inflicting suffering to all levels of Life. May their Hearts awaken to an all-encompassing purification in the Highest Light and true consciousness, so that they may know their Highest Truth, their Highest Light — so that all their actions and thoughts are transmuted into Love and honoring, kindness and compassion. May all animals, and all Beings, and all of Mother Earth bask in the One Light, as One in the Heart of all Hearts, in the Heart of God.

Today, in my Sacred Heart, I witness the purification of all minds and hearts, a purification and enlightenment, where the Garden of Eden is revealed in all Beings, and All That Is. I am of service to ensure the rebirth of the World in all its multidimensional sacredness and holiness where all truth is revealed and unfettered—a liberation of Light all encompassing.

In my awareness, I search "beyond" the world of physicality, where I perceive and witness the Love and Light that inherently reside in all that is, and from which all is born. I invoke and praise a World of Light, a pure essence of Love from which all Beings and all of Life are permeated with, born and sourced from that Light.

Today, I choose to go Home. I choose to delve within the Portal of my Heart. From my physical-emotional-spiritual senses and all of my physicality, I perceive doorways of Light where my Heart consciousness leads me. I walk through these Doorways in meditation, and in contemplation, infused by the nurturing Divine Beauty and Sacredness of Mother Earth. The boundless Love emanating from Mother Earth Garden of Eden, all of Nature's Intelligence, are a guiding source for my Heart to reach Home, Heaven on Earth, Heaven in all places and spaces — the realm where true Love, pure Love is and always will be. I then know, see, and feel my true essence as intact, as pure, as a Ray of Light forever illuminating all worlds, all Hearts and consciousness. I am a Ray of Light in the radiance of God.

Dear Father Mother God, I surrender to the boundlessness of your Love. Please attend with your unconditional Love to all the places and spaces where illusory beliefs, wounds, and weaknesses still linger. May your Healing Light strengthen my faith now and always, as I choose to be a conduit for your Divine qualities of Love to shine through me and illuminate all Hearts — in furtherance of Peace and Harmony into the World. May I awaken to the self-realization of my Light, for the whole World to be blessed with Peace, once more and furthermore in eternity.

I declare to be free from all indoctrinations, from humans' thought-forms. Anchored in my Highest Light, my minds are completely free from thoughts, inviting the Divine Mind to attend and listen to my One Sacred Heart truth, where genuine holy guidelines and true knowledge from Source, from God are revealed to me, where kindness, love, respect, honoring and compassion, beauty and grace, and joy permeate throughout eternity.

From the consciousness of my Pure Being, I delve into the realization of my spiritual sacred path which holds the true liberation of my Soul and Heart — from where my Divine Mind holds the true knowledge of my Sacred Heart, the Heart of God within, a Wisdom all encompassing. I breathe in the oneness of the sanctity of Life from which all truth and true love arise.

I surrender to a higher power, the highest power of Love, the Love of the Creator. I know in the deepest places of my Heart that all my experiences serve my highest good and the highest good of all. I let go of control and invite the highest forces of Love Light to guide me, to show me the way. I choose to reside in true consciousness, in the Heart of God. I rest in the Heart of God. I give my life to God. I let go, surrender, and rest in the pure nurturing Love of the Great Father and the Great Mother.

May I awaken from the illusory state of the material hallucination, to know the spiritual nature of Life and of my Purest Being. Delving in Compassion, Grace, and Love, I discover the essence of my Pure Being. I am the awakener, the miracle worker, co-creating with God, a shining ray of Light, a Light permeating all of Life, inviting the Garden of Eden, Heaven on Earth TO BE. I am a Force of Love and Unity.

Enlightenment is the awakening, the self-realization, the experience of truth, and pure essence of Life, true knowledge, true consciousness. It is the oneness, the experience of the Light and unconditional Love intrinsic to All That Is.

I choose enlightenment: From my physicality to my holiness, I awaken. From separation, aloneness to unity consciousness, I awaken. From pain and blame to compassionate blessings, I awaken. From fear to Love, I awaken. My nervous system is calm and my whole being is serene. There is stillness and delight. I am held within a Holy Chamber of Light. Enlightenment is the purpose of my Life.

My Heart remembers a world where Love is authentic, therefore, I am not attached to the vicissitude of the world of physicality. I assert and see truth, the Sempiternal Peace of God beyond all veils of illusion and uncertainty.

The sempiternal Peace and Love of God unites us all, in all time, space, and dimensions. That truth has lived within me and keeps permeating the consciousness of my whole beingness. That truth encompasses a universal web of Light where I rest and dwell in the miracles of infinite possibilities.

I rest and delight within the deepest chambers of my Heart where Divine consciousness resides. As I repose within that soft and gentle Holy Presence of my Heart, Life recognizes the power of the Divine in me – I am a pure conduit of God's Love, Divine qualities and Divine knowledge. I am of service in the joy of living Heaven on Earth.

The frequencies of love and compassion I exude are bouncing back to me multiplied. I have come to the self-realization of my oneness from the gentle peace within my Heart. It is only in that peace, that I find my way to freedom and love. It is through the Portal of the Heart that I may thrive and find the ultimate gift: I have decided to Love with all my Heart. Judging is not an option any longer. I am the Awakener.

In the oneness of Life, I naturally reside within the realm of unity consciousness, a flow of abondance and infinite wisdom. In that oneness there is flow, ease and grace, there is true Love. In that Oneness there is union. In that oneness I am flooded with gratitude, trusting that all the dreams God has for me are manifesting into my life in all the Love that is. In that oneness I found myself on a trajectory to greatness, fulfilment, and happiness.

My faith engages my Heart to experience God's Divine Qualities, inviting miracles into my life. In all that faith, a self-realization of oneness, expands multidimensionally. I feel safe in my physical body and with all Life. God-Given Gifts within me expand multidimensionally in all the Love that is, giving birth to additional God-Given Gifts. All these Divine Gifts epitomize my work of service that is of reverence, goodness, unity, joy and beauty, engendering blessings of peace and harmony – a flow of Love expanding to all Life. **In the oneness of Life, there is infinite flow of abundance and prosperity in every aspects of life. In that**

infinite flow of abundance, I am a Divine Conduit of Love, a Healing Light to the World.

I see and recognize the sanctity of my being, of all beings, all of life, as One Love and One Light. Within the Holy Web of Light, I am of service to all people, to all animals, to all of Nature's Intelligence, and Mother Earth in all dimensions of Life, in the highest love, joy, and reverence possible. I invite my highest Divine Angelic Guidance team to walk with me. Their love, light, wisdom, courage and strength are blessing my Heart, my Mind, and the whole world in every moment. I am infinitely grateful.

In my inherent oneness, grace and abundance already flow, therefore, I don't have to seek and create what already exists. All that is required is that I adjust my perception to what already is. I free myself from all illusory limiting beliefs. From my Heart, I then witness boundless abundance of Love, Beauty, and Grace in all that is. In that unity consciousness my Heart dwells in Bliss.

I am a Divine Angelic Being of God, living, breathing in the Garden of Eden, lovingly held in the Heart of God, with my family and friends and all beings. I see only truth – I see all people as Divine Angelic Beings of God. I see their Holy Light and Beauty as I see my Holy Light and Beauty. In my Heart, I see all people of the world in their Pure Light.

In all the Love that is, I am impervious, invincible, dwelling within the oneness consciousness of my Pure Being.

I live within the consciousness of my Pure Being, in the Oneness of the Sacred Heart, in the Garden of Eden, where dwells infinite flow of unconditional Love, Light, Bliss, Peace, Oneness, Grace, Joy, Beauty, Harmony, Goodness, infinite Holy Abundance and Prosperity.

I am a Divine Angelic Being of God, breathing in the Heart of God, in the Heart of all Hearts, where I reside now and always, safe and protected.

I am a Holy Being of Light, a powerful Divine Angelic Being of God. My power is the Love of God illuminating my pure essence, illuminating the whole World.

I am the embodiment of Love.

I surrender all my dreams to you dear God, trusting and embracing the miraculous dreams you have for me. I choose not to be consumed by my dreams, but to be nourished by them with joy, love, beauty, exhilaration, goodness, peace, and bliss. I am dreaming and living my dreams in all your Love dear God, and they nourish me. My faith in you, dear God, empowers me with a Sanctified Force of infinite possibilities within a Holy Matrix of unconditional Blissful Love. I dream the dreams you have for me, dear God. I live the dreams you have for me, dear God. They are a driven force, in the Heart of all Hearts, in the Garden of Eden where miracles unfold with harmony, in your Divine Light, dear God. The Divine Angels of the Light who are walking with me and assisting me on my sacred path, rejoice in the Love-Gratitude I emanate, which has become an eternal melody in my One Sacred Heart.

Dear Father Mother God, Creator of All That Is, you are the Creator of my destiny, of my sacred path encompassing all the dreams you have for me, in the highest Light possible. I invite you into my Heart and Mind, and into my life. Your dreams are of Love, Goodness, and Harmony. I embrace them all.

I am whole and I am free, held with unconditional Love in the vastness of Creation, held in the Heart of God, and in the Garden of Eden where my Higher Light shines in the miracles and Glory of God.

Dear Father Mother God, thank you for granting me with your infinite gifts and blessings, and divine qualities of Love. Dear God, may I rise deeper within my Pure Being, may I be the embodiment of Integrity, Honesty, Forgiveness, Love, and Compassion. May I be of service, always welcoming with bliss and gratitude the dreams you have for me.

Dear Father Mother God, dear Divine Angelic Beings of the Light, dear Masters of the White Brotherhood, dear Star Beings from the highest dimensions of Light, in your Presence I am present, in your Awareness I am aware, in your pure Consciousness I am conscious, in your Radiance I am radiant, in all your Love I am Love embodied. Thank you for leading my journey on a path of Light, of Boundless Blessings, within the pure Matrix, in the Sanctity of the One True LOVE.

From the union of the Divine Mind and Sacred Heart, I reconcile with all aspects of my beingness and life, I let go of pain and suffering. It is a time to discover my multidimensional Self in a new way, in a deeper way, from a renewed relationship with my Self, with all Beings, and all of Life.

The Divine Angels of the Light are walking with you, eager to assist you, and guide you, with unconditional Love. Their beautiful luminous wings are holding you across and above the veils of illusions, leading you on a journey of reconciliation with your pure being and all of Life, awakening your purpose and path of service, all the way to your Sacred Heart, to God, to Source, to Home.

Forever embraced by the Luminous Wings of the Angels, in Heavenly realms, the Angels invited me to sing with them, from the embodiment of my Angelic Self, in the middle of their choir, in the eternity of time, in the ONE LIGHT, in the ONE LOVE: "Om I am Elohim!"

Dear Father Mother God, dear Guardian Angels, all Angels of the Light, and Archangels, dear Luminous Masters, dear Father Sun, dear Mother Earth, dear Grandmother moon, I unify my spirit, my consciousness, all of my beingness with your Divine Love and Light to be a clear conduit of Peace, of the Sacred Light and Truth in integrity and honoring. May every word, every sentence, all messages within this book, be infused with your forces of Love from the Temple of the One Sacred Heart of Creation. Thank you, dear Angelic Divine Guides, dear Luminous Beings for blessing this holy work, and compilation with the Sanctity of your Presence and Radiance to free and awaken all Hearts, in furtherance of Peace and Harmony in all Hearts and all Life — in the Oneness of unconditional Love — for all beings and all consciousness to live and breathe from the forces of Pure Love and Reverence, now and forever, in the Eternal Peace of Creation.

In Sacred Peace!
Namaste!

About the Author

Sibli - Sarah Jeane

Sibli is an artist of Light and graphic artist, illustrator and art director, author, angelic channel-healer, and spiritual teacher. She chooses to express "Light, the Sanctity of Life", in all that she creates in furtherance of peace and harmony for all beings and our world.

Sibli has been on a spiritual quest her whole life — practicing meditation, channeling, healing modalities, yoga, breath work, and deep Heart communion with Nature's Intelligence. Embraced by the Light, Healed by God, guided by Luminous Beings in several out of body experiences, Sibli travelled into higher dimensions of Light to faraway places throughout the Universe. She experienced her angelic self, her luminescence, unity consciousness—God's unconditional pure Love, the Heart of God within her beingness and in All That Is. In Heavenly realms the Angels invited her to sing the name of God, in her Angelic Soul embodiment. These experiences are the catalyst of the Light work she has been guided to convey to the world, of service to all of Life.

From 1975 to 1997, in Europe and the U.S., after many years working in the film industry and various companies as an art director, background artist, illustrator, graphic artist, and color stylist, she was guided to dedicate her creative gifts to serve a higher purpose and be of service using her God-Given Gifts. On this journey, Sibli has been led to discover her true purpose, to be of service as an Artist of Light, a Channel-Healer, a Practitioner of Energy Medicine-Shamanic Energy Healer, an Author, teaching and helping people to release and heal pain, to embody their Angelic Self—around the world.

Sibli communicates and works daily with Angelic Beings, Masters of Light, Luminous Star Beings from higher dimensions of Light, and Nature's Intelligence.

She is extending her light work around the world with her creative art, healing-channeling gifts, and healing classes. Her creative works are Doorways of Light. You may read additional information about healing services, view galleries and artistic stores from the following website: **sibliartfromthelight.com**

Her books are doorways to the Sacred Heart to experience the God-Self **"Twelve Doorways of Light: A Portal to Your God-Self"** and **"Twelve Doorways of Light: Sacredness of**

Life". Her latest book **"Odyssey with the Angels"** epitomizes a reconciliation with life, divine channeled messages, prayers, and meditations raising your frequencies and awakening your consciousness to embody your pure being. The Angelic Luminous Beings are illuminating your path, inviting you to dream from within your One Sacred Heart where you are co-creating with God—you are discovering your soul calling, your capacity to be a conduit of Love, Peace, and Beauty.

RESOURCES

• **Contact Sibli at: sibliangelicchannel@gmail.com**

Artistic store online, galleries, order books, info healing:
sibliartfromthelight.com

Angelic Channel-Healer

Spiritual Counselor Healer - Spiritual Teacher - Author

Multidimensional Energy Healing

• **Master Practitioner of Energy Medicine**, Shamanic Energy
Healer - Soul Retrieval.

• Sibli channels, practices, and teaches a Healing Modality
named by the Angels:

"Synergism into Love, Angelic Light Codes for
Harmonization".

• **"Soul Memory Discovery"** Practitioner and Teacher.

• **"Past Life Healing"** - Past Life Regression Therapy.

• **"Theta Healing"** Practitioner and Teacher.

Sibli is a channel of service to all of Life, working in
communion with the Angels and Masters of the Light, the
Luminous Beings. From within a sacred space, she is a conduit

to assist all beings. She offers energy healing sessions and teaches in person or online — one on one, couples, and groups.

1• Sibli teaches people how to create a Sacred Space and why it is important to do so. Learn to live within a clear and sacred space, anchored within the Heart of Mother Earth. To be in communion with the Earth Being and to live with a consciousness of the Sacred, supports your work of service in love, your well-being, and balance.

2• How to clear your Energy field: How to sustain the energetic field clear and why it is important to do so. You will learn how to recognize and release intrusive energies and entities, earthbound spirits that are blocking light within your auric field. You will feel lighter, more peaceful, happier, and more connected. You will move deeper within the Heart. You will learn to release energies, which do not serve you and do not belong to you. You will learn to connect furthermore with your God-Self and raise your frequencies.

3• Heal painful unresolved issues with your loved ones who have passed on: When you clear the energetic field, you additionally release earthbound spirits into the Light of God and often, some of them, are close friends or family members. People wish to heal painful unresolved issues with their loved ones who have passed on. Within a sacred space, this is the moment to communicate from the Heart with love and reverence, to heal painful issues, to assist him or her to move into the Light with ease and grace and in peace. These are profound and touching moments and also joyous moments, when all spaces and spaces are infused with the Love, Peace, and Light of God.

4• Release and heal traumas, painful issues, PTSD, and karmic issues — DNA-RNA, cellular reprogramming — past life healing: Multidimensional energy healing, clearing your life path, healing soul loss and trauma, in this lifetime and past lives—deep energy healing and clearing in your relationships and work of service.

5• Sibli channels, practices, and teaches a Healing Modality named by the Angels "Synergism into Love": Angelic Light Codes for Harmonization", induces the body to express itself in truth, by locating specific beliefs, causing energetic blockages within the physical body and in some aspects of your life. These blockages are linked to emotional and physical pain, sometimes unresolved issues and traumas. When such painful hidden programs within the physical body are energetically located, it is possible to release them and transform them in the Healing Light—liberating the freedom of your spirit, your ability to expand in love and harmony.

6• How to clear places and spaces—workplaces and play-spaces, homes, and lands. Infuse your living spaces with blissful peace and harmony.

7• Activate your One Sacred Heart to love "your Self" and all beings, and all of Life unconditionally: Healing and unifications of all your hearts to awaken and bring into oneness your One Sacred Heart and Divine Mind is leading to an ascension and communion of Love with all of Life.

8• Heal and let go of past lives issues and traumas: A safe journey, a guided meditation, leading you to Past Life Exploration, Regression Therapy, and Energetic Release. When the pain is gone and replaced with the infinite Love Light Blessings of the Divine and of your Angelic Guides, you are completely free.

9• A Journey to embody your Higher Light, your God Self, your Angelic Self: You are raising your frequencies to be of service from the highest place of Love and Honoring.

10• How to be of service as a Light Worker in Harmony and

Honoring. Important guidelines and teachings to become a channel-healer, so that you work in integrity, allowing always the Pure Love of God's consciousness to be in charge with your Divine Guidance team. Learn to be a clear channel-healer in honoring, compassion, gratitude, and unconditional love. Learn to let go and let God. Learn to commune with the Masters of Light, Archangels, and Angels, all your Divine Guides, and Nature's Intelligence.

11 • Learn to work with St. Germain, the Angels of the Violet Flame, and the Violet Flame, the sacred flame of transmutation and purification. Receive the gift of its Divine Essence. Discover the metaphysics of this Sacred Flame: Harmonize your life, heal your relationships and bodies, raise your frequencies in all aspects of your life and contribute globally to the expansion of Light, Love, and Harmony.

12 • Learn to read energetic frequencies: Read the life force in your whole being, as well as any object, water, food, and place. Learn to raise your energetic frequency — activate and expand the "light life force" from a deeper level of your being and hearts with breath work and clearings. Become aware of your energetic frequency to live in a more conscious way of your mission and purpose — to bring forth further joy and well-being into your life.

13 • Tree of Life Activation: Within a Sacred space raise your frequencies, activate all Divine qualities of God/all Aspects of the Tree of Life within your beingness to experience your pure essence, your God-Self. Invite a flow of Love, Peace, Divine Life Force and Light to awaken and support your ascension. Anchor all Divine qualities of God and corresponding Light Rays within specific energetic centers, within the Sacred Heart, and within your whole Beingness. This process increases your capacity to Love from the Sacred Heart, allowing your creative abilities and potentialities to expand, to be of service in furtherance of Global Peace and Harmony.

14• Rejuvenate and Heal in the Heart Center of Mother Earth, the Core Crystal of Mother Earth. Travel into the Heart of Mother Earth, Garden of Eden, high dimensions of Light, supported and guided by the Luminous Angelic Beings within a Chamber of Light. Create your personal Sanctuary of Peace within the Heart of the Sacred Garden, among Nature's Sprits and the sacredness of the Unicorns. Empower your Heart's desires and dreams within these high dimensions of Light in the Heart of the Divine Mother, in the Garden of Eden. Heal within the Heart of Mother Earth in her Garden of Eden. Experience your Oneness with all Creation and your infinite Crystalline Essence within the Garden of Eden. This process opens the Heart in nurturing ways.

15• Clear, balance, and energize your Energetic Centers or Chakras by embracing the Luminous Light of the Sacred Father Sun and the nurturing Love Light of Mother Earth dwelling within her Garden of Eden. Your Chakras are power centers connected with universal energies. The Angelic Luminous Beings activate the flow of Light within your Chakras to make you whole, healthy, energized, and balanced, supporting the embodiment of your God Self, your Angelic Self, to be of service from the highest place of Love and honoring.

16• Anchor all your Senses into your One Sacred Heart, infused by Luminous Light Rays. This process and guided meditation empower your Light and awakening.

17• Hands on Healing - Energetic Healing Surgery, takes place within a Chamber of Light, in the presence of the Luminous Beings, Angels of the Light, the highest Divine Guidance Team of Healers, in the Divine Love, Light, Peace of God — Holy Healing Hands and Light heal all bodies.

Artist Services

**Artistic store online, galleries, order books, info
healing: sibliartfromthelight.com**

Graphic Design • Logos

• Book Covers, Jackets and CD Covers,

• Illustrator • Art Director •

• Paintings • Murals • Portraits •

• Realism, Symbolic, and Visionary Light Art •

Artist of Light - Graphic Artist - Illustrator - Art Director
Art Consultant for Home & Business - Decorative Art

1- Sibli creates and channels, various graphic artistic projects to support your business such as logos, business cards, posters, book covers, CD covers, artistic images and graphics to enhance your "work of service and messages" with positive uplifting energies.

2• She creates and channels "Activation-Ascension Light Art" for your home and business raising the frequencies on the Planet for all Beings (murals, posters, artistic prints on various support), energetically uplifting your living spaces.

3• Sacred Personal Empowering Painting: Within a sacred space, Sibli connects from her Heart with your Soul-Heart calling, in honoring and Love. Within a beautiful sacred space, an awareness of your Soul's Divine purpose is revealed to her Higher Self. She then artistically expresses this vision. It is an Activation-Ascension painting that is personal to your mission on the Planet—an energetic loving support of boundless Light. In the process, within a sacred space, Sibli proceeds with an energetic field clearing to open the space for you to be free to express your work of service through this new Portal of Light, this artistic image, from the highest Dimensions—in all the Love That Is.

Sibli invites you to visit her store online to decorate your living spaces with beautiful artistic objects that are uplifting, Light enhancing, harmonizing and clearing, practical and useful in your daily lives, at sibliartfromthelight.com.